#72.00

World Religions

Primary Sources

World Religions

Primary Sources

Michael J. O'Neal and J. Sydney Jones
Marcia Merryman Means, Editor

U·X·L
*An imprint of Thomson Gale,
a part of The Thomson Corporation*

THOMSON
GALE

Detroit • New York • San Francisco • New Haven, Conn. • Waterville, Maine • London

THOMSON

———✶———™

GALE

World Religions: Primary Sources

Written by Michael J. O'Neal and J. Sydney Jones
Edited by Marcia Merryman Means

Project Editor
Nancy Matuszak

Editorial
Julie L. Carnagie

Rights and Acquisitions
Edna Hedblad, Emma Hull, and Sue Rudolph

Imaging and Multimedia
Lezlie Light, Michael Logusz,
and Robyn Young

Product Design
Jennifer Wahi

Composition
Evi Seoud

Manufacturing
Rita Wimberley

LIBRARY OF CONGRESS CATALOGING-IN-PUBLICATION DATA

Jones, J. Sydney.
  World religions reference library / edited by Neil Schlager and Jayne Weisblatt;
written by J. Sydney Jones and Michael O'Neal; Nancy Matuszak, content project editor.
    p. cm. -- (World religions reference library)
  Includes bibliographical references and index.
  ISBN-13: 978-1-4144-0227-7 (Almanac : set : alk. paper) --
  ISBN-10: 1-4144-0227-9 (Almanac : set : alk. paper) --
  ISBN-13: 978-1-4144-0228-4 (Almanac : vol. 1 : alk. paper) --
  ISBN-10: 1-4144-0228-7 (Almanac : vol. 1 : alk. paper) --
  [etc.]
    1. Religions.I. O'Neal, Michael, 1949-II. Schlager, Neil, 1966-III. Weisblatt, Jayne.
  IV. Title.V. Series.
  BL74.J66 2006
  200--dc22   2006012295

ISBN-13:

978-1-4144-0229-1	978-1-4144-0232-1
(Almanac vol. 2)	(Biographies vol. 2)
978-1-4144-0230-7	978-1-4144-0233-8
(Biographies set)	(Primary Sources)
978-1-4144-0231-4	978-1-4144-0234-5
(Biographies vol. 1)	(Cumulative Index)

ISBN-10:

1-4144-0229-5	1-4144-0232-5
(Almanac vol. 2)	(Biographies vol. 2)
1-4144-0230-9	1-4144-0233-3
(Biographies set)	(Primary Sources)
1-4144-0231-7	1-4144-0234-1
(Biographies vol. 1)	(Cumulative Index)

This title is also available as an e-book.
ISBN-13: 978-1-4144-0232-1, ISBN-10: 1-4144-0612-6
Contact your Thomson Gale sales representative for ordering information.
Printed in the United States of America

10 9 8 7 6 5 4 3 2

Contents

Reader's Guide

Religion influences the views and actions of many people in the world today in both political and personal ways. In some instances religious fervor compels people to perform selfless acts of compassion, while in others it spurs them to bitter warfare. Religion opens some people to all humanity but restricts others to remain loyal to small groups.

In general, religion can be described as a unified system of thought, feeling, and action that is shared by a group and that gives its members an object of devotion—someone or something sacred to believe in, such as a god or a spiritual concept. Religion also involves a code of behavior or personal moral conduct by which individuals may judge the personal and social consequences of their actions and the actions of others. Most of the time, religion also deals with what might be called the supernatural or the spiritual, about forces and a power beyond the control of humans. In this function, religion attempts to answer questions that science does not touch, such as the meaning of life and what happens after death.

Perhaps one of the most amazing things about religion is that there is no commonly held way of looking at it. Yet most of the world's population participates in it in one way or another. Though hard to define, religion seems to be a universal experience and need. Of the nearly 6.5 billion people on Earth, only about 16 percent (about 1.1. billion) say they do not believe in a god or do not believe in a specific religion. The rest of the world's population belongs to one of more than twenty different major religions.

Features and Format

World Religions: Primary Sources offers eighteen excerpted writings, speeches, and sacred texts from across the religious spectrum. The selections are grouped into three thematic chapters: Creation Stories and Foundation Myths; Characteristics of the Divine; and Religion as a Guide to Living. The first explores the creation stories of religions, such as those relayed in Judaism's Tanakh and Islam's Qur'an, and the foundation myths, such as the one relayed by Black Elk, which provide a unifying cultural basis for many people. The second chapter, Characteristics of the Divine, explores the aspects and personalities of God or the gods as revealed through religious documents such as the *The Epic of*

Gilgamesh, Sikhism's Sri Guru Granth Sahib, and Swami Vivekananda's "Paper on Hinduism." The third chapter examines how religion provides guidelines that people can use in their everyday lives. These include selections from the Christian Bible; the Daoist text Dao De Jing; Buddhism's Dhammapada; the Avesta, the sacred scripture of Zoroastrianism; and Emma Goldman's essay "The Philosophy of Atheism."

The following additional material accompanies each excerpt:

- An **introduction** places the document and its author in a historical context.
- **Things to remember while reading** gives important background information and directs the reader to central ideas in the text.
- **What happened next** . . . gives an account of later historical events.
- **Did you know** . . . cites significant and interesting facts about the document, the author, or the events discussed.
- **Consider the following** . . . poses questions about the material for the reader to consider.
- **For More Information** lists sources for more information on the author, topic, or document.

World Religions: Primary Sources includes numerous sidebars highlighting interesting, related information. More than fifty black-and-white images illustrate the text. A glossary running alongside each primary source document defines terms, people, and ideas contained in the document. The volume begins with a timeline of events and a listing of important words to know. It concludes with a subject index of people, places, and events.

World Religions Reference Library

World Religions: Primary Sources is only one component of the three-part World Religions Reference Library. The set also includes two almanac volumes and two biographies volumes:

- *World Religions: Almanac* (two volumes) covers the history, traditions, and worldviews of dominant and less prominent religions and their sects and offshoots. This title examines the development of religions throughout history: their philosophies and practices, sacred texts and teachings, growth into modern times, influences on society and culture, and more. The set features eighteen chapters on today's prominent world religions and also explores ancient beliefs, smaller movements, and the philosophies of agnosticism and atheism. In addition, an introductory chapter explores the concept of religion in more depth.

- *World Religions: Biographies* (two volumes) presents the biographies of fifty men and women who have played a critical role in the world's religions throughout history. Among those profiled are Abraham, whose influence is seen in three of the modern world's most influential religions: Judaism, Christianity, and Islam; Muhammad, considered the final and most important prophet by Muslims; and Siddhartha Gautama, who became known as the Buddha. Modern figures include the Hindu teacher Swami Vivekananda and Baháʾuʾlláh, the founder of the Baháʾí faith. Women who made significant impacts on religion are also featured, including Mother Maria Skobtsova, an Orthodox Christian nun who worked to save many during the Holocaust.

Acknowledgments

U • X • L would like to thank several individuals for their assistance with the *World Religions: Primary Sources.* At Schlager Group, Marcia Merryman Means oversaw the editing, while Michael J. O'Neal and J. Sydney Jones wrote the text. Thanks also to Shannon Kelly, who assisted with copyediting, Nora Harris for indexing, and Gloria Lam for proofing.

Special thanks are due for the invaluable comments and suggestions provided by U • X • L's World Religions Reference Library advisors and consultants:

- George Alscer, Associate Professor and Chair of Religious Studies, Philosophy and Pastoral Ministry, Marygrove College, Detroit, Michigan.
- Janet Callahan, Ford Interfaith Network, Dearborn, Michigan.
- Mary Ann Christopher, Librarian, Yellow Springs High School, Yellow Springs, Ohio.
- Margaret Hallisey, Retired library media specialist and former board member of the American Association of School Librarians; the Massachusetts School Library Media Association; and the New England Educational Media Association.

- Fatima al-Hayani, Professor of Religious Studies, University of Toledo, Toledo, Ohio.
- Madan Kaura, Bharatyia Temple, Ford Interfaith Network, Dearborn, Michigan.
- Ann Marie LaPrise, Huron School District, Monroe, Michigan.
- Ann W. Moore, Librarian, Schenectady County Public Library, Schenectady, New York.
- Chuen Pangcham, Midwest Buddhist Meditation Center (Buddha Vihara Temple), Warren, Michigan.
- Gene Schramm, Retired professor of Semitic Languages and Near Eastern Studies, University of Michigan, Ann Arbor, Michigan.
- Cheryl Youse, Media specialist, Hatherly Elementary School, Plymouth, Michigan.

Comments and Suggestions

We welcome your comments on *World Religions: Primary Sources* and suggestions for other topics in history to consider. Please write to Editors, *World Religions: Primary Sources,* U • X • L, 27500 Drake Road, Farmington Hills, Michigan 48331-3535; call toll-free 800-877-4253; send faxes to 248-699-8097; or send e-mail via http://www.gale.com.

Timeline of Events

c. 2000 BCE Shin-eqi-unninni writes ***The Epic of Gilgamesh,*** about a king who lived in Babylonia around 2700 BCE. One story in the poem tells of a great flood, for which one man prepares by building a boat and gathering all living things into it. A similar story (Noah's Ark) would appear in the Bible.

1700–400 BCE Period during which the **Avesta,** sometimes referred to as the Zend-Avesta, the sacred scripture of Zoroastrianism, is compiled. The core of the Avesta is the Gathas, a collection of religious songs believed to have been composed by the prophet of Zoroastrianism, Zarathushtra.

c. 800 BCE The Greek poet Homer writes ***The Odyssey.*** This epic poem offers a detailed view of the role of gods in human affairs as it was conceived by ancient Greeks.

604–531 BCE Life span of Laozi, a Chinese wise man who in Daoist tradition is thought to be the author of the **Dao De Jing.** This text is one of the sacred writings of Daoism.

c. 490–c. 410 BCE Life span of Mahavira, considered the main founder of Jainism. He establishes the main beliefs of Jainism, which are passed down orally and later compiled in writings such as the Akaranga Sutra found in the **Gaina Sutras.**

c. 479–221 BCE **The Analects,** thought to be written by the Chinese philosopher and politician Confucius or his disciples, is compiled. The book is a guide to moral behavior and conduct.

440 BCE Possible date for the writing of the book of Genesis found in the **Tanakh (Hebrew Bible).** Orthodox Jews believe the book was written by Moses much earlier than this. Regardless of its date, this creation story remains a vital part of the Judeo-Christian tradition even today.

c. first century BCE Date marking the writing of **The Dhammapada,** a Buddhist text thought to contain the actual sayings of the Buddha, Siddhartha Gautama (563–483 BCE).

c. 60–100 CE Period during which the Gospel According to Saint Matthew was likely written. This text features accounts of the life and teachings of Jesus Christ, including the Sermon on the Mount. It is a key part of the Christian **Bible.**

610–632 The **Qurʾan,** the holy book of Islam, is revealed to the prophet Muhammad by the archangel Jabraʾil.

712 The Kojiki, a Japanese Shinto text, is compiled. It is the earliest surviving document written by the Japanese. Part scripture, part history, and part folktale and myth, it represents an effort to document much of the history of early Japan. It also contains an account of the creation of the world.

1603 The Sikh sacred scripture, **Shri Guru Granth Sahib,** is compiled by the guru Shri Arjan Dev Ji (1563–1606).

c. 1857 Baháʾuʾlláh, the founder of the Baháʾí faith, writes **The Hidden Words.** The purpose of the book is to take the most important elements from the teachings of all religions to find their "inner essence," or true meaning.

1889 The British scholar Thomas Henry Huxley discusses his belief in agnosticism in his essay **"Agnosticism and Christianity."**

1893 Swami Vivekananda delivers his **"Paper on Hinduism"** at the World Parliament of Religions in Chicago. His speech sparks interest in Hinduism in the Western world.

1916 The American political activist Emma Goldman writes **"The Philosophy of Atheism."** In this essay, she rejects belief in such ideas as heaven, hell, sin, and other religious ideas and principles.

1932 The publication of ***Black Elk Speaks*** brings the traditional religious practices of the Lakota Sioux tribe to a wider audience.

1988 In ***Wicca: A Guide for the Solitary Practitioner,*** Scott Cunningham offers a description of the neo-pagan religious movement known as Wicca, a form of modern witchcraft.

Words To Know

A

acupuncture: Traditional Chinese medical treatment that uses needles inserted into the body at specific locations to stimulate the body's balanced flow of energy.

adur aduran: The "fire of fires" that burns in Zoroastrian temples.

agnosticism: The view that the existence or nonexistence of God is unknown and is probably unknowable.

ahimsa: The principle of nonviolence, or not doing harm to any living creature.

Ahura Mazda: The supreme God of Zoroastrianism.

Akaranga Sutra: One of the sacred texts of Jainism, which contains the teachings of Mahavira.

Akhand Paath: Any occasion, such as a marriage or a death, when the Granth Sahib is read in its entirety.

alchemy: An ancient science that aimed to transform substances of little value into those of greater value, such as lead into gold.

Allah: The name of God in Islam, derived from the Arabic word *al-ilah,* meaning "the One True God."

Amaterasu: The Sun-goddess.

Amesha Spentas: The "Bounteous Immortals," aspects, or sides, of Ahura Mazda.

amrit: A solution of water and sugar, used in the ceremony when Sikhs are initiated into the faith.

Amrit Sanskar: The initiation ceremony for young Sikhs.

Anand Karaj: The Sikh wedding ceremony.

animism: The worship of trees, rocks, mountains, and such, which are believed to have supernatural power.

anthropomorphism: Attributing human shape or form to nonhuman things, such as the gods.

apathia: Stoic belief that happiness comes from freedom from internal turmoil.

apeiron: Anaximander's term for the first principle, an undefined and unlimited substance.

archē: The beginning or ultimate principle; the stuff of all matter, or the building block of creation.

arihant: An enlightened person.

Ark of the Covenant: A cabinet in which the Ten Commandments were kept in the First Temple of Jerusalem.

artha: Prosperity and success in material affairs.

Asatru: A neo-pagan religion based on worship of the Norse (Scandanavian) gods.

ascetic: A person who practices rigid self-denial, giving up all comforts and pleasures, as an act of religious devotion. Jain monks and nuns are ascetics.

asha: Righteousness that derives from natural law.

Ashkenazic: Term used to refer to Jews of France, Germany, and Eastern Europe.

astrology: The study of the movement of the planets and stars in relation to one another in order to predict future events.

ataraxia: Serenity, tranquility, or peace of mind.

atheism: A disbelief in the existence of God or a belief that there is no God.

atomism: The belief that matter is composed of simple, indivisible, physical particles that are too tiny to be observed by human beings.

atonement: In Christianity, the sacrifice and death of Jesus to redeem humankind from its sins.

aum: Often spelled Om, the sacred syllable and symbol of Hinduism; a symbol of the unknowable nature of Brahma.

Avesta: The chief sacred scripture of Zoroastrianism.

B

baptism: A religious ceremony in which a person is dipped in or sprinkled with water as a sign of being cleansed of sin.

bar mitzvah: The Jewish coming-of-age ceremony for boys.

bat mitzvah: The Jewish coming-of-age ceremony for girls.

belief: A conviction of the truth of a proposition either by close examination or trust.

Beltane (Beltaine): Neo-pagan holiday on April 30.

benevolence: The tendency to do good and to be kind to others.

Bhagavad Gita: A Sanskrit poem regarded as a Hindu scripture; part of the epic *Mahabharata,* which means "Great Epic of the Bharata Dynasty"; examines the nature of God and how mortals can know him.

bhakti: Devotion.

blasphemy: Disrespectful comments or actions concerning a religion or its God.

bodhisattva: A person who has attained enlightenment but, rather than entering a state of nirvana, chooses to stay behind to help others reach enlightenment.

Bon: An indigenous religion of Tibet.

Brahma: The creator-god.

The Buddha: The title of Siddhartha Gautama after he attained enlightenment.

C

caliph: One of Muhammad's successors as leader of the faith.

Candomblé: A South American religion with many similarities to Santería, often used synonymously with Santería.

canon: The official, sacred texts of a religion.

caste: Social classes in Hinduism, the dominant religion in India.

Celtic: A term referring to an ethnic group that spread throughout Europe, particularly the British Isles, and is the source of many modern neo-pagan movements.

church: From the Greek, this word refers to the community of all Christians. It is also the place where Christians go to worship.

consciousness: The condition of being aware of one's thoughts, feelings, and existence.

conservative: A movement in modern Judaism that tries to strike a balance between Orthodox and Reform Judaism.

conversion: A change in which a person adopts a new set of religious beliefs.

coven: A group of neo-pagans, such as Wiccans. Alternately referred to as circles, groves, kindreds, garths, hearths, and other terms.

covenant: In religion, a covenant refers to an agreement between God or a messenger of God and his followers.

creed: A statement of belief or basic principles.

crucifixion: The suffering and death by nailing or binding a person to a cross.

cuneiform: Sumerian writing, so-called because of its wedge-shaped marks.

D

daevas: Ancient Persian deities.

Dao: The path or way; the rhythmic balance and natural, flowing patterns of the universe.

de: Political power that is the result of a ruler's virtue and honesty.

deity: A god or goddess.

dharma: Righteousness in one's religious and personal life.

Diaspora: The scattering of the Jews throughout the world.

Digambara: Literally "sky-clad"; one of the two major sects of Jainism.

disciple: A person who accepts and assists in spreading the teachings of a leader. In the Bible, a follower of Jesus.

doctrine: A set of ideas held by a religious group.

druidism: A neo-pagan religion based in the Celtic region of the British Isles.

dynasty: A sequence of rulers from the same family.

E

Eightfold Path: The path of the Buddha's teachings that can lead to the end of suffering.

Ek Onkar: The "True God" of Sikhism.

emanation: That which inevitably flows outward from the transcendental (spiritual, beyond human experience) central principle of reality, "the One," in the Neoplatonic philosophy of Plotinus.

empiricism: Belief that knowledge comes through the senses.

enlightenment: The state of realization and understanding of life, a feeling of unity with all things.

Epicureanism: The philosophy of Epicurus and others that states that the highest good is pleasure and the avoidance of pain.

equinox: Either of two points during the year when the Sun crosses the equator and the hours of day and night are equal. The spring, or vernal, equinox occurs generally on March 21 and the autumn equinox occurs on or about September 23.

Esbat: Wiccan celebration of the full Moon.

ethics: The study of moral values and rules or a guide to such values and rules.

etiquette: Proper behavior; good manners.

Evangelical: Describing a Protestant group that emphasizes the absolute authority of the Bible and forgiveness of sin through belief in Jesus.

excommunicate: To exclude or officially ban a person from a church or other religious community.

F

faith: Belief and trust in God, accompanied by a sense of loyalty to the traditional doctrines, or principles, of religion.

Faravahar: A figure of a bird with its wings spread that is a chief symbol of Zoroastrianism.

filial piety: The respect and devotion a child shows his or her parents.

fitrah: An inborn tendency to seek the creator.

Five Classics: The original texts used by Confucius in his practices and teachings: *Liji, Shijing, Shujing, Chunqui,* and *Yijing.*

Five Pillars: The core of Islamic belief referring to declaring faith, daily prayer, charitable giving, fasting, and pilgrimage.

folk beliefs: The beliefs of the common people.

Folk (*Minzoku*) Shinto: Shinto that emphasizes folk beliefs, or common beliefs, of rural agricultural laborers.

Four Affirmations: A code of conduct by which Shintoists live, including emphases on tradition and family, nature, cleanliness, and worship of the kami.

Four Books: The most prominent of Confucian sacred texts, established by Zhu Xi: the Analects, the Mencius, *Da Xue* (Great Learning), and *Zhongyong* (Doctrine of the Mean).

Four Noble Truths: The foundations of the Buddhist religion: that all life is suffering, that desire causes suffering, that suffering can end, and that ending suffering happens by following the path of the Buddha's teachings.

G

Gahambars: Seasonal festivals.

Gathas: A portion of the Zend-Avesta that contains holy songs; believed to be the words of Zarathushtra himself.

God: The supreme or ultimate being or reality; creator of the universe.

Goddess worship: Term that refers generally to any neo-pagan practice that elevates the status of goddesses over that of gods.

Golden Temple: The chief Sikh temple, located in the city of Amritsar in India; more formally, the Sri Harmandir Sahib.

gurdwara: A Sikh temple or place of worship.

guru: A religious teacher.

H

Ha-ne-go-ate-geh: The "Evil-Minded," the evil spirit of the Iroquois nation.

Ha-wen-ne-yu: The Great Spirit of the Iroquois nation.

hadiths: The sayings of the prophet Muhammad recorded by his followers.

Haj: Pilgrimage to the holy city of Mecca.

halal: Permissible activities for Muslims.

Hanukkah: The Jewish Festival of Lights commemorating the rededication of the First Temple.

haram: Prohibited activities for Muslims.

heretic: A person whose beliefs oppose his or her religion's official doctrines, or defining principles.

Ho-no-che-no-keh: The Invisible Agents, or lesser spirits, of the Iroquois.

Holocaust: The systematic slaughter of Jews by the Nazi regime in Germany before and during World War II (1939–45).

householders: Laypeople; Jains who are not monks or nuns.

idol: A statue or other image that is worshipped as a god.

Imbolc: Neo-pagan holiday generally held on February 2 to mark the lengthening of the days and the emergence of the world from winter.

Immaculate Conception: The principle of the Roman Catholic Church that Mary, the mother of Jesus, was conceived with a soul free from original sin.

incarnation: In Christianity, the belief that God took on bodily form through Jesus, making Jesus fully human and fully divine.

indigenous: A word that describes a people, culture, or religion that is native to a particular geographical region.

indulgence: In the Roman Catholic Church, the belief that paying money to the Church would allow a person to get into heaven or be forgiven for sins that were not yet committed.

Izanagi: The male figure in the Shinto creation myth.

Izanami: The female figure in the Shinto creation myth.

J

jinja: Shrine.

jinn: Evil spirits that tempt a person away from dedication to Allah.

jinn: Literally, "conquerors"; the great teachers of Jainism who have conquered their earthly passions.

jiva: The soul.

junzi: A gentleman or superior man.

K

Ka'aba: The shrine built by the prophet Abraham in the holy city of Mecca and the focal point of pilgrimages to the city.

kama: Gratification of the senses.

kami: The gods or divinities of Shinto; the life force or spirit associated with places, natural objects, and ancestors.

kami-dana: A "kami shelf" or altar in a private home.

kara: A steel bracelet, worn by Sikhs as a symbol of God.

karma: The result of good or bad actions in this lifetime that can affect this or later lifetimes.

kasha: The white shorts worn by Sikhs as a symbol of purity.

kesh: Uncut hair, a symbol of Sikhism.

kevalnyan: Enlightenment.

Khalsa: The militant "brotherhood" of Sikhism, founded by Guru Gobind Singh.

Khanda: The emblem of Sikhism.

kirpan: A sword or dagger worn by Sikhs as a symbol of their willingness to fight to defend their faith.

Kojiki: The chief text of Shinto, a work that combines history, myth, and folk belief.

kosher: Dietary laws, referred to in Hebrew as *kashrut*.

kungha: The wooden comb used to groom hair, a symbol of Sikhism.

kushti: The sacred cord, or belt, that Zoroastrians wear.

kusti: The "holy path" one has to follow to be a Zoroastrian.

L

laity: Body of worshippers who are not members of the clergy.

li: The rules of behavior a person must follow to reach the Confucian ideal of correct living.

Logos: Word, logic, or defining pattern of the universe, similar to the Dao in Chinese philosophy.

Lughnasadh: Neo-pagan harvest festival on August 1.

Ⓜ

maat: Divine order and justice; a central concept in the religion of ancient Egypt.

Mabon: Neo-pagan celebration of the autumn equinox; the completion of the harvest season.

Magen David: The so-called Star of David, a symbol of the Jewish faith and nation.

magick: The ability to focus mental and physical energies to affect the natural world or to achieve a goal.

Mahavira: The twenty-fourth tirthankara often regarded as the founder of Jainism.

Mahavira jayanti: Mahavira's birthday, an important holy day for Jains.

mantra: A formula repeated over and over to create a trancelike state.

materialism: A belief that matter and the motion of matter constitute the universe. All phenomena, even those of mind, are the result of material interactions.

matsuri: Festival.

Mecca: A city in present-day Saudi Arabia, the holiest site of Islam, where the religion was founded.

meditation: Quiet reflection on spiritual matters.

menorah: A seven-branched candelabrum; at Hanukkah, a nine-branched candelabrum is used.

Messiah: The expected deliverer and king of the Jews, foretold by the prophets of the Old Testament; used by Christians to refer to Jesus Christ.

metaphysical: Having to do with the philosophical study of the nature of reality and existence.

metaphysics: The branch of philosophy that deals with explanations for the most general questions of being, such as what brought the world into being, and the nature of space, time, God, and the afterlife.

metempsychosis: Transmigration of souls, or the migration of the soul into a different form, animal, or object after death.

mezuzah: A small case containing Torah passages that observant Jews attach to the doorposts of their houses.

midrashim: Stories that expand on incidents in the Hebrew Bible.

Mishnah: The written text of the Talmud.

mitzvoth: The laws of Judaism contained in the Torah.

moksha: Salvation; liberation from rebirth.

monastery: A place where religious people such as monks live, away from the world and following strict religious guidelines.

monotheism: Belief in one supreme being.

morality: Following the rules of right behavior and conduct.

Moshiach: The expected Messiah in Jewish belief.

muezzin: The person who issues the call to prayer.

murti: Image of a god.

Muslim: A follower of Islam, from the Arabic phrase *bianna musliman,* meaning "submitted ourselves to God."

myth: A legendary story, often with no basis in historical fact, that frequently tells of the actions of deities and helps to explain some naturally occurring event or some supernatural occurrence.

mythology: The collected stories of a culture or religion, especially those dealing with the origins, heroes, gods, and beliefs of a group of people.

N

Naam Karam: The naming ceremony for children.

namaskar: The basic prayer of Jainism, recited each morning and at night before bedtime.

Neo-paganism: A term referring to modern religions based on ancient pagan religions.

nirvana: The end of suffering, beyond time and space; the goal of all Buddhists.

nivritti: People who choose to withdraw from the world to lead a life of renunciation and contemplation.

norito: Prayers to the kami.

O

Offering of Eightfold Puja: An important Jain temple ritual in which the worshipper makes eight offerings to the tirthankara.

Olódùmarè: The name of the supreme god in Santería.

Om: Often spelled Aum; the sacred syllable and symbol of Jainism (and Hinduism), used for purposes of meditation.

Oral Torah: Interpretations of the Torah and ways to apply their laws.

orders: Religious communities.

Original Sin: The sin that fell upon humankind when Adam and Eve ate of the forbidden fruit in the Garden of Eden; this act, in turn, led to the separation of humans from God.

orishas: Name given to the lesser gods of Santería.

orthodox: The name of one of the sects of Judaism, generally referring to traditional Jews who are conservative in their outlook.

Oshogatsu: The Shinto new year.

Ostara: Neo-pagan holiday held at the time of the spring equinox.

P

pagan: Pre-Christian or non-Christian; also referring to those who worship many gods.

pantheon: The class or collection of all gods and goddesses in a system of belief.

Parshva: The twenty-third tirthankara, who lived about 250 years before Mahavira.

Parsis (Parsees): Zoroastrians who live in India.

Paryushana: An eight-day festival, the most important holy observance for Jains during the year.

Pesach: The feast of Passover, commemorating the flight of the Jews from Egypt.

philosophical Daoism: A form of Daoism by which followers seek knowledge and wisdom about the unity of everything in existence and how to become closer to it.

philosophy: The study of morals and reality by logical reasoning to gain a greater understanding of the world.

polytheism: A religion worshiping many gods.

pravritti: People who choose to live in the world rather than withdraw from it.

prophecy: Prediction of future events.

prophet: A person chosen to serve as God's messenger.

pu: Uncarved or unformed; the state of simplicity to which Daoists try to return.

puja: Worship.

purusharthas: The four aims of Hinduism or "the doctrine of the four-fold end of life."

Purva: The original Jain sacred texts, now lost.

pyramid: A stone tomb constructed to house a deceased pharaoh of Egypt.

Q

qi: The breath of life or vital energy that flows through the body and the earth.

Qur'an: The sacred scriptures of Islam; contains the revelations given to the prophet Muhammad revealed to him beginning in 610.

R

ra'kah: A unit of prayer.

rationalism: Belief that knowledge can come exclusively from the mind.

reform: One of the sects of Judaism, generally used to refer to the less traditional branch of the faith.

Regla de Ocha: The formal name for the Santerían religion.

Rehit Maryada: The Sikh code of ethical conduct.

religious Daoism: A form of Daoism that recognizes gods, ancestor spirits, and life after death.

ren: Empathy, the ability to feel for and sympathize with others; the highest Confucian ideal.

Resurrection: The rising of Jesus Christ from the dead three days after his Crucifixion, or death on a cross.

Rig Veda: The central scripture of Hinduism, a collection of inspired hymns and songs.

Rosh Hoshanah: The Jewish "New Year."

S

Sabbat: Holidays practiced by Wiccans throughout the year, including the summer and winter solstices, the vernal and autumnal equinoxes, and four additional holidays between these four.

sacrament: A sacred rite, or ceremony.

sadhana: Ascetic person.

saint: A deceased person who has been recognized for living a virtuous and holy life.

salat: Daily prayer.

salvation: The deliverance of human beings from sin through Jesus Christ's death on the cross.

Samhain (Samhuinn): Neo-pagan holiday celebrated on October 31.

samsara: The ongoing cycle of birth, life, death, and rebirth.

Samyak charitra: Right conduct; one of the Three Jewels of Jain ethical conduct.

Samyak darshana: Right faith, or right perception; one of the Three Jewels of Jain ethical conduct.

Samyak jnana: Right knowledge; one of the Three Jewels of Jain ethical conduct.

Sanskrit: An ancient Indo-European language that is the language of Hinduism, as well as of much classical Indian literature.

Santería: The "way of the saints"; an African-based religion practiced primarily in Cuba and other Central and South American countries.

Santero: A practitioner of Santería.

saum: Fasting.

sect: A small religious group that has branched off from a larger established religion.

Sect (*Kyoha*) Shinto: Shinto as it is practiced by a number of sects, or groups, formed primarily in the nineteenth century.

secular: Worldly things, of the physical world, as opposed to religious and spiritual.

Sedreh-pushi: The Zoroastrian initiation rite.

Sephardic: Term used to refer to Jews of North Africa, the Middle East, Spain, and Portugal.

Shahadah: The Islamic declaration of faith. It consists of the words "*Ashahadu an la ilaha ill Allah wa ashahadu ann Muhammadar Rasulullah,*" or "I declare there is no god except God, and I declare that Muhammad is the Messenger of God."

shaman: In indigenous tribes, an intermediary between the gods and the tribal members; also one who controls various spiritual forces, can look into the future, and can cure the ill with magic.

shamanism: A term used generally to refer to indigenous religions that believe in an unseen spirit world that influences human affairs.

shariʾah: Islamic law.

Shiʾite: One of the main sects of Islam; from the phrase *Shiʾat Ali,* or the party of ʾAli.

Shinbutsu bunri: The separation of Shinto and Buddhism when Shinto was declared the official state religion.

Shinbutsu shugo: The combination of Shinto and Buddhism.

Shinto: Literally, "the way of the gods" or "the way of the kami."

Shiva: The destroyer god, embodying the erotic and sexual.

Shivaism: A major sect of Hinduism, which sees Shiva ("the Destroyer") as the central god.

Shrine (*Jinja*) Shinto: The traditional, mainstream practice of Shinto, with emphasis on the local shrine.

skepticism: Doubt or disbelief toward a particular proposition or object.

Skepticism: A philosophical system that doubted the possibility of ever discovering real truth through the senses.

Socratic: Having to do with the philosopher Socrates and his method of asking questions of students to develop an idea.

solstice: The points in the year when the day is longest (the summer solstice, generally on June 21) and the shortest (the winter solstice, generally on December 21).

Sophists: A group of traveling teachers in ancient Greece who doubted the possibility of knowing all the truth through the physical senses.

State Shinto: Shinto as it was practiced after it was declared the official state religion in the late nineteenth century until 1945.

Stoicism: The philosophical system that holds that people should pursue the knowledge of human and divine things through the use of logical systems. It also says that humans may not be able to control natural events, but that they can control the way they react to them.

stupas: Originally a mound marking the spot where the Buddha's ashes were buried. Rock pillars carved with the words of the Buddha are also sometimes called stupas.

Sufism: A trend in or way of practicing Islam; characterized by an ecstatic, trancelike mysticism.

Sunnah: The example of the prophet Muhammad, containing the *hadiths,* or sayings; provides guidance to everyday questions of faith and morality.

Sunni: The main sect of Islam.

supernatural: That which is beyond the observable world, including things relating to God or spirits.

supreme being: The central God responsible for creating the cosmos.

sura: Any chapter in the Qur'an.

Susano-o: The Shinto god of violence and the ruler of the oceans.

Svetambara: Literally, "white-clad"; one of the two main sects of Jainism.

swastika: A pictorial character that symbolizes the eternal nature of Brahma because it points in all directions; also used as the official emblem of the Nazi Party during World War II (1939–45).

T

takhts: Seats of spiritual authority in Sikhism. The "Five Takhts" are gurdwaras located in India.

Talmud: Traditions that explain and interpret the Torah.

Tanakh: The chief Jewish scripture; the Hebrew Bible.

tawba: Repentance.

theism: Belief in the existence of gods or God.

theocracy: A form of government in which God or some supreme deity is the ruler. God's laws are then interpreted by a divine king or by a priest class.

theology: The study of God and of religions truths.

Three Jewels: The Jain code of ethical conduct, consisting of right faith, right knowledge, and right conduct.

Tian: Heaven, or the principle of ordering the universe.

Tipitaka: The Buddhist sacred texts accepted by all branches of Buddhism.

tirthankara: Literally, "makers of the ford,"; those souls who have attained enlightenment and have been freed from the cycle of death and rebirth; the twenty-four leaders of Jainism.

Torah: The first five books of the Tanakh: Genesis, Exodus, Leviticus, Numbers, and Deuteronomy.

***tori*:** The gate that marks the entrance to a shrine. Its shape is regarded as a symbol of Shinto.

totem: Some sort of object or, perhaps, animal that assumes a spiritual symbolism for a clan or tribe.

transcendent: Going beyond the ordinary, beyond the universe and time, into spiritual dimensions.

Trinity: In Christianity, the union of the Father, Son, and Holy Spirit as three divine persons in one God.

Tsukiyomi: The Shinto moon-god and the ruler of night.

U

***ujiko*:** A "named child" whose name is entered at birth at the local Shinto shrine.

Upanishads: The core of Hindu philosophy; collections of texts, originally part of the Vedas, that explain such core Hindu beliefs as karma, reincarnation, nirvana, the soul, and Brahman.

urvan: The soul.

V

Vaishnavaism: A major sect of Hinduism, which sees Vishnu ("the Preserver") as the central god.

Vedas: The chief sacred scriptures of Hinduism; knowledge, wisdom, or vision.

Virgin Birth: The Christian belief that Jesus Christ was the Son of God and born of a virgin mother.

Vishnu: Also called Krishna; the preserver-god.

Vodou: An African-based religion practiced primarily in Haiti and in other Central and South American countries.

Vodouisant: An uninitiated practitioner of Vodou.

W

Wakan: The incomprehensibility of life and death for the Sioux.

Wakan tanka: The world's motivating force for the Sioux.

wen: The arts of music, poetry, and painting.

Wicca: The name of a neo-pagan religion that generally worships the God and the Goddess.

wu wei: Nonaction, or deliberate and thoughtful action that follows the Dao.

Y

Yahweh: One of the names for God in the Tanakh.

yazata: Guardian angel.

Yin and yang: Literally, "shady" and "sunny"; terms referring to how the universe is composed of opposing but complementary forces.

Yom Kippur: The Day of Atonement.

Z

zakat: Annual charitable giving.

ziggurat: A stepped foundation or structure that held a shrine or temple in the Mesopotamian religion.

Zionism: A movement that began in the nineteenth century to find a permanent home for Jews.

Creation Stories and Foundation Myths

Nearly every culture in the world has a creation myth. A creation myth is a story that explains the origins of the world, the creation of humans, and the relationship between a god or gods and humans. In these stories, the origins of the world are generally the act either of a single supreme being (in the case of monotheistic religions, which believe in a single god) or of a group of gods (in the case of polytheistic religions, which believe in more than one god). One noteworthy exception among major religions is Buddhism, whose scriptures, or holy writings, often refer to "beginningless time." This suggests that Buddhists do not believe in a single creation event or a single creator-god.

Foundation myths differ from creation myths in that they do not necessarily focus on the creation of the world, but they have many characteristics in common with creation myths. Foundation myths in some way define the cultures that produced them. As a foundation myth develops over time, it becomes a way for people to understand the nature of the world they live in and their place within that world. It provides support for the culture's way of viewing the world, in much the same way that the foundation of a house supports the structure.

These creation and foundational stories are often referred to as "myths," a word that implies something fanciful or untrue. Theologians (those who study religious beliefs and practices) and other scholars, however, use the word *myth* in a way that is not intended to dismiss a narrative as untrue. Rather, the word suggests a culture's specific way of explaining the world and its origins, expressed in terms that were understandable even to people in a culture with no written language. Used this way, *myth* connects more with "story," "narrative," or "explanation" than with "untruth." A myth expresses a deeper, more fundamental truth that actual facts do not always capture.

In the major monotheistic religions of Judaism, Christianity, and Islam, creation is seen as what theologians call *ex nihilo. Ex* means

An African Creation Story

Virtually every culture in the world has a creation story that explains how the world came about. The cultures of Africa present a rich collection of such stories. Here is one from the Fulani people of Mali.

> At the beginning there was a huge drop of milk
>
> Then Doondari (God) came and he created the stone.
>
> Then the stone created iron;
>
> And iron created fire;
>
> And fire created water;
>
> And water created air.
>
> The Doondari descended a second time. And he took the five elements
>
> And he shaped them into man.
>
> But man was proud.
>
> Then Doondari created blindness and blindness defeated man.
>
> But when blindness became too proud, Doondari created sleep, and sleep defeated blindness;
>
> But when sleep became too proud, Doondari created worry, and worry defeated sleep;
>
> But when worry became too proud, Doondari created death, and death defeated worry.
>
> But when death became too proud, Doondari descended for the third time,
>
> And he came as Gueno, the eternal one
>
> And Gueno defeated death.

"Unit Three: Exploring Africa through the Humanities. Module Fourteen: Religion in Africa." *Exploring Africa.* http://exploringafrica. matrix.msu.edu/curriculum/lm14/ creationstories.html.

"out of" and *nihilo* means "nothing." In other words, it is believed that nothing existed before God, who not only formed and structured the universe but also created from nothing the materials of which the universe is made. This process is seen as having occurred over a period of time, often expressed as "days." This reference of *day* is generally interpreted in symbolic terms to refer to some span of time. In the book of Genesis in the Christian and Judaic scriptures, for example, creation occurred in stages over a six-"day" period, with God resting on the seventh day. This is depicted in the Hebrew Bible, the **Tanakh (Hebrew Bible).** The creation account in the **Qur'an,** the scripture of Islam, is similar: "Allah is He Who created the heavens and the earth and what is between them in six periods." Allah is Islam's name for God.

Common themes

Despite the difference in creation myths throughout the world, they tend to have a number of elements or themes in common. The first of these elements is the idea of creation as a kind of birth, often from an egg. For example, in some versions of the Japanese Shinto religion's creation myth, contained in the sacred text called **Tales from the Kojiki,** the chaotic mass of elements that existed at the time of creation was in the shape of an egg. In Greek mythology, the god of love, Eros, emerged from an egg laid by the bird Nyx. The shell pieces became Gaia, the goddess of Earth, and Uranus, the god of the sky. The egg especially stands out in the creation myths of early Chinese Daoists, who told the story of a great cosmic egg from which the god Pangu emerged when the shell split. The top half of the shell became the sky, and the bottom half became Earth.

A second common theme found in creation myths is the concept that the universe has both a father and a mother. Again, in Greek mythology, Gaia and Uranus produced children, who in turn produced grandchildren, giving rise to plants, the stars, and other elements of creation. In the Shinto creation myth, Izanagi and Izanami gave birth to the islands of Japan and then gave birth to Amaterasu, the sun goddess, and Tsuki-Yumi, the moon god. Among the Aborigines of Australia, the Father of All Spirits awakened the Sun Mother and gave her instructions for waking the spirits and giving them life and form. She repeatedly tried to follow his instructions, but when she returned to the Father, he told her to do more, until he was finally pleased with her work. Similarly, Wiccans worship a god and a goddess, masculine and feminine principles of creation and renewal.

Common to most creation myths is the notion of a supreme being. The creation accounts of Judaism, Christianity, and Islam see a single supreme god as responsible for all creation. Similarly, Zoroastrianism attributes creation to its supreme deity, Ahura Mazda; the ancient Babylonians to Marduk; and Hindus to Krishna, the "cause of all causes." Interestingly, while the Church of Christ of Latter-day Saints (also known as Mormons) is Christian, its followers believe that the physical universe is eternal, so it was not created by a supreme being; God, however, organized and arranged the physical universe in the act of creation.

Yet another theme that runs through the world's creation myths is the question of whether creation took place from above or below. In Shinto, for example, creation took place from above, in a world beyond the clouds. In the Sioux foundational myth relayed in **Black Elk Speaks,** a record of the tales told by a holy man of the Oglala Lakota Sioux, Black Elk narrates a vision of a cloud world where he encounters the Six Grandfathers who empower him. In contrast, the creation and foundational myths of the Bushmen of Africa and of the Hopi Indians of North America both depict creation as occurring from below. The Bushmen, for example, believe that in times past people and animals lived below Earth but that the god Kaang planned a place of happiness for them on Earth's surface. He planted a large tree with branches that spread over Earth and then dug a large hole through which people climbed to the surface. The Hopi believe that they climbed a pine tree to reach the world's surface, to escape an unbearable world below. They also believe that life on Earth may be part of an ongoing process of climbing to achieve yet a better world.

A related theme is that of the "diver" myth, which sees creation as somehow having been pulled out from chaos or muck. In Shinto, for example, the gods Izanagi and Izanami dipped a spear into the muck and pulled it out. The drops that fell from the spear became the Japanese islands. Similarly, the Iroquois believe that a Sky Woman fell to Earth, which was covered by water. After the water animals seized her and took her to the bottom, she brought up mud, which she spread on the back of a turtle and which grew into the North American continent.

Creation without a god

Of course, not all people believe in a god or gods. Some people, called atheists, do not believe in a god at all. Others, called agnostics, say that they are not sure whether a god exists. Agnostics typically argue that no concrete evidence proves that there is a god who created the world. Thomas Henry Huxley, a nineteenth-century British biologist, is an example of a prominent intellectual (a person who engages in study, reflection, or contemplation) who was an agnostic, a term he himself coined. A biologist studies the processes of plant and animal life. In his essay "**Agnosticism and Christianity**," he argues his position that "it is wrong for a man to say that he is certain of the objective truth of any proposition unless he can produce evidence which logically justifies that certainty." In Huxley's view, there simply is no evidence that supports the existence of a creator-god.

During the nineteenth century, many scientists were studying geology and other branches of science that indicated that evolution, not creation, was the driving force behind the creation of the world and of humankind. Evolution is the theory that living beings evolved, or changed, over time to take on the forms we know today. This contrasts with the belief that God created all beings. Perhaps because he was a biologist, Huxley viewed issues involving creation, the soul, the afterlife, and other religious concepts from the standpoint of a scientist rather than a believer.

All these creation and foundational myths represent an effort on the part of the cultures that produce them to find a link between the present and the past, including the past of their ancestors. It is a part of being human for people to question where they came from and where they are going. Creation and foundational myths attempt to answer these questions in ways that reflect the cultural realities of a people at a given time and in a given place. Even science shares this wonder.

Tanakh (Hebrew Bible)

"Bereshit—Genesis," from the The Holy Scriptures,
available online from the Jewish Virtual Library at
http://www.jewishvirtuallibrary.org/jsource/Bible/Genesistoc.html
Written in about the first century BCE
Published in 1917 by the Jewish Publication Society

"IN THE beginning G-d created the heaven and the earth."

Non-Jews use the word *Bible* to refer to the Judeo-Christian scriptures, and Christians divide it into the Old and New Testaments. Jews, however, refer to their sacred scripture as Tanakh. This word comes from the Hebrew letters used to refer to its three parts. The first part is the Torah, which comprises five books: Genesis, Exodus, Leviticus, Numbers, and Deuteronomy. The second is called Nevi'im, or Prophets, and includes twenty-one books, such as I Kings, II Kings, Isaiah, Jeremiah, and others. The third is called Ketuvim, or Writings, and consists of a number of the more "literary" or story-like books, including Psalms, Proverbs, Ecclesiastes, and others. The Tanakh is also referred to as the Hebrew Bible. For Christians, the Hebrew Bible is the Old Testament.

The epic story of creation is contained in the first book of the Hebrew Bible. This book, consisting of fifty chapters, is generally called Genesis, but in the Hebrew tradition it is called Bereshit (sometimes spelled Bereishit; pronounced Buh-RAY-sheet). This word means "in the beginning" and is taken from the book's opening words: *Bereshit Bara Elokim Et Hashamayim Veet Haaretz,* meaning "In the beginning God created heaven and earth."

The account of the creation of the world and of human beings is detailed in the first two chapters of Genesis, ending with the fourth verse of chapter 2. In vivid, simple language, it tells of the creation of

The Jewish Shabbat

Central to the Jewish tradition is Shabbat, the source of the English word *Sabbath*. While usually the word is interpreted as "rest," it comes from a Hebrew word meaning something closer to "cease" and is typically interpreted to mean "cease working," just as God ceased his creative activity. Shabbat commemorates God's "resting" on the seventh day after six days of creation. It is the only Jewish holiday mentioned in the Old Testament. Indeed, the seventh day of creation is regarded as the first celebration of Shabbat, and the obligation to celebrate Shabbat is one of the Ten Commandments.

In strict Jewish tradition, Jews are obligated to honor Shabbat by not engaging in any creative activity, or any activity that somehow affects or changes the environment. For example, writing would be considered a violation of Shabbat. In modern life, however, many Jews have modified their interpretation of activities that would be a violation of Shabbat; thus, creative writing might be considered a "leisure" activity that would add to the holiness of Shabbat.

Shabbat begins at sundown on Friday, when the new day is thought to begin, and continues until sundown on Saturday, when the day ends. Christianity moved its Sabbath to Sunday as part of its break with Jewish traditions. This order was made by the Church Council of Laodicea in 364 CE.

light and darkness on day one; of the firmament (the sky) on day two; of the seas and dry land as well as plants and trees on day three; of the sun, moon, stars, seasons, day, and years on day four; of sea creatures and birds on day five; and of land animals and man on day six. On the seventh day, God rested.

The creation story contains a number of important principles that survive in the Judeo-Christian tradition. First, Judaism believes in a creator-god, who made all there is. Second, the story of creation emphasizes that all God created was good. Third, the greatest of all God's creations was humankind. Fourth, humans are distinguished from all other creatures because they are made in God's likeness—they have the potential to achieve God's goodness and creative energy—and because they have "dominion" over the rest of God's creatures, that is, they have control over their environment. Finally, the pattern of six days of work followed by a day of rest formed the pattern for working life throughout the history of the Western world.

Things to remember while reading the excerpt from the Tanakh (Hebrew Bible):

- The account of creation in Genesis establishes Judaism as possibly the world's first monotheistic religion, though historians of religion continue to debate this question. Monotheism (*mono-*, meaning "one") refers to the concept of a single creator-god.

- It is conventional to number the chapters and verses of the Jewish scripture as well as the Christian New Testament. Thus, the first line of the excerpt would be referred to as Genesis 1:1, meaning Genesis, chapter 1, verse 1. The verse numbers generally, but not always, correspond to a single sentence. The numbering of verses is standard, so that readers of any edition of the Bible can find chapters and verses without having to refer to differing page numbers.

- In the excerpt from Genesis, the name "God" is written "G-d." Omitting letters from God's name is a common practice in Jewish tradition out of a concern that the written name of God could be defaced or erased or that the document could be destroyed. Accordingly, Jews avoid writing the complete name of God, often writing G-d or YHVH or YHWH rather than Yahweh. Modern-day rabbis have had to deal with the emergence of the computer and the fact that God's name can be deleted from a computer text. They have determined that this is not an "erasure" or "defacement," because a computer text has no permanence.

- The "days" mentioned in the creation account in Genesis are generally not regarded as literal twenty-four-hour days. Jewish tradition accepts the idea that notions of time are relative and that the word *day* was used because it would be simple to understand. The use of day, then is not inconsistent with modern scientific views that Earth was formed over a period of millions of years.

• • •

Excerpt from the Holy Scriptures

Genesis: Chapter 1

1 IN THE beginning G-d created the heaven and the earth.

2 Now the earth was unformed and **void,** and darkness was upon the face of the deep; and the spirit of G-d hovered over the face of the waters.

Void: Empty.

3 And G-d said: "Let there be light" And there was light.

4 And G-d saw the light, that it was good; and G-d divided the light from the darkness.

5 And G-d called the light Day, and the darkness He called Night And there was evening and there was morning, one day.

6 And G-d said: "Let there be a **firmament** in the midst of the waters, and let it divide the waters from the waters."

Firmament: The sky, the heavens.

7 And G-d made the firmament, and divided the waters which were under the firmament from the waters which were above the firmament; and it was so.

8 And G-d called the firmament Heaven. And there was evening and there was morning, a second day.

9 And G-d said: "Let the waters under the heaven be gathered together unto one place, and let the dry land appear." And it was so.

10 And G-d called the dry land Earth, and the gathering together of the waters called He Seas; and G-d saw that it was good.

11 And G-d said: "Let the earth put forth grass, herb yielding seed, and fruit-tree bearing fruit after its kind, wherein is the seed thereof, upon the earth." And it was so.

12 And the earth brought forth grass, herb yielding seed after its kind, and tree bearing fruit, wherein is the seed thereof, after its kind; and G-d saw that it was good.

13 And there was evening and there was morning, a third day.

14 And G-d said: "Let there be lights in the firmament of the heaven to divide the day from the night; and let them be for signs, and for seasons, and for days and years;

15 and let them be for lights in the firmament of the heaven to give light upon the earth." And it was so.

16 And G-d made the two great lights: the greater light to rule the day, and the lesser light to rule the night; and the stars.

17 And G-d set them in the firmament of the heaven to give light upon the earth,

18 and to rule over the day and over the night, and to divide the light from the darkness; and G-d saw that it was good.

19 And there was evening and there was morning, a fourth day.

20 And G-d said: "Let the waters swarm with swarms of living creatures, and let **fowl** fly above the earth in the open firmament of heaven."

Fowl: Birds, especially game birds.

21 And G-d created the great sea-monsters, and every living creature that creepeth, wherewith the waters swarmed, after its kind, and every winged fowl after its kind; and G-d saw that it was good.

22 And G-d blessed them, saying: "Be fruitful, and multiply, and fill the waters in the seas, and let fowl multiply in the earth."

23 And there was evening and there was morning, a fifth day.

24 And G-d said: "Let the earth bring forth the living creature after its kind, cattle, and creeping thing, and beast of the earth after its kind." And it was so.

25 And G-d made the beast of the earth after its kind, and the cattle after their kind, and every thing that creepeth upon the ground after its kind; and G-d saw that it was good.

In the creation story of the Tanakh, God rested on the seventh day. Jews rest on this day, called Shabbat, to follow God's model and devote their time to Him. © DAVID H. WELLS/CORBIS.

26 And G-d said: "Let us make man in our image, after our likeness; and let them have dominion over the fish of the sea, and over the fowl of the air, and over the cattle, and over all the earth, and over every creeping thing that creepeth upon the earth."

27 And G-d created man in His own image, in the image of G-d created He him; male and female created He them.

28 And G-d blessed them; and G-d said unto them: "Be fruitful, and multiply, and **replenish** the earth, and **subdue** it; and have dominion over the fish of the sea, and over the fowl of the air, and over every living thing that creepeth upon the earth."

Replenish: To fill up or to restore a supply.

Subdue: To bring under control.

29 And G-d said: "Behold, I have given you every herb yielding seed, which is upon the face of all the earth, and every tree, in which is the fruit of a tree yielding seed—to you it shall be for food;

30 and to every beast of the earth, and to every fowl of the air, and to every thing that creepeth upon the earth, wherein there is a living soul, I have given every green herb for food." And it was so.

31 And G-d saw every thing that He had made, and, behold, it was very good. And there was evening and there was morning, the sixth day.

Genesis: Chapter 2

Host: A large number.

1 And the heaven and the earth were finished, and all the **host** of them.

2 And on the seventh day G-d finished His work which He had made; and He rested on the seventh day from all His work which He had made.

Hallowed: Made holy.

3 And G-d blessed the seventh day, and **hallowed** it; because that in it He rested from all His work which G-d in creating had made.

4 These are the generations of the heaven and of the earth when they were created, in the day that **HaShem** G-d made earth and heaven.

HaShem: Literally, "the name," or another name for the Lord God.

• • •

What happened next . . .

The book of Genesis contains many of the most famous stories from the Tanakh. These stories remain important parts of the cultural heritage of the West. The first eleven chapters recount the general history of humankind over a period of thousands of years. They begin with creation of the physical world and go on to the creation of humans. After chapter 11, the emphasis in Genesis begins to change. Instead of focusing on all of humankind, Genesis concentrates on major individuals. With Abraham, the founder of Judaism, and his descendants, God hoped to renew the world through his chosen people, the Jews.

Genesis contains at least four important themes in Jewish history. The first is the concept of election, or the belief that God chooses special people to carry out his work on Earth. Thus, the Jewish people, and Christians as well, see Abraham as the founder of the Jewish nation. The second major theme is the concept of covenant. This refers to agreements between God and human beings, such as God's promise never to send another flood. This sense of covenant governed all human relationships and made both moral and ritual demands on the Jewish people.

The third theme is law. The best example is the Ten Commandments, but the Torah (the first five books of the Hebrew Bible) contains other examples of laws. All are based on the belief in one supreme God and humankind's covenants with Him. The final theme is exodus, the most prominent example of which is contained in the second book of the Torah, titled Exodus (or Shemot). The escape of Jews from bondage in Egypt and their return to the Promised Land (the land of Canaan, now Israel) is a key event in Jewish history. This event is still remembered in the yearly feast of Passover.

Did you know . . .

- Traditionally, it was believed that Moses was the author of Genesis, but modern biblical scholarship has determined that the book's authorship is unknown. For centuries, the oldest manuscripts of Genesis, and of the other books of the Hebrew Bible, dated to the ninth century. Then, in 1947, the Dead Sea Scrolls, which include the books of the Hebrew Bible, were discovered by a shepherd boy in a cave near Qumran, Israel, near the northwestern coast of the Dead Sea. These scrolls were hidden by members of the clergy to protect them from invading Romans. With the discovery of the Dead Sea Scrolls, the earliest manuscript versions of the Hebrew Bible known to survive now date to the first century BCE.

- The creation account of Genesis is similar to the creation stories told in numerous other cultures. Many folk stories worldwide feature a creator-god who creates the world by divine command and forms the human being in his image from clay. One remarkably similar account is the Babylonian Genesis, written late in the second millennium BCE in honor of the god Marduk. The Babylonian epic Atrakhasis also contains elements strikingly similar to events in Genesis.

Consider the following . . .

- Some religions view the physical universe as eternal. Summarize ways in which Genesis provides a different view of the physical universe.
- Explain the sequence of creation, as outlined in Genesis.
- Explain what Genesis means when it says that God gave humans "dominion" over the rest of creation.

For More Information

BOOKS

Alter, Robert, ed. *Genesis: Translation and Commentary*. Rev. ed. New York: Norton, 1997.

"Bereshit—Genesis." In *The Holy Scriptures*. Philadelphia: Jewish Publication Society, 1917. This excerpt can also be found online at http://www.jewishvirtuallibrary.org/jsource/Bible/Genesistoc.html.

Brodie, Thomas L. *Genesis as Dialogue: A Literary, Historical, and Theological Commentary*. New York: Oxford University Press, 2001.

Sarna, Nahum M. *Understanding Genesis: The World of the Bible in the Light of History*. New York: Schocken, 1966.

Tov, Emmanuel. *Textual Criticism of the Hebrew Bible*. 2nd ed. London and New York: Augsburg Fortress, 2001.

WEB SITES

"Genesis." *The Hebrew Bible in English. Mechon Mamre*. http://www.mechon-mamre.org/e/et/et0.htm (accessed on June 5, 2006).

Jacob, Benno, and Emil G. Hirsch. "Genesis: The Book of." *JewishEncyclopedia.com*. http://www.jewishencyclopedia.com/view.jsp?artid=137&letter=G&search=Genesis (accessed on June 5, 2006).

Tales from the Kojiki

"Japanese Creation Myth," from Tales from the Kojiki,
in Reading about the World, *available online at*
http://www.wsu.edu:8080/~wldciv/world_civ_reader/world_civ_reader_1/kojiki.html
Kojiki compiled by O No Yasumaro in the eighth century
Book by Genji Shibukawa
Translated by Yaichiro Isobe
Published in 1999 by Harcourt Brace Custom Publishing

> "Before the heavens and the earth came into existence, all was a chaos, unimaginably limitless and without definite shape or form."

The Kojiki, an eighth-century Shinto text, is the earliest surviving document written by the Japanese. Shinto is a native Japanese religion that focuses on the worship of natural spirits called *kami*. Until the end of World War II in 1945, Shinto was the state religion of Japan. Part holy text, part history, and part folktale (a story passed on through oral traditions, usually containing a timeless truth, custom, or belief) and myth, it represents an effort to document much of the history of early Japan. It also contains an account of the creation of the world, one that in many respects is similar to creation accounts contained in the scriptures, or holy texts, of other world religions.

Kojiki means "Record of Ancient Matters." The book consists of 180 sections. The first third gives an account of the creation of the world (and of the Japanese islands, in particular), the birth of the gods and goddesses, and the descent of the gods and goddesses to Japan. The remaining sections list the line of succession of the Japanese emperors, linking these emperors to the gods and goddesses. These sections also record taboos (social or religious bans or restrictions), rituals, and ceremonies that were important to Shinto. Over the centuries, the Kojiki has become an important part of Japanese/Shinto mythology and helps define the Japanese worldview.

The Shinto creation story relates the activities of Izanagi and Izanami, a god and goddess who created the Japanese islands out of chaos, a state of disorder or formlessness. Shinto recognizes both a male and a female principle, or element, in creation. This is in contrast to religions such as Christianity and Judaism, which see creation as the work of a male god alone. The story notes, however, that because Izanami spoke ahead of her husband at their wedding ceremony, the ceremony had to be repeated so that the male god was given priority over the female goddess. This male prominence is an important feature of historic Japanese culture and can still be found in the twenty-first century. The islands of Japan were seen as the god and goddess's children. So, too, were the kami, especially the spirits that ruled the islands. Later, the two gods produced additional gods, including Kagutsuchi, the fire god. The creation story goes on to recount Izanami's death and Izanagi's pursuit of her to the underworld, or the Nether Regions.

The creation account of the Kojiki contains a number of elements that are important to Japanese culture. The chief one is the concept of the "world." While people who practice Shinto can be found worldwide, Shinto is truly a Japanese religion. In this way it differs from religions such as Christianity, which is not identified with any particular culture or country. In order to understand why Shinto is so uniquely Japanese, it is necessary to understand the history of the Kojiki's composition.

The Kojiki is as much a political document as it is a holy work. During the seventh century Japan was greatly influenced by its much larger neighbor, China, and many elements of Japanese culture reflect this influence. The Chinese had been thorough and careful about recording their history. Under their influence Japanese writers began to do the same, although none of their works from the seventh century survive.

Then, in 673, the emperor Tenmu seized the throne of Japan. Tenmu ordered a history compiled, similar to the kinds of histories produced in China. He believed that the records of many of his courtiers (attendants), imperial officials, and the chief families in the realm had been either misrepresented or changed. His goal was to produce a history that would justify his rule by showing that he was a descendant of the gods. He commissioned a court reciter, Hieda no Are, to begin memorizing a family tree and a collection of stories. Hieda no Are was the perfect person for the job, for he had a flawless memory. He could recite with complete accuracy any written text that he had looked at once.

Tenmu died in 686. For years the family histories and stories that Hieda no Are had compiled existed solely in the court reciter's memory. Finally in 712, during the reign of the empress Genmei, the material that Hieda no Are had memorized was compiled and written down by O No Yasumaro. Those stories formed the basis of the Kojiki. In 720 a second text, called the Nihonshoki, containing more stories that Hieda no Are had memorized, was also written down. These two books are the earliest surviving texts of any kind written by the Japanese.

The Kojiki was written partly to prove that the Japanese emperor was divine and partly to assert the superiority of Japanese culture. For this reason the Kojiki's concept of "the world" was limited to the Japanese islands. When Izanagi and Izanami create "the world," their creation was only the islands of Japan, not the rest of the world. In this respect, though, the creation account of the Kojiki is like those of other cultures in the world. The seventh-century Japanese people only knew their own home regions well. They had little contact with people from other islands or other regions. It was natural that, in their view, "the world" was their homeland and that "the people" were their neighbors.

Japan's geography helps explain some of the creation elements found in the Kojiki. Japan is an island nation, and much of its land is dominated by mountains. The sea cuts the many islands of Japan off from the rest of the world. So the story of creation told in the Kojiki takes place on a high plain, lifted above the surrounding oceans.

Shinto Kami

Shinto believes in *kami*, a word usually translated as "divinities" or "gods." Trying to define kami is difficult, however. They include not only the original creator-gods but also a host of lesser gods that, in turn, can include the spirits of ancestors and natural forces.

The origins of kami can be found in early Japanese history. Japanese society was divided into separate clans. Each of these clans was headed by a chieftain, and each clan worshipped a kami. Part of the chieftain's job was to oversee the ceremonies devoted to the kami. When one clan overran another, the kami of the defeated clan became subject to that of the conquering clan. In this way the hierarchy (classification of a group according to rank) of the kami was shifted about. Later, when the Japanese began to form a centralized government with a supreme emperor at its head, this belief helped support the emperor's authority. Because the emperor descended directly from Amaterasu, the sun goddess, the emperor's clan was more powerful than any other clan and thus possessed the right to rule Japan.

According to Shinto belief, because the world is the creation of Amaterasu, all things are part of her divinity. A better translation of the word kami would be "the sacredness in things" or even "life forces." The kami include ancestral spirits, social organization, and the natural forces that control disease and health, death and life, the stars and planets, and the physical world. Kami represent the Shinto view that the world is basically sacred and anything can be the object of worship.

Things to remember while reading the excerpt from Tales from the Kojiki:

- Despite the fact that Shinto defines the Japanese character, it has been heavily influenced by cultures from the Asian mainland. Shinto originated among the peoples of Korea and Mongolia and was exported to Japan by immigrants. In the eighth century early Shinto absorbed many influences from China, including other religions, such as Buddhism and Daoism.

- Izanagi and Izanami are regarded in the Kojiki as having introduced death to the world. In giving birth to the fire god, Izanami is severely burned and dies. She leaves her husband, Izanagi, lonely in the world, so he searches for her in Hades, or the land of the dead, where she is horribly deformed. The Shinto concept of death, however, is that one's spirit goes to a realm that is little different from this life. The afterlife is seen as neither a heaven nor a hell. In contrast to such religions as Islam and Christianity, Shinto places most of its emphasis on happiness in this life. There is little emphasis on preparing for a life after death.

Eon: A period of time equal to a thousand million years or, simply, an extremely long time.

Materialized: Took physical shape.

Opaque: Preventing the passage of light, not transparent.

Precipitated: Condensed into solid form.

Medusa-like: Similar to Medusa, a female monster in Greek mythology who had living snakes for hair.

Succession: A sequence in which one thing directly follows another.

Bade: Instructed, ordered.

Nebulous: Hazy or blurred, not clearly defined.

Consolidate: To combine into a whole, to unify.

Terra firma: Solid earth.

• • •

Excerpt from Tales from the Kojiki

The Beginning of the World

Before the heavens and the earth came into existence, all was a chaos, unimaginably limitless and without definite shape or form. **Eon** followed eon: then, lo! out of this boundless, shapeless mass something light and transparent rose up and formed the heaven. This was the Plain of High Heaven, in which **materialized** a deity called Ame-no-Minaka-Nushi-no-Mikoto (the Deity-of-the-August-Center-of-Heaven)....

In the meantime what was heavy and **opaque** in the void gradually **precipitated** and became the earth, but it had taken an immeasurably long time before it condensed sufficiently to form solid ground. In its earliest stages, for millions and millions of years, the earth may be said to have resembled oil floating, **medusa-like,** upon the face of the waters....

Many gods were thus born in **succession,** and so they increased in number, but as long as the world remained in a chaotic state, there was nothing for them to do. Whereupon, all the Heavenly deities summoned the two divine beings, Izanagi and Izanami, and **bade** them descend to the **nebulous** place, and by helping each other, to **consolidate** it into **terra firma.** "We bestow on you," they said, "this precious treasure, with which to rule the land, the creation of which we command you to perform." So saying they handed them a spear called Ama-no-Nuboko, **embellished** with costly gems. The divine couple received respectfully and ceremoniously the sacred weapon and then withdrew from the presence of the Deities, ready to perform their **august commission.** Proceeding **forthwith** to the Floating Bridge of Heaven, which lay between the heaven and the earth, they stood awhile to gaze on that which lay below. What they **beheld** was a world not yet condensed, but looking like a sea of filmy fog floating to and fro in the air, exhaling the **while** an inexpressibly fragrant odor. They were, at first, **perplexed** just how and where to start, but at length Izanagi suggested to his companion that they should try the effect of stirring up the **brine** with their spear. So saying he pushed down the jeweled shaft and found that it touched something. Then drawing it up, he examined it and observed that the great drops which fell from it almost immediately **coagulated** into an island, which is, to this day, the Island of Onokoro. Delighted at the result, the two deities descended forthwith from the Floating Bridge to reach the miraculously created island. In this island they **thenceforth** dwelt and made it the basis of their subsequent task of creating a country. Then wishing to become **espoused,** they erected in the center of the island a pillar, the Heavenly August Pillar, and built around it a great palace called the Hall of Eight Fathoms. Thereupon the male Deity turning to the left and the female Deity to the right, each went round the pillar in opposite directions. When they again met each other on the further side of the pillar, Izanami, the female Deity, speaking first, exclaimed: "How delightful it is to meet so handsome a youth!" To which Izanagi, the male Deity, replied: "How delightful I am to have fallen in with such a lovely maiden!" After having spoken thus, the male Deity said that it was not in order that woman should anticipate man in a greeting. Nevertheless, they fell into **connubial** relationship, having been instructed by two **wagtails** which flew to the spot. Presently the Goddess bore her divine **consort** a son, but the baby was weak and boneless as a **leech.** Disgusted with it, they abandoned it on the waters, putting it in a boat made of reeds. Their second offspring was as disappointing as the first. The two Deities, now sorely disappointed at their failure and full of **misgivings,** ascended to Heaven to inquire of the Heavenly Deities the causes of their misfortunes. The latter performed the ceremony of **divining** and said to them: "It is the woman's fault. In turning round the Pillar, it was not right and proper that the female Deity should in speaking have taken **precedence** of the male. That is the reason." The two Deities saw the truth of this divine suggestion, and made up their minds to **rectify** the error. So, returning to the earth again, they went once more around the Heavenly Pillar. This time Izanagi spoke first saying: "How delightful to meet so beautiful a maiden!"

Bestow: Give.

Embellished: Decorated.

August: Very important.

Commission: A task, a duty to perform a specific piece of work.

Forthwith: Immediately.

Beheld: Saw.

While: A certain length of time.

Perplexed: Puzzled, confused.

Brine: Water with salt in it.

Coagulated Changed from a liquid into a thicker substance.

Thenceforth: From that time onward.

Espoused: Married.

Connubial: Relating to marriage.

Wagtails: A kind of songbird with a long tail.

Consort: A spouse, a husband or a wife.

Leech: A bloodsucking worm.

Misgivings: Doubts or uneasiness.

Divining: Predicting the future through mystical or supernatural knowledge.

Precedence: Priority or superiority in rank or position.

Rectify: To correct.

Izanami and Izanagi stand on the Floating Bridge of Heaven as they prepare to dip their spear into the brine and pull out the island of Onokoro.
© PETER HARHOLDT/CORBIS.

"How happy I am," responded Izanami, "that I should meet such a handsome youth!" This process was more appropriate and in accordance with the law of nature. After this, all the children born to them left nothing to be desired. First, the island of Awaji was born, next, Shikoku, then, the island of Oki, followed by Kyushu; after that, the island Tsushima came into being, and lastly, Honshu, the main island of Japan. The name of Oyashi-ma-kuni... was given to these... islands. After this, the two Deities became the parents of numerous smaller islands destined to surround the larger ones.

The Birth of the Deities

Begetting: Giving birth to.

Preside: Rule.

Procreation: Having children.

Befell: Happened to.

Having, thus, made a country from what had formerly been no more than a mere floating mass, the two Deities, Izanagi and Izanami, [set] about **begetting** those deities destined to **preside** over the land, sea, mountains, rivers, trees, and herbs....

The process of **procreation** had, so far, gone on happily, but at the birth of Kagutsuchi-no-Kami, the deity of fire, an unseen misfortune **befell** the divine mother, Izanami. During the course of her **confinement,** the goddess was so severely burned by the flaming child that she **swooned** away. Her divine consort, deeply alarmed, did all in his power to **resuscitate** her, but although he succeeded in restoring her to consciousness, her appetite had completely gone. . . . Her **demise** marks the **intrusion** of death into the world. Similarly the **corruption** of her body and the grief **occasioned** by her death were each the first of their kind.

By the death of his faithful spouse Izanagi was now quite alone in the world. In conjunction with her, and in accordance with the instructions of the Heavenly Gods, he had created and consolidated the Island Empire of Japan. In the fulfillment of their divine mission, he and his heavenly spouse had lived an ideal life of mutual love and cooperation. It is only natural, therefore, that her death should have dealt him a truly **mortal** blow.

. . . In a fit of uncontrollable grief, he stood sobbing at the head of the **bier.** . . . Meanwhile Izanami, for whom her divine husband pined so bitterly, had **quitted** this world for good and all and gone to the Land of Hades.

Izanagi's Visit to the Land of Hades

. . . Unable any longer to bear his grief, he resolved to go down to the Nether Regions in order to seek for Izanami and bring her back, at all costs, to the world. He started on his long and **dubious** journey. . . . Far ahead of him, he **espied** a large castle. "That, no doubt," he **mused** in delight, "may be where she resides."

Summoning up all his courage, he approached the main entrance of the castle. Here he saw a number of gigantic demons, some red, some black, guarding the gates with watchful eyes. He retraced his steps in alarm, and stole round to a gate at the rear of the castle. He found, to his great joy, that it was apparently left unwatched. He crept **warily** through the gate and peered into the interior of the castle, when he immediately caught sight of his wife standing at the gate at an inner court. The delighted Deity loudly called her name. "Why! There is some one calling me," sighed Izanami-no-Mikoto, and raising her beautiful head, she looked around her. What was her amazement but to see her beloved husband standing by the gate and gazing at her intently! He had, in fact, been in her thoughts no less constantly than she in his. With a heart leaping with joy, she approached him. He grasped her hands tenderly and murmured in deep and earnest tones: "My darling, I have come to take thee back to the world. Come back, I pray thee, and let us complete our work of creation in accordance with the will of the Heavenly Gods—our work which was left only half accomplished by thy departure. How can I do this work without thee? Thy loss means to me the loss of all." This appeal came from the depth of his heart.

Confinement: The period before, during, and just after childbirth.

Swooned: Fainted.

Resuscitate: To revive or bring back from the brink of death.

Demise: Death.

Intrusion: An unwelcome entrance or presence.

Corruption: The state of being ruined or made rotten.

Occasioned: Caused.

Mortal: Powerful, severe.

Bier: A stand on which a coffin is placed.

Quitted: Left.

Dubious: Uncertain.

Espied: Caught sight of.

Mused: Thought.

Summoning up: Calling upon.

Warily: Cautiously.

The goddess sympathized with him most deeply, but answered with tender grief: "Alas! Thou hast come too late. I have already eaten of the furnace of Hades. Having once eaten the things of this land, it is impossible for me to come back to the world." So saying, she lowered her head in deep despair.

Entreat: Plead with, beg.

"Nay, I must **entreat** thee to come back. Canst not thou find some means by which this can be accomplished?" exclaimed her husband, drawing nearer to her. After some reflection, she replied: "Thou hast come a very, very long way for my sake. How much I appreciate thy devotion! I wish, with all my heart, to go back with thee, but before I can do so, I must first obtain the permission of the deities of Hades. Wait here till my return, but remember that thou must not on any account look inside the castle in the meantime." "I swear I will do as thou **biddest**," **quoth** Izanagi, "but **tarry** not in thy quest." With **implicit** confidence in her husband's pledge, the goddess disappeared into the castle.

Biddest: Ask, request.

Quoth: Said.

Tarry: Delay.

Implicit: Unspoken but understood.

Injunction: Command or ban.

Waned: Faded.

Uncanny: Mysterious, creepy.

Apprehension: Fear, dread.

Ghastly: Horrible, frightening.

Naught: Nothing.

For sooth: Indeed, truly.

Perfidy: Betrayal.

Izanagi observed strictly her **injunction.** He remained where he stood, and waited impatiently for his wife's return. Probably to his impatient mind, a single heart-beat may have seemed an age. He waited and waited, but no shadow of his wife appeared. The day gradually wore on and **waned** away, darkness was about to fall, and a strange unearthly wind began to strike his face. Brave as he was, he was seized with an **uncanny** feeling of **apprehension.** Forgetting the vow he had made to the goddess, he broke off one of the teeth of the comb which he was wearing in the left bunch of his hair, and having lighted it, he crept in softly and glanced around him. To his horror he found Izanagi lying dead in a room: and lo! a **ghastly** change had come over her. She, who had been so dazzlingly beautiful, was now become **naught** but a rotting corpse, in an advanced stage of decomposition. . . . The sound he made awakened Izanami from her death-like slumber. **"For sooth!"** she cried: "he must have seen me in this revolting state. He has put me to shame and has broken his solemn vow. Unfaithful wretch! I'll make him suffer, for his **perfidy.**"

Then turning to the Hags of Hades, who attended her, she commanded them to give chase to him. At her word, an army of female demons ran after the Deity.

• • •

What happened next . . .

Izanagi, pursued by the demons and by Izanami herself, fled. The two stood face to face at the entrance to the underworld, where they agreed to divorce. They decided that Izanagi would rule the realm of the living and that Izanami would rule that of the dead. After Izanagi returned to

Earth, he bathed in a stream, where he purified himself. Out of his eyes and nose, three major deities emerged: Amaterasu, the sun goddess and ruler of heaven; Tsuki-Yumi, the moon god and ruler of night; and Sus-ano-o, the god of violence and ruler of the ocean. Afterward, Izanagi returned to heaven and remained there. Izanami continued to rule over the underworld.

Did you know...

- In the Nihonshoki, the other major Shinto text from this era, the creation story is told again. In this version, however, some of the elements that reflect poorly on Izanami are not included. She does not corrupt the original wedding ceremony, nor is she banished to the underworld. This version of the story never became as popular as the version in the Kojiki.

- The story of the journey to the underworld is remarkably similar to a story told in Greek mythology. Like Izanagi, the Greek god Orpheus also made the mistake of looking at his mate against her wishes when he sought her in the underworld. Izanami made an error similar to that of the Greek goddess Persephone by eating the food of the underworld, forcing her to remain in the world of the dead.

- Records from the tenth century show that several shrines were built to Izanagi and Izanami in the Kinki area of Japan, an area that encompasses the cities of Kyoto, Osaka, and Kobe. Later, the Taga shrine was built for the worship of Izanagi in Omi, which is now the Shiga prefecture, or district, and this shrine be-came the most popular place for worshipping the couple.

Consider the following...

- Explain the view of divinities that emerges from the Kojiki. Note, for example, how they are similar to or different from people.

- Discuss how and why it would have been important to Japanese rulers during this period to encourage a myth that equates the cre-ation of the world with the creation of Japan.

- The Kojiki has been described as being as much folklore as it is scripture. In other words, it is a collection of stories that were passed along orally and developed over time. Other scriptures, such as the Islamic Qur'an, are seen not as cultural stories but as the direct revelation of God to one of his prophets. Explain how the excerpt can be seen as either a story or as a scripture.

For More Information

BOOKS

Chamberlain, Basil Hall. *Kojiki: Records of Ancient Matters.* Reissued ed. North Clarendon, VT: Tuttle Publishing, 2005.

Davis, F. Hadland. *Myths and Legends of Japan.* New York: Dover, 1992.

Philippi, Donald L., trans. *Kojiki.* Tokyo: University of Tokyo Press, 1982.

Shibukawa, Genji. *Tales from the Kojiki.* Translated by Yaichiro Isobe. In *Reading about the World,* vol. 1. Edited by Paul Brians et al. San Diego, CA: Harcourt Brace Custom Publishing, 1999. This excerpt can also be found online at http://www.wsu.edu:8080/~wldciv/world_civ_reader/world_civ_reader_1/kojiki.html.

Qur'an

"The Adoration," from The Holy Qur'an,
available online from the Online Book Initiative, University of Michigan,
at http://www.hti.umich.edu/cgi/k/koran/koran-idx?type=DIV0&byte=645764
Written in the seventh century
Translated by M. H. Shakir
Published in 1983 by Tahrike Tarsile Qur'an, Inc

"Allah is He Who created the heavens and the earth and what is between them in six periods. ..."

The Qur'an (often written as "Koran" in English) is the holy book of Islam. *Qur'an* is an Arabic word that means "the recitation." Muslims, the followers of Islam, believe that the Qur'an is the literal word of God. God is called Allah in Islam. The Qur'an was revealed to the Prophet Muhammad (c. 570–632) by the archangel Jabra'il (Gabriel) beginning in 610 and continuing until Muhammad's death.

Muslims hold to a number of core beliefs. Each of these core beliefs is reflected in the excerpt from the Qur'an, titled "The Adoration." This excerpt contains verses that describe creation and the relationship between creation and Allah.

1. Belief in a single God, named Allah, a name from the Arabic *al-ilah,* meaning "the One True God." Allah created the heaven and the earth over a period of six days. As described in "The Adoration," this six-day period of creation is virtually the same as that described in the Judaic-Christian biblical book of Genesis. Unlike some religions Islam believes that God created the physical universe. The physical universe is not eternal but exists only because Allah willed it.

2. Belief in angels. Muslims believe that the Qur'an was revealed to Muhammad by the archangel Jabra'il, the angel who communicates

revelations, or divine truths, to the prophets. The other major angels include Mika'il, the angel who controls the weather; Israfil, the angel who will blow the horn to signal the end of the universe; and Azra'il, the Angel of Death, who is referred to in "The Adoration." Like Christianity and Judaism, Islam recognizes that God has not withdrawn from his creation but communicates with people through angels.

3. Belief in the revealed books of God. The Qur'an does not contain just a philosophy of life. The commandments, or demands, it imposes on Muslims are laws, not recommendations or suggested ways to lead a happier life on Earth.

4. Belief in God's many prophets, including Abraham, Moses, and Jesus Christ. ("And certainly We gave the Book to Musa [Moses], so be not in doubt concerning the receiving of it, and We made it a guide for the children of Israel.") The concept of prophets suggests a God who is in constant communication with the world he created.

5. Acceptance that the world will end and that Allah will measure and judge human affairs. In contrast to such religions as Shinto, for example, Islam sees a God who judges human conduct. People have free will, so they can choose to follow Allah or not. Daily activities in Islam are classified according to whether they are sinful or not. The term *halal* refers to permitted activities, while *haram* refers to activities that are prohibited. All actions are judged according to the Islamic halal and haram. Those considered haram are sinful.

6. Belief in life after death. Islam sees heaven as a paradise. The word used most frequently in the Qur'an for heaven can literally be translated into English as "garden." Muslims view paradise as union with God, a place of unimaginable joy. While hell is a place of punishment and torment, Islamic scholars disagree about whether the punishments of hell are eternal. Some believe that they are, but others believe that Allah, in his mercy, eventually will release souls from hell.

The Qur'an consists of 114 *suras,* or chapters, and totals just over 6,200 *ayat,* or verses, though sometimes a different number is given, because Islamic scholars dispute the authoritativeness, or accuracy, of a few verses. While it is conventional in Western translations to number the suras, Muslims do not refer to them by number but rather by name, such as "The Adoration." Nonetheless, "The Adoration" is sura 32, and each verse in the sura is also numbered.

Muslims believe that the true Qur'an can only be read in Arabic. They try to memorize at least a portion of the holy text as part of their devotion to Islam. © JAMES MARSHALL/CORBIS.

The Qur'an was written in a combination of prose and rhymed poetry. The language, classical Arabic, continues to be used as a literary language. Spoken Arabic is different from the language of the Qur'an. All Muslims are expected to memorize at least a portion of the Qur'an and to be familiar enough with the language to understand the meaning. Some Muslims memorize the entire Qur'an—which is the most memorized book in the world—and they are known as *Hafiz*, or "Guardian." Muslims do not regard translations of the Qur'an as the actual Qur'an. They believe that because Allah's word was revealed in Arabic, translations are more like commentaries or interpretations. The fact that the words in English can differ across translations suggests that the English translations cannot be considered the revealed word of Allah. Allah is the creator, and what he created through Muhammad was the Qur'an in the original language. For this reason, most translations are given a title such as *The Holy Qur'an* or some other variant, to distinguish them from the true Qur'an.

Things to remember while reading the excerpt from the Holy Qur'an:

- The Qur'an became the single most important unifying factor in the early history of Islam. At a time when the region of the Middle East was populated by competing tribes, the Qur'an forged unity among them.

- The Qur'an is not written with a single narrative thread that runs from the beginning to the end. It is not meant to be read in a linear fashion, meaning from beginning to end. Readers are to memorize, meditate on, and discuss the Qur'an, and the process of trying to understand it can take a lifetime.

- The suras (often written as *surrah*) are not arranged in chronological order, or the order in which they were revealed to Muhammad. Rather, they are arranged roughly according to size, with the longest ones appearing early in the Qur'an and the shortest ones at the end.

- At the heart of the Qur'an is a quest for unity. All of life is seen as divine. Allah is shown in "The Adoration" to be a God of unity and completeness, and the purpose of the Qur'an is to teach people that sense of unity and completeness, called *tawhid,* or "making one."

- The "We" that is frequently used in "The Adoration" refers to Allah himself.

• • •

Excerpt from the Holy Qur'an

"The Adoration"

Beneficent: Good.

In the name of Allah, the **Beneficent,** the Merciful.

[**32.1**] Alif Lam Mim.

[**32.2**] The revelation of the Book, there is no doubt in it, is from the Lord of the worlds.

[**32.3**] Or do they say: He has forged it? Nay! it is the truth from your Lord that you may warn a people to whom no warner has come before you, that they may follow the right direction.

[**32.4**] Allah is He Who created the heavens and the earth and what is between them in six periods, and He mounted the throne (of authority); you have not besides Him any guardian or any **intercessor,** will you not then mind?

Intercessor: One who prays or makes a plea on behalf of another.

[**32.5**] He regulates the affair from the heaven to the earth; then shall it ascend to Him in a day the measure of which is a thousand years of what you count.

[**32.6**] This is the Knower of the unseen and the seen, the Mighty the Merciful,

[**32.7**] Who made good everything that He has created, and He began the creation of man from dust.

[**32.8**] Then He made his **progeny** of an **extract** of water held in light **estimation.**

Progeny: Children, descendants.

[**32.9**] Then He made him complete and breathed into him of His spirit, and made for you the ears and the eyes and the hearts; little is it that you give thanks.

Extract: An essence or concentrate, a small part of another material.

[**32.10**] And they say: What! when we have become lost in the earth, shall we then certainly be in a new creation? Nay! they are disbelievers in the meeting of their Lord.

Estimation: Opinion, assessment.

[**32.11**] Say: The angel of death who is given charge of you shall cause you to die, then to your Lord you shall be brought back.

[**32.12**] And could you but see when the guilty shall hang down their heads before their Lord: Our Lord! we have seen and we have heard, therefore send us back, we will do good; surely (now) we are certain.

[**32.13**] And if We had pleased We would certainly have given to every soul its guidance, but the word (which had gone forth) from Me was just: I will certainly fill hell with the **jinn** and men together.

Jinn: A type of invisible spirit; also called "genie."

[**32.14**] So taste, because you neglected the meeting of this day of yours; surely We **forsake** you; and taste the **abiding chastisement** for what you did.

Forsake: Abandon, desert.

Abiding: Long-lasting.

[**32.15**] Only they believe in Our communications who, when they are reminded of them, fall down making **obeisance** and celebrate the praise of their Lord, and they are not proud.

Chastisement: Scolding or punishment.

Obeisance: A movement of the body that indicates respect, like a bow.

[**32.16**] Their sides draw away from (their) beds, they call upon their Lord in fear and in hope, and they spend **(benevolently)** out of what We have given them.

Benevolently: Kindly or generously.

[**32.17**] So no soul knows what is hidden for them of that which will refresh the eyes; a reward for what they did.

[**32.18**] Is he then who is a believer like him who is a **transgressor**? They are not equal.

Transgressor: Sinner or one who disobeys a law.

[**32.19**] As for those who believe and do good, the gardens are their abiding-place; an entertainment for what they did.

The name Allah is embroidered onto a cloth. Allah revealed the Qur'an to the prophet Muhammad. © KAZUYOSKI NOMACHI/ CORBIS.

Abode: Residence, place where one lives.

[32.20] And as for those who transgress, their **abode** is the fire; whenever they desire to go forth from it they shall be brought back into it, and it will be said to them: Taste the chastisement of the fire which you called a lie.

[32.21] And most certainly We will make them taste of the nearer chastisement before the greater chastisement that **haply** they may turn.

Haply: By chance, perhaps.

[32.22] And who is more unjust than he who is reminded of the communications of his Lord, then he turns away from them? Surely We will give punishment to the guilty.

[32.23] And certainly We gave the Book to Musa, so be not in doubt concerning the receiving of it, and We made it a guide for the children of Israel.

Imams: Muslim scholars or leaders.

[32.24] And We made of them **Imams** to guide by Our command when they were patient, and they were certain of Our communications.

[32.25] Surely your Lord will judge between them on the day of resurrection concerning that wherein they differ.

[**32.26**] Does it not point out to them the right way, how many of the generations, in whose abodes they go about, did We destroy before them? Most surely there are signs in this; will they not then hear?

[**32.27**] Do they not see that We drive the water to a land having no **herbage,** then We bring forth thereby seed-produce of which their cattle and they themselves eat; will they not then see?

Herbage: Herbaceous, or herblike, plants such as grass.

[**32.28**] And they say: When will this judgment take place, If you are truthful?

[**32.29**] Say: On the day of judgment the faith of those who (now) disbelieve will not profit them, nor will they be **respited.**

Respited: Given rest or relief.

[**32.30**] Therefore turn away from them and wait, surely they too are waiting.

• • •

What happened next . . .

The Qur'an that is read and recited in the modern day is little different from the Qur'an from the seventh century and the years following Muhammad's death. Muhammad himself was illiterate; he could not read or write. His revelations were recorded by his followers, who acted as his secretaries. At that time, though, writing down the Qur'an and compiling it in book form were not thought of as important, for the goal of all Muslims was to memorize it.

During the rule of the first Muslim caliph (a successor to Muhammad as leader of Islam), Abu Bakr, a number of prominent Muslims who had memorized the Qur'an were killed in a rebellion. Abu Bakr was worried that the Qur'an could be lost, so he had one of Muhammad's chief secretaries, or scribes, record it on paper, a technique newly introduced from China. Later, the third caliph, Uthman (often spelled Usman) ibn Affan, learned that many non-Arabs were writing down their own versions of the Qur'an, with varying spellings and pronunciation marks. Uthman was concerned that among all these competing versions, the true Qur'an would be lost. Accordingly, he ordered production of an official version, with one copy sent to every major Muslim city. Scribes in those cities produced additional copies for use in that city, and faulty copies were ordered to be burned. Two of these official copies, called the Usmani Qur'ans, are preserved today in museums in Turkey and in Tashkent, Uzbekistan, and they are the source of the text used in modern times.

The Qur'an and The Hadith

While the Qur'an is the central scripture of Islam, Muslims also turn to the hadith for guidance. The hadith is a compilation of Muhammad's sayings, preserved to show how to live the details of Islam in daily life. While the Qur'an is written in a poetic, literary style, with emphasis on repeated sounds and other poetic devices both to inspire the reader and to make memorization easier, the hadith is written in a simpler, more everyday style. One example is "Learning is a duty on every Muslim, male and female." These sayings, which number about 2,600, were written down by Muhammad's followers. The hadith forms the basis of another text that is important to Islam, the Sunnah, or "the Way of the Prophet," used to refer to Muhammad's life example.

Did you know . . .

- Many of the beliefs held by Muslims, including belief in a single supreme God and the existence of angels, heaven, hell, and the final judgment are remarkably similar to concepts held by Jews and Christians.

- Muslims are required to ensure that they are in a ritually pure state before touching the Qur'an. To do so, they wash their hands, face, and feet. Any copy of the Qur'an is to be handled with extreme care and reverence. Worn-out or damaged copies are to be buried or burned.

- The *sahaba* were the "companions" of Muhammad. One could be considered a sahaba if he or she heard, saw, or spent time with Muhammad. The number of such sahaba ran to more than a hundred thousand, although only a few hundred spent any significant time with the prophet. These people are regarded as the earliest Islamic scholars, for they heard Muhammad's message directly from him. They included people from all different races and backgrounds. It was the sahaba who recorded the sections of the Qur'an as Muhammad revealed them

- Although Muslims agree on central issues of faith, there are minor points of disagreement, particularly over details of how a person should conduct his or her daily affairs. This disagreement arises because some of the verses of the Qur'an are open to differing interpretations. Muslims accordingly follow one of five different legal traditions, which provide guidance on these matters. Named for their originators, they are the Hanafi, the Ja'fari, the Hanbali, the Maliki, and the Shafi. One or the other of these legal traditions tends to predominate in a particular Muslim country or region. For example, Hanafi tends to prevail in Pakistan and northern Egypt, whereas Shafi holds sway in Syria and Iraq.

Consider the following ...

- Summarize the image and characteristics of Allah that are presented in "The Adoration."

- List some of the similarities between Islamic belief, as contained in "The Adoration," and the beliefs of other religious traditions with which you may be familiar.

- Explain what, according to Islamic belief, will happen on the day of judgment.

For More Information

BOOKS

"The Adoration." In *The Holy Qur'an.* Translated by M. H. Shakir. Elmhurst, NY: Tahrike Tarsile Qur'an, Inc., 1983. This excerpt can also be found online at http://www.hti.umich.edu/cgi/k/koran/koran-idx?type=DIV0&byte= 645764.

McAuliffe, Jane Dammen, ed. *Encyclopaedia of the Qur'an.* Leiden, Netherlands: Brill, 2002–2004.

Pickthall, Marmaduke (Muhammad). "Surah as-Sajdah (Prostration)." In *The Meaning of the Glorious Qur'an.* Beltsville, MD: Amana Publications, 2005. This source can also be found online at http://www.al-sunnah.com/call_to_ islam/quran/pickthall/surah32.html.

Robinson, Neal. *Discovering the Qur'an.* Washington, DC: Georgetown University Press, 2002.

Watt, W. Montgomery, and Richard Bell. *Introduction to the Qur'an.* Edinburgh, Scotland: Edinburgh University Press, 2001.

Yusuf Ali, Abdullah. "Surah 32: The Prostration, Worship, Adoration." In *The Holy Qur'an.* Elmhurst, NY: Tahrike Tarsile Qur'an, 1987.

WEB SITES

Qur'an. IslamOnline.net. http://www.islamonline.net/surah/english/quran.shtml (accessed on June 5, 2006).

"Qur'an Transliteration." *Transliteration.org.* http://transliteration.org/quran/ home.htm (accessed on June 5, 2006).

Black Elk Speaks

"The Great Vision," from Black Elk Speaks:
Being the Life Story of a Holy Man of the Oglala Sioux,
available online from Black Elk's World at http://blackelkspeaks.unl.edu/index2.htm
By John G. Neihardt
Originally published in 1932
Reprinted in 2004 by University of Nebraska Press

"Behold them yonder where the sun goes down, the thunder beings! You shall see, and have from them my power; and they shall take you to the high and lonely center of the earth that you may see: even to the place where the sun continually shines, they shall take you there to understand."

Black Elk (1863–1950) was born as Hehaka Sapa and was also known as Nicholas Black Elk (his Christian name after he was baptized). He was a traditional healer and holy man among the Oglala Lakota, a tribe that is part of the Great Sioux Nation. Born on the Little Powder River just west of present–day South Dakota, he came of age during the final years of the wars between the U.S. government and the Sioux. One of the major events in this conflict is the Battle of Little Bighorn in 1876, famous as "Custer's last stand," a reference to General George Armstrong Custer, who led the ill-fated U.S. Seventh Cavalry troops at the Battle of Little Big Horn in 1876. The tragic events at Wounded Knee are also important in the conflict. Some three hundred Sioux and their leader, Sitting Bull, were massacred by U.S. troops at their South Dakota reservation near Wounded Knee in 1890. A reservation is land within the United States set aside for the use of native peoples.

Black Elk was baptized a Catholic at the Holy Rosary Mission near Pine Ridge, South Dakota, in 1904. Although he practiced Catholicism, he remained part of an underground movement to preserve Sioux culture and religious beliefs during a time when the U.S. government officially banned Native American religious practices. The government at the time pursued a policy that tried to transform Native Americans into farmers and landowners who would fit into white America.

In time Black Elk grew increasingly fearful that the Sioux would be absorbed into white culture and that people would forget that the Lakota existed. He joined other Sioux in efforts to record both his personal history and that of the Lakota nation. When author John Neihardt appeared on the reservation to gather material for a long narrative poem about the American West, Black Elk met with him and shared his story. The result was Neihardt's widely popular 1932 book, *Black Elk Speaks: Being the Life Story of a Holy Man of the Oglala Sioux.* Most of the book consists of Black Elk's words, arranged and edited by Neihardt. The book was essentially a warning to the Lakota nation of the constant danger of losing its traditions and ceasing to exist as a distinct people.

Black Elk Speaks is not a creation story but is what is often called a foundation myth. A foundation myth functions in a way similar to a creation story. Like the creation stories of many of the world's religions, it is a tale passed orally through generations. And, like creation stories, it contains elements that define the culture that produced it. Different nations use their foundation myths to preserve their cultural identities: the nature of their community, taboos (bans or restrictions), codes of appropriate behavior, and their relationship with the spiritual world.

All cultures have foundational myths that shape the way the culture looks at the world and its place in creation. In the United States, stories of the Old West, the fierce independence of its gunslingers, ranchers, cowboys, and sheriffs, provides a foundational myth for the nation. This foundational myth, however, is often at odds with the worldview of the Native American tribes that were forced off their traditional lands as the United States spread westward.

In "The Great Vision," Black Elk recalls a vision he had when he was nine years old. A voice tells him that his Grandfathers are waiting for him. He is taken to a cloud world, where a bay horse, a horse of a reddish-brown color with a black mane and tail, tells him his history and that of the Sioux people. In each direction—north, south, east, and west—are twelve horses that will take Black Elk to a council of his six Grandfathers. Each of the Grandfathers then tells him a story about the people and gives him a symbolic object. In essence, the vision

An Oglala Sioux man stands before tepees at Pine Ridge Reservation in South Dakota, 1891. The tepee's circular shape is sacred, symbolizing the unity of the people.
NATIONAL ARCHIVES AND RECORDS ADMINISTRATION.

depicts the four stages of humankind as the Sioux knew it, from its happy beginnings, through its difficulties in the present and near future, to a return (in the remainder of the vision, not included in the excerpt) to a final state of happiness and prosperity.

Black Elk's vision contains a number of symbols that are important to the Sioux. One is the number four: there are four seasons, four directions, and four stages in the life of the Sioux. Also symbolic is the number twelve: in each of the four directions, twelve horses, all of the same color, greet Black Elk. The North, associated with snow and white horses, represents winter and death; the South is associated with yellow, the flowering stick, and maturity; the East, with greenness, spring, and youth; and the West, with black, black horses, and old age.

Another important symbol is that of the hoop, or circle. Native Americans did not adopt the circle for practical purposes. For example, they did not use the wheel. Instead, the circle symbolized the unity of the people. The Lakota were imagined as united, as in a circle, just as the four directions were seen as part of a vast circle that has no beginning or ending. This symbolism was used in Sioux living arrangements, where the people lived in tepees that were circular at the base. Tepees in a village

The Sioux and the Black Hills

The Black Hills of South Dakota are sacred to the Sioux. Sioux legend has it that when the universe was created, each part of it was given a song, but only in the Black Hills can the song be found in its entirety. The Sioux see the Black Hills as the "heart" of their world.

The Sioux also see the hills as a reclining female figure that provides life, and they are said to return to the hills as children return to their mothers' arms. The Sioux believe that they originally came from the Black Hills. Because it was at Bear Butte on the eastern edge of the Black Hills that the creator-god first gave his instructions to them, the butte is an especially sacred place. Each year, many Sioux (along with the Cheyenne, another Native American nation that fought alongside the Sioux at the Little Big Horn) return to Bear Butte for religious and spiritual observances. Finally, it is believed that the souls of the Sioux dead reside in the Black Hills.

were arranged in a ring. Efforts made by whites to force the Sioux to live in square or rectangular cabins were resisted—to the puzzlement of whites, who did not understand the significance of the circle to Native Americans.

Some readers have questioned the validity, the genuineness, of Black Elk's vision. They point out that the vision had taken place many decades before Black Elk reported it to Neihardt. They suggest that some of the details of the vision may have been the result of hindsight, looking back at the history of the Sioux people in the years between the vision and its recording on paper. Others, however, note that many of the symbols used in the vision, as well as throughout the book—have universal significance and that many other religious traditions are built on faith in the visions of their prophets and holy figures.

Things to remember while reading the excerpt from *Black Elk Speaks:*

- The name *Sioux* comes from a French word, *nadouessioux.* The word is actually offensive, for it was an insulting term that meant "little snakes." In the modern world, the Sioux prefer the names Dakota, Nakota, and Lakota. These are names given to different tribal groups based on geography and language. "Sioux" is often still used, however, by those outside the tribal groups to refer to them collectively.
- The Sioux see the universe as incomprehensible, beyond our understanding and certain knowledge. Their religious view is that life, growth, and death are mysteries that cannot be explained. The word *wakan* is used to suggest this mysteriousness and unpredictability. It also indicates the idea of a force that gives life to the universe, called *Wakan Tanka,* and is represented by the six Grandfathers.
- *Black Elk Speaks* is regarded as a holy text among the Sioux nation, for it recorded the history of the people and has served as inspiration for the people to preserve their culture and religious traditions.

• • •

Excerpt from *Black Elk Speaks*

"The Great Vision"

What happened after that until the summer I was nine years old is not a story. There were winters and summers, and they were good; for the **Wasichus** had made their **iron road** along the Platte and traveled there. This had cut the bison [buffalo] herd in two, but those that stayed in our country with us were more than could be counted, and we wandered without trouble in our land. . . .

When we had camped again, I was lying in our tepee and my mother and father were sitting beside me. I could see out through the opening, and there two men were coming from the clouds, headfirst like arrows slanting down, and I knew they were the same that I had seen before. Each now carried a long spear, and from the points of these a jagged lightning flashed. They came clear down to the ground this time and stood a little way off and looked at me and said: "Hurry! Come! Your Grandfathers are calling you!"

. . . Then the two men spoke together and they said: "Behold him, the being with four legs!"

I looked and saw a bay horse standing there, and he began to speak: "Behold me!" he said. "My life history you shall see." Then he wheeled about to where the sun goes down, and said: "Behold them! Their history you shall know."

I looked, and there were twelve black horses **yonder** all **abreast** with necklaces of bison hoofs, and they were beautiful, but I was frightened, because their manes were lightning and there was thunder in their nostrils.

Then the bay horse wheeled to where the great white giant lives (the north) and said: "Behold!" And yonder there were twelve white horses all abreast. Their manes were flowing like a blizzard wind and from their noses came a roaring, and all about them white geese soared and circled.

Then the bay wheeled round to where the sun shines continually (the east) and **bade** me look; and there twelve **sorrel** horses, with necklaces of elk's teeth, stood abreast with eyes that glimmered like the daybreak star and manes of morning light.

Then the bay wheeled once again to look upon the place where you are always facing (the south), and yonder stood twelve **buckskins** all abreast with horns upon their heads and manes that lived and grew like trees and grasses.

And when I had seen all these, the bay horse said: "Your Grandfathers are having a council. These shall take you; so have courage."

Wasichus: White people.

Iron road: Railroad.

Yonder: In the distance.

Abreast: Side by side in a straight line.

Bade: Instructed.

Sorrel: A light brown color; sorrel horses have white manes and tails.

Buckskins: Yellow-colored horses with black tails and manes.

Then all the horses went into formation, four abreast—the blacks, the whites, the sorrels, and the buckskins—and stood behind the bay, who turned now to the west and neighed; and yonder suddenly the sky was terrible with a storm of plunging horses in all colors that shook the world with thunder, neighing back.

Now turning to the north the bay horse whinnied, and yonder all the sky roared with a mighty wind of running horses in all colors, neighing back.

And when he whinnied to the east, there too the sky was filled with glowing clouds of manes and tails of horses, in all colors singing back. Then to the south he called, and it was crowded with many colored, happy horses, nickering.

Then the bay horse spoke to me again and said: "See how your horses all come dancing!" I looked, and there were horses, horses everywhere—a whole skyful of horses dancing round me.

"Make haste!" the bay horse said; and we walked together side by side, while the blacks, the whites, the sorrels, and the buckskins followed, marching four by four.

I looked about me once again, and suddenly the dancing horses without number changed into animals of every kind and into all the **fowls** that are, and these fled back to the four quarters of the world from whence the horses came, and vanished.

Fowls: Birds, especially game birds.

Then as we walked, there was a heaped up cloud ahead that changed into a tepee, and a rainbow was the open door of it; and through the door I saw six old men sitting in a row.

The two men with the spears now stood beside me, one on either hand, and the horses took their places in their quarters, looking inward, four by four. And the oldest of the Grandfathers spoke with a kind voice and said: "Come right in and do not fear." And as he spoke, all the horses of the four quarters neighed to cheer me. So I went in and stood before the six, and they looked older than men can ever be—old like hills, like stars.

The oldest spoke again: "Your Grandfathers all over the world are having a council, and they have called you here to teach you." His voice was very kind, but I shook all over with fear now, for I knew that these were not old men, but the Powers of the World. And the first was the Power of the West; the second, of the North; the third, of the East; the fourth, of the South; the fifth, of the Sky; the sixth, of the Earth. I knew this, and was afraid, until the first Grandfather spoke again: "Behold them yonder where the sun goes down, the thunder beings! You shall see, and have from them my power; and they shall take you to the high and lonely center of the earth that you may see: even to the place where the sun continually shines, they shall take you there to understand."

John G. Neihardt

BLACK ELK SPEAKS

And as he spoke of understanding, I looked up and saw the rainbow leap with flames of many colors over me.

Now there was a wooden cup in his hand and it was full of water and in the water was the sky.

"Take this," he said. "It is the power to make live, and it is yours."

Now he had a bow in his hands. "Take this," he said. "It is the power to destroy, and it is yours."

Then he pointed to himself and said: "Look close at him who is your spirit now, for you are his body and his name is Eagle Wing Stretches."

And saying this, he got up very tall and started running toward where the sun goes down; and suddenly he was a black horse that stopped and turned and looked at me, and the horse was very poor and sick; his ribs stood out.

Then the second Grandfather, he of the North, arose with a herb of power in his hand, and said: "Take this and hurry." I took and held it toward the black horse yonder. He fattened and was happy and came prancing to his place again and was the first Grandfather sitting there.

The second Grandfather, he of the North, spoke again: "Take courage, younger brother," he said; "on earth a nation you shall make live, for yours shall be the power of the white giant's wing, the cleansing wing." Then he got up very tall and started running toward the north; and when he turned toward me, it was a white goose wheeling. I looked about me now, and the horses in the west were thunders and the horses of the north were geese. . . .

And now it was the third Grandfather who spoke, he of where the sun shines continually. "Take courage, younger brother," he said, "for across the earth they shall take you!" Then he pointed to where the daybreak star was shining, and beneath the star two men were flying. "From them you shall have power," he said, "from them who have awakened all the beings of the earth with roots and legs and wings." And as he said this, he held in his hand a peace pipe which had a spotted eagle outstretched upon the stem; and this eagle seemed alive, for it was poised there, fluttering, and its eyes were looking at me. "With this pipe," the Grandfather said, "you shall walk upon the earth, and whatever sickens there you shall make well." Then he pointed to a man who was bright red all over, the color of good and of plenty, and as he pointed, the red man lay down and rolled and changed into a bison that got up, and galloped toward the sorrel horses of the east, and they too turned to bison, fat and many.

And now the fourth Grandfather spoke, he of the place where you are always facing (the south), whence comes the power to grow. "Younger brother," he said, "with the powers of the four quarters you shall walk, a relative. Behold, the living center of a nation I shall give you, and with it many you shall save." And I saw that he was holding in his hand a bright red stick that was alive, and as I looked it sprouted at the top and sent forth branches, and on the branches many leaves came out and murmured and in the leaves the birds began to sing. And then for just a little while I thought I saw beneath it in the shade the circled villages of people and every living thing with roots or legs or wings, and all were happy. "It shall stand in the center of the nation's circle," said the Grandfather, "a cane to walk with and a people's heart; and by your powers you shall make it blossom."

Then when he had been still a little while to hear the birds sing, he spoke again: "Behold the earth!" So I looked down and saw it lying yonder like a hoop of peoples, and in the center bloomed the holy stick that was a tree, and where it stood there crossed two roads, a red one and a black. "From where the giant lives (the north) to where you always face (the south) the red road goes, the road of good," the Grandfather said, "and on it shall your nation walk. The black road goes from where the thunder beings live (the west) to where the sun continually shines (the east), a fearful road, a road of troubles and of war. On this also you shall walk, and from it you shall have the power to destroy a people's foes. In four **ascents** you shall walk the earth with Power."

I think he meant that I should see four generations, counting me, and now I am seeing the third.

Then he rose very tall and started running toward the south, and was an elk; and as he stood among the buckskins yonder, they too were elks.

Now the fifth Grandfather spoke, the oldest of them all, the Spirit of the Sky. "My boy," he said, "I have sent for you and you have come. My power you shall see!" He stretched his arms and turned into a spotted eagle hovering. "Behold," he said, "all the wings of the air shall come to you, and they and the winds and the stars shall be like relatives. You shall go across the earth with my power." Then the eagle soared above my head and fluttered there; and suddenly the sky was full of friendly wings all coming toward me.

Now I knew the sixth Grandfather was about to speak, he who was the Spirit of the Earth, and I saw that he was very old, but more as men are old. His hair was long and white, his face was all in wrinkles and his eyes were deep and dim. I stared at him, for it seemed I knew him somehow; and as I stared, he slowly changed, for he was growing backwards into youth, and when he had become a boy, I knew that he was myself with all the years that would be mine at last. When he was old again, he said: "My boy, have courage, for my power shall be yours, and you shall need it, for your nation on the earth will have great troubles. Come."

Ascents: Climbs or advances, rising upward.

• • •

What happened next . . .

The remainder of the narrative outlines Black Elk's career as a healer and holy man. He discusses his first cure, and he shares additional visions he had of the spiritual world. He also talks about the events surrounding the tragedy at Wounded Knee in South Dakota. At the end of his narrative, he takes the book's author back to the place where he had the vision detailed in "The Great Vision." There he comments on the destiny of the Sioux people, who live, he says, in a state of despair. He calls on Grandfather and says: "With tears running, O Great Spirit, Great Spirit, my Grandfather—with running tears I must say now that the tree has never bloomed. A pitiful old man, you see me here, and I have fallen away and have done nothing. Here at the center of the world, where you took me when I was young and taught me; here, old, I stand, and the tree is withered, Grandfather, my Grandfather!"

Did you know . . .

- The horse held an important place among the Sioux. Although the largest branch of the Sioux nation, the Lakota, originally came from the forests of Minnesota, they moved to the Great Plains in the seventeenth century. When they acquired horses, around 1750, they formed the basis of the horse culture of the Plains. Today many Sioux believe that the horse helps define them as a people, and horses are important symbols of the Sioux nation.

- One Native American religious practice banned by the U.S. government was the Ghost Dance, which was inspired by a vision of a Paiute Indian prophet named Wovoka. Wovoka was known among the Sioux as the Messiah. At a time when Sioux fortunes seemed at their lowest, Wovoka reported that through the Ghost Dance, Indian dead would be brought back to life, the buffalo herds would return, and the white man would leave Indian country. Black Elk attended Ghost Dances himself in 1890. The Ghost Dance was a ritual designed to reconnect the Sioux with their past. Unlike the normally fast-paced dances of other rituals, the Ghost Dance was a slow-moving, shuffling dance. It took place over four or five days and was accompanied by chanting and singing, with no drumming. Both men and women took part in the dance.

- While many objects are sacred in Sioux religion, the Sacred Pipe holds special meaning. It symbolizes the unity of the Sioux people with the earth of which the pipe is made. It is believed that when people pray with the Sacred Pipe, the spirits will come. Care of the Sacred Pipe, given to the Sioux by White Buffalo

Woman, is in the hands of a keeper; in 2005 the keeper was Arval Looking Horse.

Consider the following...

- Explain the position and role of each of the Six Grandfathers in Black Elk's vision.
- Sioux religious belief focuses on many elements of the natural world, including the seasons, the directions, and creatures such as the buffalo, horses, and birds. Explain why they might be important elements in a traditional religious community.
- Compare Sioux spirituality with the spirituality of any other religious community with which you may be familiar.

For More Information

BOOKS

Costello, Damian. *Black Elk: Colonialism and Lakota Catholicism.* Maryknoll, NY: Orbis Books, 2005.

Holler, Clyde. *The Black Elk Reader.* Syracuse, NY: Syracuse University Press, 2000.

Holloway, Brian. *Interpreting the Legacy: John Neihardt and "Black Elk Speaks."* Boulder: University Press of Colorado, 2003.

Neihardt, John G. "The Great Vision." In *Black Elk Speaks: Being the Life Story of a Holy Man of the Oglala Sioux.* New York: William Morrow, 1932. Reprint, Lincoln, Nebraska: University of Nebraska Press, 2004. This excerpt is also available online at http://blackelkspeaks.unl.edu/index2.htm.

WEB SITES

Oglala Sioux Tribe. http://www.lakotamall.com/oglalasiouxtribe/index.htm (accessed on June 5, 2006).

"Sioux Religion." *Overview of World Religions.* http://philtar.ucsm.ac.uk/encyclopedia/nam/sioux.html (accessed on June 5, 2006).

Collected Essays, vol. 5: Science and Christian Tradition

"Agnosticism and Christianity," from Collected Essays, *vol. 5:*
Science and Christian Tradition, *available online from the Huxley File,*
http://aleph0.clarku.edu/huxley/CE5/Agn-X.html
By Thomas Henry Huxley
Published in 1894 by D. Appleton and Company

"It is wrong for a man to say that he is certain of the objective truth of any proposition unless he can produce evidence which logically justifies that certainty."

Thomas Henry Huxley (1825–1895) was a biologist and one of the leading English intellectuals of the nineteenth century. A biologist is a scientist who studies plant and animal life in the environment. Huxley is perhaps best remembered in the twenty-first century for coining the terms *agnostic* and *agnosticism*. These terms have since been used to refer to uncertainty about the existence of gods, an afterlife, the soul, and similar religious concepts. For Huxley, however, the words had a more complex meaning. He outlined this meaning in his essay "Agnosticism and Christianity," written in 1889. Put simply, Huxley was not prepared to accept the existence of a creator-god who made the world in a period of "days."

Agnosticism, for Huxley, was an intellectual position. It implied skepticism, meaning a refusal to take anything on faith without logical examination of evidence. He began to show his skepticism even as a child, when he recorded in his diary doubts and uncertainties about such matters as the soul, morality, and the church. The Huxley File Web site explains that, as a young adult, Huxley quoted approvingly in his diary the German poet and playwright Johann Goethe: "An active skepticism is that which unceasingly strives to overcome itself and by

Thomas Henry Huxley coined the term "agnosticism," which to him meant a skepticism towards accepting anything, such as the existence of God, without a logical examination of evidence. HIP/ART RESOURCE, NY.

well-directed research to attain to a kind of conditional certainty." In other words, a skeptic is someone who tries to discover the truth through research. A skeptic also arrives at conditional certainty, meaning that his or her belief could change with new evidence.

As an adult, Huxley was an active participant in the debates that surrounded the appearance in 1859 of Charles Darwin's *On the Origin of Species.* This book introduced readers to the theory of natural selection. This theory states that animals on Earth, including humankind, slowly changed, or evolved, over time through a random process and that those who were the most fit adapted and survived, while the weak died out. Darwin's theory was controversial because it eliminated the need to believe in divine, or godlike, intervention to explain the emergence of different species of animals. Along with other nineteenth-century books about biology (the study of plant and animal life and their processes) and geology (the study of the history of Earth and its processes, mainly through the evidence of rocks), it shook the foundations of religious faith. It cast into doubt the traditional Judeo-Christian view of creation as described in the biblical book of Genesis, the view that God created Earth and all things on it. The theory of natural selection challenged this by proposing that living creatures changed randomly over time, influenced only by their environment.

Because of Darwin's works and the interpretations of scientists like Huxley, it seemed that nineteenth-century science was turning away from the concept of a creator-god or gods and seeing natural processes as the way in which the world and humankind came into being. The suggestion that humans may have evolved over time from apes into the beings they are today challenged the basic Judeo-Christian belief that God created humankind in His own image. Science seemed to be replacing the faith in creation.

At the height of Huxley's career, from the 1860s through the 1880s, the findings of modern science and the teachings of religion seemed to be at war with each other. Religion insisted that there was a creator-god.

Science seemed to be denying that claim. Huxley was on the front lines of this war. As a strong supporter of Darwin he came to be called "Darwin's bulldog." In 1860 Huxley took part in a debate with the Anglican bishop Samuel Wilberforce at Oxford University. Wilberforce, along with many members of the clergy, opposed Darwin's ideas. At one point he turned to Huxley and asked disapprovingly, "Is it on your grandfather's or your grandmother's side that you claim descent from a monkey?" Huxley gave an equally disapproving reply, scolding Wilberforce for interfering in scientific areas about which he knew little and distracting attention from the real issues of the debate.

In 1869 Huxley was invited to join a new group called the Metaphysical Society, created to discuss "metaphysical and theological matters in a scientific manner." Metaphysics is the branch of philosophy that examines the nature of reality, especially reality that cannot be perceived by the senses. At an early meeting of the group, each member was asked to state his religious or philosophical affiliation or membership. Huxley had none, so he replied "agnostic," the opposite of gnostic (one who claims to understand divine mysteries), and the word was born.

Agnosticism, as Huxley defined it, was a form of intellectual honesty, a demand for evidence and rational thought, a refusal to accept ideas on faith. Toward the end of "Agnosticism and Christianity," he summarized his position by saying that agnosticism "is not a creed 'statement of belief', but a method." He went on to say that at the basis of agnosticism is a single principle. That principle says that in intellectual matters, a person has to follow reason as far as it will go, "without regard to any other consideration." Another way of putting it is that a person should not say that conclusions about God are certain when they cannot be demonstrated. Huxley concluded, "That I take to be the agnostic faith, which if a man keep whole . . . , he shall not be ashamed to look the universe in the face, whatever the future may have in store for him."

Huxley was not opposed to religion. As a member of London's board of education, for example, he proposed that students be required to read the Bible, the holy book of Christianity, for its moral and ethical instruction, as well as for its literary value. He did not reject the miracles recorded in the Bible; he asked whether evidence showed that they could have and did happen. He also had little use for atheists (those who did not believe in God), and he rejected charges that he was a "materialist," someone who believes only in the physical, material world and not in abstract concepts such as morality and ethics, or a code of principles.

Huxley's Letter to Darwin

Huxley was immediately impressed with the views that Charles Darwin expressed in *On the Origin of Species* and wrote the following letter to him on November 23, 1859:

> I finished your book yesterday.... No work on Natural History Science I have met with has made so great an impression on me & I do most heartily thank you for the great store of new views you have given me....
>
> As for your doctrines I am prepared to go to the stake if requisite [required]....
>
> I trust you will not allow yourself to be in any way disgusted or annoyed by the considerable abuse & misrepresentation which unless I greatly mistake is in store for you.... And as to the curs [mongrels] which will bark and yelp—you must recollect that some of your friends at any rate are endowed with an amount of combativeness which (though you have often & justly rebuked [scolded] it) may stand you in good stead—
>
> I am sharpening up my claws and beak in readiness.

University of California Museum of Paleontology, "Thomas Henry Huxley," http://www.ucmp.berkeley.edu/history/thuxley.html.

He did not oppose the study of theology as long as it was conducted in a scientific manner.

Things to remember while reading the excerpt from *Collected Essays*, vol. 5: *Science and Christian Tradition*

- Huxley coined the word *agnostic* as the opposite of *gnostic,* or one who claims to understand divine mysteries.

- The definition of "agnosticism" is stated by Huxley "that it is wrong for a man to say that he is certain of the objective truth of any proposition unless he can produce evidence which logically justifies that certainty." He does not say that he does not believe in God or religion. His point always was that the existence of God cannot be proved rationally.

- Huxley refers to a "metaphysical Nifelheim" when he talks about the realm of spiritual matters where, over history, one doctrine slays, or replaces, another. Nifelheim, often spelled Niflheim, refers to the outer region of cold and darkness in Norse mythology. It is the abode of Hel, the goddess of the dead. His allusion suggests that the realm of religion is a mysterious, frightening realm where belief systems come and go.

• • •

Excerpt from *Collected Essays*, vol. 5: *Science and Christian Tradition*

"Agnosticism and Christianity"

The present discussion has arisen out of the use, which has become general in the last few years, of the terms "Agnostic" and "Agnosticism." The people who call themselves "Agnostics" have been charged with doing so because they have not the courage to declare themselves "**Infidels.**" It has been **insinuated** that they have adopted a new name in order to escape the unpleasantness which attaches to their proper **denomination.** To this wholly **erroneous imputation,** I have replied by showing that the term "Agnostic" did, as a matter of fact, arise in a manner which **negatives** it; and my statement has not been, and cannot be, **refuted.** Moreover, speaking for myself, and without **impugning** the right of any other person to use the term in another sense, I further say that Agnosticism is not properly described as a "negative" **creed,** nor indeed as a creed of any kind, except in so far as it expresses absolute faith in the **validity** of a principle, which is as much ethical as intellectual. This principle may be stated in various ways, but they all amount to this: that it is wrong for a man to say that he is certain of the objective truth of any proposition unless he can produce evidence which logically justifies that certainty. This is what Agnosticism **asserts;** and, in my opinion, it is all that is essential to Agnosticism. That which Agnostics deny and **repudiate,** as immoral, is the contrary doctrine, that there are propositions which men ought to believe, without logically satisfactory evidence; and that **reprobation** ought to attach to the **profession** of disbelief in such inadequately supported propositions. The **justification** of the Agnostic principle lies in the success which follows upon its application, whether in the field of natural, or in that of civil, history; and in the fact that, so far as these topics are concerned, no sane man thinks of denying its validity.

Still speaking for myself, I add, that though Agnosticism is not, and cannot be, a creed, except in so far as its general principle is concerned; yet that the application of that principle results in the denial of, or the **suspension** of judgment concerning, a number of propositions respecting which our contemporary **ecclesiastical** "gnostics" profess entire certainty. And, in so far as these ecclesiastical persons can be justified in their old-established custom (which many nowadays think **more honoured in the breach than the observance** of using **opprobrious** names to those who differ from them, I fully admit their right to call me and those who think with me "Infidels"; all I have ventured to urge is that they must not expect us to speak of ourselves by that title.

The extent of the region of the uncertain, the number of the problems the investigation of which ends in a verdict of not proven, will vary according to the knowledge and the intellectual habits of the individual Agnostic. I do not very much care to speak of anything as "unknowable." What I am sure about is that there are many topics about which I know nothing; and which, so far as I can see, are out of reach of my **faculties.** But whether these things are knowable by any one else is exactly one of those matters which is beyond my knowledge, though I may have a tolerably strong

Infidels: People with no religious beliefs.

Insinuated: Suggested.

Denomination: Identifying term by which someone is classified.

Erroneous imputation: Incorrect attribution or suggestion, often offensive or insulting.

Negatives: Shows to be false.

Refuted: Proved incorrect.

Impugning: Attacking.

Creed: System of beliefs or principles.

Validity: Soundness.

Asserts: Declares.

Repudiate: Reject.

Reprobation: Criticism.

Profession: A statement of opinion.

Justification: A defense, a statement in explanation.

Suspension: Postponement.

Ecclesiastical: Associated with a church.

More honoured in the breach than the observance: Widely ignored.

Opprobrious: Scornful, critical.

Faculties: Powers of perception or understanding.

Nebulous: Vague.

Theism: Belief in the existence of a god.

Nifelheim, or Niflheim: The home of the dead in Norse mythology.

Innumerable: Countless.

Mystifications: Confusions.

Tell: Become apparent.

Inevitable: Unavoidable.

Theology: The study of religion and religious truth.

Ecclesiasticism: Excessive devotion to church practices.

Idiosyncrasy: A quirk, a way of thinking or behaving that is particular to a person.

Impartial: Neutral, not having an opinion for or against something.

Arrest: Holding off, slowing down.

Emissaries: Representatives.

Attainment: Achievement.

Ascertainment: Discovering with certainty.

opinion as to the probabilities of the case. Relatively to myself, I am quite sure that the region of uncertainty—the **nebulous** country in which words play the part of realities—is far more extensive than I could wish. Materialism and Idealism; **Theism** and Atheism; the doctrine of the soul and its mortality or immortality appear in the history of philosophy like the shades of Scandinavian heroes, eternally slaying one another and eternally coming to life again in a metaphysical "**Nifelheim.**" It is getting on for twenty-five centuries, at least, since mankind began seriously to give their minds to these topics. Generation after generation, philosophy has been doomed to roll the stone uphill; and, just as all the world swore it was at the top, down it has rolled to the bottom again. All this is written in **innumerable** books; and he who will toil through them will discover that the stone is just where it was when the work began.... More and more eyes have been cleansed of the films which prevented them from seeing it; until now the weight and number of those who refuse to be the prey of verbal **mystifications** has begun to **tell** in practical life.

It was **inevitable** that a conflict should arise between Agnosticism and **Theology;** or rather, I ought to say, between Agnosticism and **Ecclesiasticism**. For Theology, the science, is one thing; and Ecclesiasticism, the championship of a foregone conclusion as to the truth of a particular form of Theology, is another. With scientific Theology, Agnosticism has no quarrel. On the contrary, the Agnostic, knowing too well the influence of prejudice and **idiosyncrasy,** even on those who desire most earnestly to be **impartial,** can wish for nothing more urgently than that the scientific theologian should not only be at perfect liberty to thresh out the matter in his own fashion; but that he should, if he can, find flaws in the Agnostic position; and, even if demonstration is not to be had, that he should put, in their full force, the grounds of the conclusions he thinks probable. The scientific theologian admits the Agnostic principle, however widely his results may differ from those reached by the majority of Agnostics.

But, as between Agnosticism and Ecclesiasticism, or, as our neighbours across the Channel call it, Clericalism, there can be neither peace nor truce. The Cleric asserts that it is morally wrong not to believe certain propositions, whatever the results of a strict scientific investigation of the evidence of these propositions. He tells us "that religious error is, in itself, of an immoral nature." He declares that he has prejudged certain conclusions, and looks upon those who show cause for **arrest** of judgment as **emissaries** of Satan. It necessarily follows that, for him, the **attainment** of faith, not the **ascertainment** of truth, is the highest aim of mental life. And, on careful analysis of the nature of this faith, it will too often be found to be, not the mystic process of unity with the Divine,

understood by the religious **enthusiast;** but that which the candid simplicity of a Sunday scholar once defined it to be. "Faith," said this unconscious **plagiarist** of **Tertullian,** "is the power of saying you believe things which are incredible."

Now I, and many other Agnostics, believe that faith, in this sense, is an **abomination;** and though we do not **indulge** in the luxury of self-righteousness so far as to call those who are not of our way of thinking hard names, we do feel that the disagreement between ourselves and those who hold this doctrine is even more moral than intellectual. It is desirable there should be an end of any mistakes on this topic. If our clerical opponents were

Enthusiast: Strong supporter.

Plagiarist: A person who uses another's ideas as his or her own.

Tertullian: An early Christian church leader (c. 155–230).

Abomination: Something that is unbearable and without acceptance.

Indulge: Give oneself freely to, allow free rein.

Delusion: A mistaken belief.

Antipodal: Directly contrasting or conflicting.

Lay: Not belonging to the clergy.

Contrived: Labored or struggled.

Distinctive: Helping to distinguish, or tell apart, one thing from another.

Jurisprudence: A branch of philosophy that has to do with the law.

In the teeth of: Despite or in defiance of.

Despicable: Offensive, repulsive.

Implicitly: Understood without being stated outright.

Explicitly: Clearly expressed or stated.

Exposition: Explanation.

Doctrine: A set of guidelines or beliefs.

Henceforward: From now on.

Materialists: Those who value money and possessions or who believe that the physical world is the only one there is.

Idealists: Those who live by high standards or believe that the material world does not exist on its own, apart from the mind, or consciousness, of persons who live in the world.

clearly aware of the real state of the case, there would be an end of the curious **delusion,** which often appears between the lines of their writings, that those whom they are so fond of calling "Infidels" are people who not only ought to be, but in their hearts are, ashamed of themselves. It would be discourteous to do more than hint the **antipodal** opposition of this pleasant dream of theirs to facts.

The clerics and their **lay** allies commonly tell us, that if we refuse to admit that there is good ground for expressing definite convictions about certain topics, the bonds of human society will dissolve and mankind lapse into savagery. There are several answers to this assertion. One is that the bonds of human society were formed without the aid of their theology; and, in the opinion of not a few competent judges, have been weakened rather than strengthened by a good deal of it. Greek science, Greek art, the ethics of old Israel, the social organisation of old Rome, **contrived** to come into being, without the help of any one who believed in a single **distinctive** article of the simplest of the Christian creeds. The science, the art, the **jurisprudence,** the chief political and social theories, of the modern world have grown out of those of Greece and Rome—not by favour of, but **in the teeth of,** the fundamental teachings of early Christianity, to which science, art, and any serious occupation with the things of this world, were alike **despicable.**

Again, all that is best in the ethics of the modern world, in so far as it has not grown out of Greek thought, or Barbarian manhood, is the direct development of the ethics of old Israel. There is no code of legislation, ancient or modern, at once so just and so merciful, so tender to the weak and poor, as the Jewish law; and, if the Gospels are to be trusted, Jesus of Nazareth himself declared that he taught nothing but that which lay **implicitly,** or **explicitly,** in the religious and ethical system of his people. . . .

I trust that I have now made amends for any ambiguity, or want of fulness, in my previous **exposition** of that which I hold to be the essence of the Agnostic **doctrine. Henceforward,** I might hope to hear no more of the assertion that we are necessarily **Materialists, Idealists,** Atheists, Theists, or any other *ists,* if experience had led me to think that the proved falsity of a statement was any guarantee against its repetition. And those who appreciate the nature of our position will see, at once, that when Ecclesiasticism declares that we ought to believe this, that, and the other, and are very wicked if we don't, it is impossible for us to give any answer but this: We have not the slightest objection to believe anything you like, if you will give us good grounds for belief; but, if you cannot, we must respectfully refuse, even if that refusal should wreck morality and insure our own damnation several times over. We are quite content to leave that to the decision of the future. The course of the past has impressed us with the firm **conviction** that no good ever comes of falsehood, and we feel **warranted** in refusing even to experiment in that direction.

Conviction: Firmly held belief.

Warranted: Justified.

• • •

What happened next...

Huxley was pleased that his invention of the term *agnostic* took hold and was used by others. The word appeared in print in a journal the same year he first used it (1869), and numerous writers used it in their books and essays.

In his 1879 autobiography, Darwin himself described himself as an agnostic. In the twentieth century one of the most prominent persons to carry on the agnostic tradition in England was the philosopher Bertrand Russell (1872–1970). He outlined his position in a 1927 pamphlet called *Why I Am Not a Christian,* a 1947 pamphlet called *Am I an Atheist or an Agnostic? A Plea for Tolerance in the Face of New Dogmas,* and a 1953 essay entitled "What Is an Agnostic?"

Agnosticism is now used to describe a series of related beliefs. While agnosticism still is used to describe a state between belief and disbelief, modern thinkers blur the distinctions that Huxley tried to make between agnosticism, atheism, and other forms of questioning dogmatic beliefs.

Did you know...

- Agnosticism was a logical consequence of the development of the scientific method, the set of principles and procedures scientists follow to increase knowledge, in the seventeenth and eighteenth centuries. One example of the newfound reliance on the methods of science was the philosophical movement called Positivism. Positivism was an effort to apply the methods of science not just to the study of physical matter but to social and historical problems as well.
- Huxley was a well-known biologist. He was the first to propose that birds evolved from dinosaurs and was England's leading expert on reptile fossils.
- Huxley's grandson was Aldous Huxley (1894–1963), the British author of *Brave New World,* a 1932 novel about the dehumanizing effects of scientific progress.

Consider the following...

- Explain the difference between agnosticism and atheism. Respond to the belief that agnostics are really atheists but do not want to admit it.

- How would Huxley respond to the idea that science and religion are always going to be in conflict with one another?

- Explain what Huxley meant when he wrote that "agnosticism is not a creed but a method."

For More Information

BOOKS

Flint, Robert. *Agnosticism.* Honolulu, HI: University Press of the Pacific, 2004.

Huxley, Thomas. "Agnosticism and Christianity" In *Collected Essays,* vol. 5, *Science and Christian Tradition.* New York: D. Appleton and Company, 1894. This excerpt can also be found online at http://aleph0.clarku.edu/huxley/CE5/Agn-X.html.

Huxley, Thomas. *Collected Essays of Thomas Huxley: Science and Christian Tradition Part Five.* Whitefish, MT: Kessinger Publishing, 2005.

Nielsen, Kai. "Agnosticism." In *Dictionary of the History of Ideas.* Detroit, MI: Thomson Gale, 2003. This article can also be found online at http://etext.lib.virginia.edu/cgi-local/DHI/d hi.cgi?id=dv1-03.

White, Paul. *Thomas Huxley: Making the "Man of Science."* Cambridge, UK: Cambridge University Press, 2003.

WEB SITES

Blinderman, Charles, and David Joyce, "Verbal Delusions: The Bible." *The Huxley File.* http://aleph0.clarku.edu/huxley/guide15.html (accessed on June 5, 2006).

Smart, J. J. C. "Atheism and Agnosticism." *Stanford Encyclopedia of Philosophy.* http://plato.stanford.edu/entries/atheism-agnosticism (accessed on June 5, 2006).

2

Characteristics of the Divine

Perhaps no other questions have engaged the minds of people since the beginning of history more than those having to do with God. These questions include: How many gods exist? Is God a "person" or an abstract concept? What is the nature of God? What is the relationship between God and the world He (or She) created, including human beings? Most of the world's scriptures and sacred texts try to provide answers to these and other questions about God.

The number of gods in existence

One of the first questions concerns how many gods exist. In connection with this question, theologians (people who study God and religion) use two major terms to describe the world's religions: monotheistic and polytheistic. Less frequently, they also use two other terms, duotheistic and henotheistic.

A monotheistic religion (from *mono–,* meaning "one") is one that believes in a single, supreme God. The principal monotheistic religions include Judaism, Christianity, and Islam. One of the chief beliefs of Islam, for example, is that there is a single God, called Allah, and this belief is reinforced on nearly every page of Islam's sacred scripture, the Qur'an. Sikhism, too, is a monotheistic religion. In "Jup," the first section of Sikhism's sacred scripture, the **Sri Guru Granth Sahib,** the first words are "One Universal Creator God."

In contrast, a polytheistic religion (from *poly–,* meaning "many") believes in more than one god. The ancient Greeks and Romans, with their pantheons of gods and goddesses, are examples of cultures whose religion was polytheistic. A pantheon refers to the officially recognized gods of a people. "Athena Inspires the Prince," an excerpt from the Greek poet Homer's ***The Odyssey,*** makes clear that the ancient Greeks believed in numerous gods, each of which had control over some aspect of creation, such as the seas.

A duotheistic religion (from *duo–,* meaning "two") is also polytheistic, because its members believe in more than one god. These religions, however, do not worship a large number of gods or even several gods. Rather, they worship a pair of gods, often a masculine god and a feminine god. As Scott Cunningham states in **Wicca: A Guide for the Solitary Practitioner,** Wicca, with its belief in a male god and a female goddess, is considered a duotheistic religion. This belief in two gods stems from ancient religions that, for example, worshipped the Sun and the Moon and saw both a feminine and a masculine principle at work in the natural world.

Finally, a henotheistic religion can be thought of as a cross between monotheism and polytheism. Such a religion worships one supreme God but does not deny that other gods exist. Sometimes believers worship these other gods as manifestations, or representations or expressions, of the supreme God. One example of a henotheistic religion is that of the ancient Egyptians. For the Egyptians, a god such as Amon was considered an attribute of the supreme god Ra; that is, he was thought to represent a trait or feature of Ra. Thus, Amon was often referred to as Amon-Ra.

Hinduism is also henotheistic. Hindus worship a single God, Brahma, who has no specific form, but they see other gods and goddess as forms or qualities of Brahma. Drawing on this belief, Hindus tend not to see their version of God as superior in any way to any other versions of God. For Hindus, all of the world's gods are manifestations, or appearances, of the same divine being or spirit. Swami Vivekananda emphasizes this belief in his **"Paper on Hinduism."** He writes that the "contradictions" among the gods of Hinduism, Islam, Christianity, and other religions are only "apparent," meaning that they seem to be contradictions but are not really so under the surface. He says that the light of religious truth, including different ideas of the nature of God, "is the same light coming through glasses of different colors." He goes on to say, "The Lord has declared to the Hindu in His incarnation as Krishna: 'I am in every religion as the thread through a string of pearls.'" In other words, while Hindus may see God in a certain way, the points of view of other religions are no less truthful or valid. All gods are manifestations of the same eternal and unchanging force.

Characteristics of god

A second major question studied by theologians concerns the characteristics of God. These features can apply either to one supreme God in monotheistic religions or to multiple gods and goddesses in polytheistic religions. Among monotheistic religions, God is typically seen as pure, eternal, and the source of all creation. People can come to know Him only by listing His many characteristics: His power, virtue, greatness, beauty, and so on. Listing these traits is one of the chief purposes of Sikhism's "Jup," as well as of the Qur'an of Islam. Other traits often assigned to a single, supreme God include His being all powerful, all knowing, present everywhere, and all good. Many religions, including Christianity, place a great deal of emphasis on the belief that God is loving and cares very much about the welfare of the humans He created.

One major question religions face is whether God is a "person." People are male or female, and they identify themselves with names. Many cultures picture their God as a person. An example is Ahura Mazda, the name for God in Zoroastrianism, an ancient religion from what is now Iran. Ahura Mazda is identified as male. Christianity also identifies God as male. The religion of Wicca identifies both male and female gods. Examples include the male gods Apollo and Tammuz and the female goddesses Hecate and Ceriddwen.

The notion of God as a person often leads both monotheistic and polytheistic religions to assign human characteristics to God. In the Jewish sacred scripture, the Tanakh (referred to by Christians as the Old Testament), God is a humanlike being who often has to be appeased (soothed or calmed) because He grows angry with humans. He shows Himself to humans to provide them with laws to live by and to make contracts, or agreements, with them. Humans can sometimes even negotiate with Him to arrive at agreements. Similarly, the gods in **The Epic of Gilgamesh** are depicted as "persons" who grow angry with humans and send a great flood to destroy humankind. Finally, the gods of Homer's *The Odyssey* have distinct humanlike personalities and meddle freely in human affairs as though they were humans themselves. Thus, in "Athena Inspires the Prince," the chief god, Zeus, is portrayed much as a human king, with the ability to govern, reward good conduct and punish evil, dispense justice, and protect cities and homes, while Athena acts like a human counselor and friend to Telemachus.

Other religions, in contrast, see God as a force, without any specific form or humanlike characteristics. Although this point of view can be found worldwide, it is especially prominent among Eastern religions such as Buddhism and Hinduism. These religions view God as an ultimate, eternal reality that exists beyond the suffering and change of the physical world. God is not identified as a specific "person." As the "Jup" notes, "By thinking, He cannot be reduced to thought." Similarly, Swami Vivekananda highlights the eternal nature of God in Hinduism when he writes, "God is the ever-active providence [fate], by whose power systems after systems are being evolved out of chaos [disorder], made to run for a time, and again destroyed." For Hindus, God is not a person but a creative principle, a force that is eternally at work in the universe.

God's relationship with humans

A third question that arises in connection with God concerns the nature of His relationship with creation and specifically with humans. Among monotheists a distinction is sometimes made between two types of belief, theism and deism. Theists believe that God is the ongoing sustainer of the universe He created. Thus, God remains involved with day-to-day human affairs. Deists, in contrast, believe that God withdrew from the world He created; the figure of speech often used to express this idea is that God is like a watchmaker (or clockmaker) who built the watch, wound it up, and then let it operate on its own. These differing views about God's involvement with creation are not necessarily associated with any particular religion. Muslims, the followers of Islam, would be considered theists, believing that God remains intimately involved with the daily affairs of creation and of humans. Judaism and Christianity lean toward the theistic view, but many Jews and especially Christians adopt a more deistic view. They believe that God created the world and set it in motion, but they do not believe that God involves Himself in the day-to-day affairs of His creation.

Polytheistic religions, too, often see the gods and goddesses as having an ongoing relationship with humans. Many polytheistic religions emerged from cultures that were not literate (that is, they did not read or write) and that did not understand science. They attributed natural forces to the work of gods and goddesses. In an arid country, for example, a rain god or rain goddess may have been credited with bringing rain as a sign of his or her favor, while drought was seen as a sign of his or her anger. In more fertile countries, gods and goddesses were thought to control the harvest of crops. The ancient Sumerians, who produced the Gilgamesh epic, were entirely dependent on the cycles of nature. They saw their gods as beings who could, for example, reward humankind with bountiful crops, but who could also punish humankind with crop failure through flood, fire, or other disasters.

Some people believe that there is no God (or gods). They argue that God is an invention of the human imagination. Most of the world's people, however, disagree. They may differ about the number of gods, the nature of God, and the ways in which they describe him (or her). They may see God as an active participant in the world's affairs or as a passive observer of creation. They may see God as a person or as a creative force. Most people have a very human need to seek truth through spirituality. The ongoing debate over the nature of God reflects this need.

The Epic of Gilgamesh

Tablet XI of The Epic of Gilgamesh,
available online from the Academy for Ancient Texts at
http://www.ancienttexts.org/library/mesopotamian/gilgamesh/tab11.htm
By Shin-eqi-unninni
Written around 2750 to 2500 BCE
Translated by Maureen Gallery Kovacs
Originally published in 1989 by Stanford University Press

> "I watched the appearance of the weather—
>
> the weather was frightful to behold!
>
> I went into the boat and sealed the entry."

The Babylonian *Epic of Gilgamesh,* written sometime around 2750 to 2500 BCE (before the Common Era), is the world's first known epic poem. An epic poem is typically a long story that records the adventurous deeds of heroic, often partly divine, persons. These deeds were important to the culture that produced the epic because they had historical, religious, or legendary significance. *The Epic of Gilgamesh* is also one of the world's earliest surviving written texts. Its author, Shin-eqi-unninni, is the earliest known named author of a surviving text. The epic was composed and written down in ancient Mesopotamia, an area that lies mostly in modern Iraq. The area was called the Fertile Crescent because of its rich agricultural lands.

Mesopotamia was not really a country as we understand the word today. Instead, it was a large region made up of areas dominated by different peoples. One of those areas was Sumer, located between the Tigris and Euphrates rivers in what is now the southern part of Iraq. The people of Sumer, called Sumerians, developed one of the world's earliest civilizations, because of the fertile soil left behind by the flooding of the two rivers. By about 3000 BCE the region had about twelve independent cities, each ruled by its own king, called a *lugal.* The Sumerians developed a code of law, had a fixed social structure, and traded with other parts of the known world, mostly to acquire lumber and stone in exchange for foodstuffs.

The major contribution of the Sumerians to civilization, though, was the development of writing. The earliest Sumerians used a form of writing called pictographs, or writing in which symbols were essentially pictures of the things they represented. Sumerian writing later developed into a form based on ideographs. An ideograph is a more symbolic or abstract representation than a pictograph. Still later, the Sumerians developed a form of writing based partially on an alphabet.

The Epic of Gilgamesh is a good example of this kind of writing. It was recorded on twelve clay tablets using a form of writing modern historians call *cuneiform,* from a Latin word meaning "wedge-shaped." The Sumerians were the first to develop this form of writing, which they made using a stylus (a pen-like instrument) made of reed or bone to impress the written characters into wet clay, which was then dried or baked to make a permanent record. Cuneiform writing was used by many ancient civilizations in Mesopotamia and the surrounding areas for several thousand years, much longer than our modern alphabet has been in existence.

The Gilgamesh epic was originally written in the Sumerian language, which bears no resemblance to any other known language in the world. The version that survives, however, was written later in the Akkadian language. Akkadian was a Semitic language (related to Hebrew and Arabic) spoken by the Babylonians. These people were natives of Babylon, a town to the north of Sumer on the Euphrates River.

The twelve clay tablets that contain the epic were discovered in the city of Nineveh (in modern Iraq) in the ruins of the library of Ashurbanipal, who was king of Assyria from 669 to 633 BCE. The library was destroyed by Persian invaders in 612 BCE, and all of the tablets were damaged, some more than others. No complete text of the epic remains. In many instances where portions of the text were lost, scholars have been able to suggest missing words and phrases. These added words and phrases are shown in parentheses in Tablet XI, excerpted here. When a word is followed by a question mark set in parentheses, scholars are not sure of the word they have chosen for their translation. When a word is followed by an exclamation point set in parentheses, scholars are sure of the translation but unsure of

the meaning of the passage. Other sections of the epic, however, remain forever lost.

Tablet I introduces Gilgamesh, the heroic king of Uruk in Babylonia, who lived around 2700 BCE. Many legends grew up around Gilgamesh, some of which were recorded in other poems. In Tablet XI, Gilgamesh is speaking to an immortal human named Utanapishtim, asking him why he cannot die. Utanapishtim reveals to the hero the secret of his immortality by telling his story.

Utanapishtim says that in the city of Shuruppak, on the banks of the Euphrates River, the gods held a meeting and decided to destroy humans

Finding Gilgamesh's Tomb

The Epic of Gilgamesh, like Homer's *Iliad,* may be based in part on historical events and characters. In 2003 German archaeologists working in the southern part of Iraq announced that they had uncovered traces of buildings like those the epic describes. The ruins were in the middle of the old bed of the Euphrates River, right where the epic places them. Jorg Fassbinder, a spokesman for the German team, told the BBC World Service that traces of the buildings were located using a technique that measures changes in tiny magnetic fields embedded in the soil. Although the German experts said that it is highly unlikely that the ancient buildings could ever be linked directly to Gilgamesh, the discovery is significant because it illustrates the link between literature and history in the region.

with a great flood. The gods agreed not to reveal their plan, but Ea, one of the gods who created humans, whispered the secret to the walls of Utanapishtim's house. Ea told the walls to build a great boat and to gather all living things into it, and Utanapishtim overheard. Utanapishtim built the boat, loaded it with silver, gold, and living things, and launched it. Soon a storm, with the thunder god Adad inside, broke out, lasting for seven days and seven nights. After the storm ended, Utanapishtim opened a window on the boat to discover that Earth was flooded and that all humans had been turned to stone.

The boat drifted until it came to rest on Mount Nimush, where it rested for seven days. Utanapishtim then offered a sacrifice to the gods, who smelled the odor of the sacrifice and gathered around him. The gods, particularly Enlil, the storm god, were enraged that a human had escaped the flood. Enlil accused Ea of treachery, but Ea pleaded with him to show mercy on Utanapishtim and his family. Enlil relented and granted immortality to Utanapishtim.

Things to remember while reading the excerpt from *The Epic of Gilgamesh:*

- Gilgamesh is believed to be a historical king of Uruk, not a fictional creation. He ruled Uruk sometime around 2700 BCE. The modern country Iraq is considered by some historians to get its name from Gilgamesh's kingdom of Uruk.

- Much of the history of the Sumerians was dictated, or determined, by geography. The land was very fertile, so the Sumerians were able to grow plenty of food crops. On the other hand, that fertility was due to the frequent flooding of the Tigris and Euphrates, which regularly renewed the soil but also caused great destruction. The fertile land also caused them to be invaded often by other people who wanted their wealth. Because of these difficulties, there was a strain of pessimism, or negativity and gloom, that ran through Sumerian thought.

- The Sumerians were a polytheistic culture, meaning that they believed in more than one god. They believed that the gods created the world and standards that people had to live by. In addition to the sky god Anu, they recognized the storm god Enlil, a normally kind god who made the land fertile and gave the Sumerians the plow. Enlil, however, was at times terrifying, forced to carry out the wishes of other gods when they were displeased with humans. Enlil was also known as the punisher. There were also many other gods that Sumerians recognized.

• • •

Excerpt from *The Epic of Gilgamesh*

Tablet XI: The Story of the Flood

Gilgamesh spoke to Utanapishtim, the Faraway:

"I have been looking at you,
but your appearance is not strange—you are like me!
You yourself are not different—you are like me!
My mind was **resolved** to fight with you,
(but instead?) my arm lies useless over you.
Tell me, how is it that you stand in the Assembly of the Gods,
and have found life!"

Utanapishtim spoke to Gilgamesh, saying:

"I will reveal to you, Gilgamesh, a thing that is hidden,
a secret of the gods I will tell you!
Shuruppak, a city that you surely know,
situated on the banks of the Euphrates,
that city was very old, and there were gods inside it.
The hearts of the Great Gods moved them to **inflict** the Flood.
Their Father **Anu uttered** the oath (of secrecy),
Valiant **Enlil** was their Adviser,
Ninurta was their **Chamberlain,**
Ennugi was their Minister of Canals.
Ea, the Clever Prince(?), was under oath with them
so he repeated their talk to the reed house:
'Reed house, reed house! Wall, wall!
O man of Shuruppak, son of Ubartutu:
Tear down the house and build a boat!
Abandon wealth and seek living beings!
Spurn possessions and keep alive living beings!
Make all living beings go up into the boat.
The boat which you are to build,
its dimensions must measure equal to each other:

Resolved: Made up one's mind to do, reached a decision.

Inflict: To cause something harmful.

Anu: Father of all the gods in Sumerian mythology.

Uttered: Spoke.

Enlil: The storm god of Sumer, the god who punishes humans who displease the gods.

Ninurta: The god of rain, war, thunderstorms, and floods.

Chamberlain: An official who manages a royal household.

Ennugi: The Sumerian god in charge of canals, bringing water to dry regions.

Ea: One of the gods who created humans and gave them souls.

Spurn: Reject or refuse.

Apsu: The underwater palace of the god Ea.

Heed: Pay attention to, listen.

Populace: The people.

Reside: Live.

Abundance: A large quantity, plenty.

Profusion: An ample amount, a large quantity.

Myriad: Many.

Pitch: A black, oily substance used to seal and waterproof various objects.

Cubits: The number of measurements from the length of the bent elbow to the end of the middle finger of the hand, approximately 18 inches per cubit.

Punting poles: Long straight poles used to move a boat through the water by pushing.

Bitumen: A black asphalt substance used as cement or sealer.

Kiln: Oven.

Porters: People hired to carry burdens or baggage.

Casks: Barrels.

Consumed: Eaten or used up.

its length must correspond to its width.
Roof it over like the **Apsu.**'
I understood and spoke to my lord, Ea:
'My lord, thus is the command which you have uttered
I will **heed** and will do it.
But what shall I answer the city, the **populace,** and the
Elders!'
Ea spoke, commanding me, his servant:
'You, well then, this is what you must say to them:
"It appears that Enlil is rejecting me
so I cannot **reside** in your city (?),
nor set foot on Enlil's earth.
I will go down to the Apsu to live with my lord, Ea,
and upon you he will rain down **abundance,**
a **profusion** of fowl, **myriad**(!) fishes.
He will bring to you a harvest of wealth,
in the morning he will let loaves of bread shower down,
and in the evening a rain of wheat!"'
Just as dawn began to glow
the land assembled around me—
the carpenter carried his hatchet,
the reed worker carried his (flattening) stone,
    . . . the men . . .
The child carried the **pitch,**
the weak brought whatever else was needed.
On the fifth day I laid out her exterior.
It was a field in area,
its walls were each 10 times 12 **cubits** in height,
the sides of its top were of equal length, 10 times in cubits each.
I laid out its (interior) structure and drew a picture of it(?).
I provided it with six decks,
thus dividing it into seven (levels).
The inside of it I divided into nine (compartments).
I drove plugs (to keep out) water in its middle part.
I saw to the **punting poles** and laid in what was necessary.
Three times 3,600 (units) of raw **bitumen** I poured into the bitumen
    kiln,
three times 3,600 (units of) pitch . . . into it,
there were three times 3,600 **porters** of **casks** who carried (vegeta-
    ble) oil,
apart from the 3,600 (units of) oil which they **consumed**(!)
and two times 3,600 (units of) oil which the boatman stored
    away.
I butchered oxen for the meat(!),
and day upon day I slaughtered sheep.

I gave the workmen(?) ale, beer, oil, and wine, as if it were river
    water,
so they could make a party like the New Year's Festival.
...and I set my hand to the oiling(!).
The boat was finished by sunset.
The launching was very difficult.
They had to keep carrying a runway of poles front to back,
until two-thirds of it had gone into the water(?).
Whatever I had I loaded on it:
whatever silver I had I loaded on it,
whatever gold I had I loaded on it.
All the living beings that I had I loaded on it,
I had all my **kith and kin** go up into the boat,
all the beasts and animals of the field and the craftsmen I
had go up.
Shamash had set a stated time:
'In the morning I will let loaves of bread shower down,
and in the evening a rain of wheat!
Go inside the boat, seal the entry!'
That stated time had arrived.
In the morning he let loaves of bread shower down,
and in the evening a rain of wheat.
I watched the appearance of the weather—
the weather was frightful to behold!
I went into the boat and sealed the entry.
For the **caulking** of the boat, to Puzuramurri, the boatman,
I gave the palace together with its contents.
Just as dawn began to glow
there arose from the horizon a black cloud.
Adad rumbled inside of it,
before him went **Shullat and Hanish,**
heralds going over mountain and land.
Erragal pulled out the mooring poles,
forth went Ninurta and made the **dikes** overflow.
The **Anunnaki** lifted up the torches,
setting the land ablaze with their flare.
Stunned shock over Adad's deeds overtook the heavens,
and turned to blackness all that had been light.
The...land shattered like a...pot.
All day long the South Wind blew...,
blowing fast, **submerging** the mountain in water,
overwhelming the people like an attack.
No one could see his fellow,
they could not recognize each other in the **torrent.**
The gods were frightened by the Flood,
and retreated, ascending to the heaven of Anu.

Kith and kin: Immediate family and other relatives.

Shamash: The god of the sun and of justice, in charge of determining day and night.

Caulking: Sealing up cracks to prevent leaking.

Adad: The god of thunder.

Shullat and Hanish: Lesser gods of storms and bad weather; they predicted bad weather and served the god Adad.

Heralds: Messengers, bearers of news.

Erragal: God of the under-world; god of war and plague.

Dikes: Bank of Earth used to control or keep back water.

Anunnaki: Gods of the underworld.

Submerging: Causing something to sink below the surface of water.

Torrent: A rush of liquid.

Cowering: Moving back in fear.

Crouching: Bending down low, squatting.

Ishtar: Goddess of love and war.

Catastrophe: Disaster, tragedy.

Parched: Dry.

Terrain: A piece of land.

Vent: An opening for air.

Leagues: Measures of about three miles each.

Perch: Place for a bird to sit.

The gods were **cowering** like dogs, **crouching** by the
    outer wall.
Ishtar shrieked like a woman in childbirth,
the sweet-voiced Mistress of the Gods wailed:
'The olden days have alas turned to clay,
because I said evil things in the Assembly of the Gods!
How could I say evil things in the Assembly of the Gods,
ordering a **catastrophe** to destroy my people!!
No sooner have I given birth to my dear people
than they fill the sea like so many fish!'
The gods—those of the Anunnaki—were weeping with her,
the gods humbly sat weeping, sobbing with grief(?),
their lips burning, **parched** with thirst.
Six days and seven nights
came the wind and flood, the storm flattening the land.
When the seventh day arrived, the storm was pounding,
the flood was a war—struggling with itself like a woman
writhing (in labor).
The sea calmed, fell still, the whirlwind (and) flood stopped up.
I looked around all day long—quiet had set in
and all the human beings had turned to clay!
The **terrain** was as flat as a roof.
I opened a **vent** and fresh air (daylight!) fell upon the side of
my nose.
I fell to my knees and sat weeping,
tears streaming down the side of my nose.
I looked around for coastlines in the expanse of the sea,
and at twelve **leagues** there emerged a region (of land).
On Mt. Nimush the boat lodged firm,
Mt. Nimush held the boat, allowing no sway.
One day and a second Mt. Nimush held the boat, allowing
no sway.
A third day, a fourth, Mt. Nimush held the boat, allowing
no sway.
A fifth day, a sixth, Mt. Nimush held the boat, allowing
no sway.
When a seventh day arrived
I sent forth a dove and released it.
The dove went off, but came back to me;
no **perch** was visible so it circled back to me.
I sent forth a swallow and released it.
The swallow went off, but came back to me;
no perch was visible so it circled back to me.
I sent forth a raven and released it.
The raven went off, and saw the waters slither back.
It eats, it scratches, it bobs, but does not circle back to me.

Then I sent out everything in all directions and **sacrificed** (a sheep).
I offered incense in front of the mountain-**ziggurat.**
Seven and seven cult vessels I put in place,
and (into the fire) underneath (or: into their bowls) I poured reeds, cedar, and myrtle.
The gods smelled the **savor,**
the gods smelled the sweet savor,
and collected like flies over a (sheep) sacrifice.
Just then **Beletili** arrived.
She lifted up the large flies (beads) which Anu had made for his enjoyment(!):
'You gods, as surely as I shall not forget this **lapis lazuli** around my neck,
may I be mindful of these days, and never forget them!
The gods may come to the incense offering,
but Enlil may not come to the incense offering,
because without considering he brought about the Flood
and **consigned** my people to **annihilation**.'
Just then Enlil arrived.
He saw the boat and became furious,
he was filled with rage at the **Igigi** gods:
'Where did a living being escape?
No man was to survive the annihilation!'
Ninurta spoke to Valiant Enlil, saying:
'Who else but Ea could devise such a thing?
It is Ea who knows every **machination!'**
Ea spoke to Valiant Enlil, saying:
'It is yours, O Valiant One, who is the **Sage** of the Gods.
How, how could you bring about a Flood without consideration
Charge the **violation** to the violator,
charge the offense to the offender,
but be **compassionate lest** (mankind) be cut off,
be patient lest they be killed.
Instead of your bringing on the Flood,
would that a lion had appeared to diminish the people!
Instead of your bringing on the Flood,
would that a wolf had appeared to diminish the people!
Instead of your bringing on the Flood,
would that famine had occurred to slay the land!
Instead of your bringing on the Flood,
would that **(Pestilent) Erra** had appeared to ravage the land!
It was not I who revealed the secret of the Great Gods,
I (only) made a dream appear to **Atrahasis,** and (thus) he heard the secret of the gods.

Sacrificed: Made a ritual offering to a god, especially of a killed animal.

Ziggurat: A Mesopotamian temple tower.

Savor: Aroma.

Beletili: A minor Sumerian deity, who is believed to have been a fertility goddess.

Lapis lazuli: A deep-blue semiprecious stone.

Consigned: Delivered or handed over.

Annihilation: Complete destruction.

Igigi: Spirits that appear as stars in the sky.

Machination: Scheme, plot, or crafty action.

Sage: Wise person.

Violation: Crime or a breaking of laws or rules.

Compassionate: Showing sympathy for the suffering of others.

Lest: In order to prevent something from happening.

Pestilent: Damaging or deadly.

Erra: Form of Erragal as a thunder god.

Atrahasis: Hero of an Akkadian epic (c. 1700 BCE) that also tells the story of the Flood.

The Epic of Gilgamesh was inscribed on this tablet in the seventh century BCE. It relays the mythic story of the king Gilgamesh and his interaction with the gods of Mesopotamia. THE GRANGER COLLECTION, NEW YORK. REPRODUCED BY PERMISSION.

Deliberation: Careful thought or planning, discussion.

Now then! The **deliberation** should be about him!'"

• • •

What happened next...

In the remaining portion of Tablet XI, Utanapishtim gives Gilgamesh a chance at immortality. He tells the hero that if he can stay awake for six days and seven nights, he, too, will be immortal. Gilgamesh agrees to try, but as soon as he sits down, he falls asleep. Utanapishtim is convinced that all humans are liars. If Gilgamesh falls asleep, Utanapishtim believes Gilgamesh will say he stayed awake. To prove that Gilgamesh will lie, Utanapishtim arranges a test. He has his wife bake a loaf of bread each day, which he places at Gilgamesh's feet. As Gilgamesh continues to sleep, the loaves of bread gather, untouched. When Utanapishtim awakens Gilgamesh, the hero insists that he only dozed off for a moment, but he is grieved when Utanapishtim points out the loaves of bread, which grew progressively stale with each passing day.

Utanapishtim's wife persuades him to have mercy on Gilgamesh, so he gives the hero another chance. He tells Gilgamesh of a plant that will restore his youth, but the plant is at the bottom of the ocean. Gilgamesh plucks the plant, but he is not certain that he trusts it, so he resolves to take it back to Uruk to test it on an old man. Along the way, however, a snake eats the plant. (This act suggests that snakes gained the ability to be reborn, which they seem to do when they shed their skin.) This leaves Gilgamesh grief-stricken because he has lost his chance at immortality.

Did you know...

- The ancient Sumerians believed that their fate depended entirely on the will of the gods. They saw their lives as a cycle, with the gods granting and then withdrawing their favor. This view is probably a reflection of nature's cycle of flooding followed by growth. When the land flooded, the Sumerians believed that they had angered the gods, who submerged the land to show their displeasure. But when the crops grew, the people thought that they had won back the gods' favor.

- The last Sumerian dynasty fell about 2000 BCE. After a period of about one hundred years, a group called the Amorites gained control of the area encompassing Mesopotamia. Little is known about the religious beliefs of the Amorites, though it is thought that they adopted many of the religious beliefs of the Sumerians. The Amorites introduced the supreme god Marduk to the Sumerians. Like the Sumerians, the Amorites were not concerned with life after death; their focus was on this world.

- *The Epic of Gilgamesh* is not the only surviving epic from this region of the world. There is also the Babylonian epic Enuma Elish, a creation story at the center of which is the creator-god Marduk. In this epic, humans are depicted as slaves of the gods. At one point Marduk says, "Let me create a primeval man./The work of the gods shall be imposed (on him), and so they shall be at leisure." Other Mesopotamian epics and poems speaks of events similar to those in the Judeo-Christian Bible, including the temptation by the serpent in the Garden of Eden.

Consider the following...

- Explain how weather, climate, and geography could influence and shape the view of the world held by ancient peoples.

- Compare the account of the flood in Tablet XI of the Gilgamesh epic with a flood story from another culture or religious tradition, focusing on similarities and differences. An example is the flood survived by Noah and his family in the biblical book of Genesis.

- Explain why the writer of the epic of Gilgamesh placed so much emphasis on the dimensions and methods of construction of the ark.

For More Information

BOOKS

Foster, Benjamin R., Douglas Frayne, and Gary M. Beckman. *The Epic of Gilgamesh*. New York: Norton, 2001.

Heidel, Alexander. *Gilgamesh Epic and Old Testament Parallels*. Chicago: University of Chicago Press, 1963.

Kluger, Rivkah Schärf. *The Archetypal Significance of Gilgamesh: A Modern Ancient Hero*. Einsiedeln, Switzerland: Daimon, 2004.

Kovacs, Maureen Gallery, trans. *The Epic of Gilgamesh*. Palo Alto, CA: Stanford University Press, 1990. This excerpt can also be found online at http://www.ancienttexts.org/library/mesopotamian/gilgamesh/tab11.htm.

Tigay, Jeffrey H. *The Evolution of the Gilgamesh Epic*. Wauconda, IL: Bolchazy-Carducci Publishers, 2002.

WEB SITES

Brown, Arthur A. "Storytelling, the Meaning of Life, and *The Epic of Gilgamesh*." *Exploring Ancient World Cultures*. http://eawc.evansville.edu/essays/brown.htm (accessed on June 5, 2006).

The Epic of Gilgamesh. *Academy for Ancient Texts*. http://www.ancienttexts.org/library/mesopotamian/gilgamesh/index.html (accessed on June 5, 2006).

The Odyssey

Book I: "Athena Inspires the Prince," from The Odyssey,
from the Ancient History Sourcebook, available online at
http://www.fordham.edu/halsall/ancient/odysseyBL.html
Written by Homer circa 800 BCE
Translated by Samuel Henry Butcher and Andrew Lang

"How vainly mortal men do blame the gods! For of us they say comes evil, whereas they even of themselves through the blindness of their own hearts, have sorrows beyond that which is ordained."

"Athena Inspires the Prince" is the first of twenty-four books in *The Odyssey*, an ancient epic poem of some twelve thousand lines thought to have been written by the Greek poet Homer. Epic poetry is lengthy poetry telling tales of heroic deeds. Virtually nothing is known about Homer and his life or about the circumstances surrounding the composition of the poem. It was probably developed orally over a period of years and may have been first written down many centuries later.

The poem survived on ancient scrolls of papyrus (a kind of paper made from the papyrus plant, primarily in Egypt) and then in handwritten manuscripts in books called codices. A codex is a collection of ancient texts in manuscript form. Codices are more than one codex. These manuscripts had been preserved in the library at Byzantium (present-day Constantinople in Turkey) by the Greeks. After Byzantium was conquered by the Ottoman Turks in 1453, the library became more available to the Western world. At this time *The Odyssey*, along with many other ancient texts, became more widely known in the West. *The Odyssey* and its companion poem, *The Iliad*, are the oldest surviving works of

Greek literature. They are regarded as two of the most influential works in the foundation of Western literature.

Odysseus' long journey home *The Odyssey* can be read as the sequel to Homer's *Iliad*. The latter epic tells the adventurous story of the Trojan War, a war between Troy and ancient Greece. This war begins when Paris, the son of the king of Troy, wins the love of Helen, the wife of Menelaus, the king of Sparta in Greece, and takes her with him back to Troy. *The Iliad* focuses on just a few weeks during the tenth and last year of that war. One of the major characters in *The Iliad* is Odysseus, a warrior-king and general from the Greek state of Ithaca.

At the beginning of "Athena Inspires the Prince," Homer calls upon the Muse of epic poetry (one of nine goddesses who inspire artistic creation) to guide him in telling the story of a man who has survived hardship and experienced the twists and turns of fate. That man is Odysseus, who has been away from his wife and his kingdom for many years. Odysseus fought at Troy for ten years before he began his long journey home. At the start of *The Odyssey,* Odysseus has spent seven years on the island of Ogygia. There, Odysseus, the only Greek who has not yet returned home from the war, is being held by Calypso, a nymph who has cast a spell over him because she wants Odysseus as her husband.

Odysseus had angered the sea god Poseidon (the brother of Zeus, the king of the gods) by blinding Polyphemus the Cyclops, Poseidon's son. Poseidon was responsible for making Odysseus's return home so difficult. At the same time Odysseus's wife, Penelope, is being courted at home in Ithaca by a large number of suitors, who feast and drink in Odysseus's home at his expense and who each hope to marry Penelope and become king. Penelope's situation remains uncertain because she does not have any reliable information about the fate of her husband.

Reputation, revenge, and power The first book of *The Odyssey* introduces a number of themes that run through the poem. One is the value of maintaining a good reputation, both with humans and with the gods. This theme illustrates that the people of Homer's time thought of their relationship with the gods in very human terms. Book I states that Odysseus is held in high regard by all the gods except Poseidon.

A second theme is the role of revenge in achieving justice. In ancient times, when societies did not have police, a court system, or prisons, individuals found justice for perceived wrongs themselves, and the gods, who had human characteristics, often helped them to do so. Telemachus, the son of Penelope and Odysseus, is hesitant to take action against the men who would seize the crown by marrying his mother. Athena, however, "inspires the prince" to act against them.

A final theme is power—how it is earned and how it is maintained. The youthful Telemachus has not yet gained the right to the throne of Ithaca. He is challenged by Antinous, one of the suitors, but he lacks support in establishing his claim to kingship. He is roused to make a stand, though, by Athena and begins to take steps to strengthen and secure his power. Again, for the people of Homer's time, success in life could be achieved only with the aid of the gods, who were all too happy to become involved in human affairs.

Characteristics of the gods *The Odyssey* provides modern readers with a rich portrait of the characteristics of the gods and the roles they play in human affairs as they were conceived by the ancient Greeks. Greek religion was polytheistic, meaning that the people believed in more than one god. Chief among the Greek gods is Zeus, son of Cronus, the king of the Titans. On reaching adulthood, Zeus leads a revolt against the Titans and takes away the throne from Cronus with the help of his brothers Poseidon and Hades. From his position on Mount Olympus, Zeus observes the affairs of humans. He sees everything, governs all human actions, rewards good conduct and punishes evil, dispenses justice, and protects cities and homes. Nonetheless, Zeus recognizes that humans play a part in determining their own fates.

In Greek myth, numerous lesser gods and goddesses have their own spheres of influence and often quarrel among themselves. Legend has it that Athena had no mother. She sprang directly from the forehead of Zeus. She is a goddess of warfare, but, more importantly, she also represents practical wisdom, restraint, and reason. In *The Iliad,* she inspires the Greek heroes, and her name is equated with military skill, excellence in combat, victory, and glory, as opposed to mere lust for blood, represented by the god Ares. In this role, she becomes Odysseus's guardian, and in her relationship with Telemachus she acts as the goddess of good counsel, practical insight, and cautious self-control.

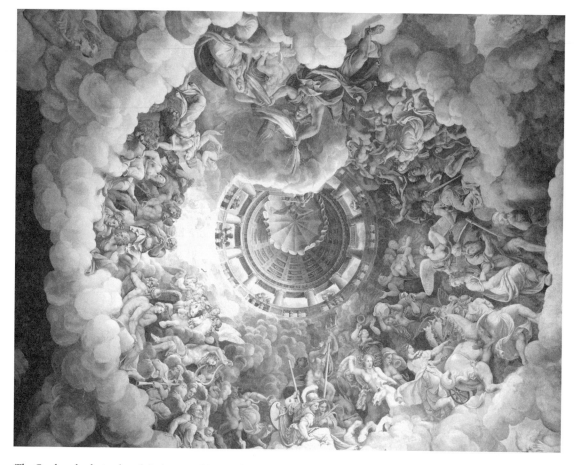

The Greek gods, depicted at their home on Mount Olympus, had many of the same passions and faults as humans. They often involved themselves in human affairs, as in the case of Odysseus, told in **The Odyssey.** THE ART ARCHIVE/PALAZZO DEL TE MANTUA/DAGLI ORTI (A).

Things to remember while reading the excerpt from *The Odyssey*:

- As the daughter of the sky god Zeus, Athena is one of the twelve Olympians, the gods and goddesses who live on Mount Olympus. The other Olympians, besides Zeus and Athena, include Aphrodite, the goddess of love; Hermes, the messenger god; Poseidon, the god of the sea; and others.

- Athena presents herself to Telemachus in disguise. She enters Ithaca in the form of Mentes, one of Odysseus's old friends, and meets with Telemachus. She tells the prince that Odysseus will return but that in the meantime Telemachus has to stand up to the suitors who are harassing his mother. Only in this way can he hope to inherit the kingdom from his father. Because Athena presents herself as a male friend of Telemachus's father rather than as a woman, Telemachus will be more likely to take her counsel.

- Telemachus's mother, Penelope, is surrounded by men from the kingdom who want to take Odysseus's place as king. Because she is a woman, Penelope cannot reign as the ruler of Ithaca herself. She has earned her position in life from her husband. The men believe that because Odysseus is gone, Penelope will marry one of them so that she can keep her position as queen.

• • •

Excerpt from *The Odyssey*

"Athena Inspires the Prince"

Tell me, **Muse,** of that man, so ready at need, who wandered far and wide, after he had **sacked** the sacred **citadel** of Troy, and many were the men whose towns he saw and whose mind he learnt, yea, and many the woes he suffered in his heart upon the deep, **striving** to win his own life and the return of his company. Nay, but even so he saved not his company, though he desired it **sore.** For through the blindness of their own hearts they perished, fools, who **devoured** the oxen of **Helios Hyperion:** but the god took from them their day of returning. Of these things, goddess, daughter of Zeus, **whencesoever** thou hast heard thereof, declare thou even unto us.

Now all the rest, as many as fled from sheer destruction, were at home, and had escaped both war and sea, but Odysseus only, craving for his wife and for his homeward path, the lady **nymph** Calypso held, that fair goddess, in her hollow caves, longing to have him for her lord. But when now the year had come in the courses of the seasons, wherein the gods had **ordained** that he should return home to Ithaca, not even there was he quit of **labours,** not even among his own; but all the gods had pity on him save Poseidon, who raged continually against godlike Odysseus, till be came to his own country. **Howbeit** Poseidon had now departed for the distant Ethiopians, the Ethiopians that are **sundered** in **twain,** the **uttermost** of men, abiding some where Hyperion sinks and some where he rises. There he looked to receive his **hetacomb** of bulls and rams, there he made merry sitting at the feast, but the other gods were gathered in the halls of Olympian Zeus. Then among them the father of gods and men began to speak, for he **bethought** him in his heart of noble Aegisthus, whom the

Muse: A Greek goddess who oversees art, song, poetry, and science.

Sacked: Destroyed.

Citadel: Fortress, castle.

Striving: Trying with great effort.

Sore: Greatly.

Devoured: Consumed, ate.

Helios Hyperion: The Greek sun god.

Whencesoever: From whatever place.

Nymph: A woodland or water-dwelling goddess.

Ordained: Decided.

Labours: Burdens.

Howbeit: However.

Sundered: Broken.

Twain: Two.

Uttermost: Greatest.

Hetacomb: Sacrifice.

Bethought: Thought.

Spake: Spoke.

Perish: Die.

Rent: Torn; broken.

Happless: Unlucky.

Affliction: Torment.

Seagirt: Surrounded by ocean or sea.

Naval: Center.

Habitation: Home.

Atlas: One of the Titans, or giant gods who ruled Earth until overthrown by Zeus.

Assunder: Apart.

Guileful: Deceptive.

Wooing: Convincing.

Yearning: Longing.

Wroth: Angry.

Girdler: Supporter.

Quenchless: Never satisfied.

Cyclops: One-eyed giant.

Unerring: Unfailing.

Rouse: Wake.

Might: Strength.

Achaeans: Greek armies.

Wooers: Those hoping to marry Odysseus's wife.

Thronging: Large.

Kine: Cattle.

Shambling gait: Slow, dragging walk.

Peraventure: By chance.

son of Agamemnon, farfamed Orestes, slew. Thinking upon him he **spake** out among the Immortals:

"Lo you now, how vainly mortal men do blame the gods! For of us they say comes evil, whereas they even of themselves through the blindness of their own hearts, have sorrows beyond that which is ordained. . . .

And the goddess, grey-eyed Athene [Athena], answered him, saying: "O father, our father Cronides, throned in the highest; that man assuredly lies in a death that is his due; so **perish** likewise all who work such deeds! But my heart is **rent** for wise Odysseus, that **happless** one, who far from his friends this long while suffereth **affliction** in a **seagirt** isle, where is the **naval** of the sea, as woodland isle, and therein a goddess hath her **habitation**, the daughter of the wizard **Atlas** who knows the depths of every sea, and himself upholds the tall pillars which keep earth and sky **assunder**. His daughter it is that holds the hapless man in sorrow: and ever with soft and **guileful** tales she is **wooing** him to forgetfulness of Ithaca. But Odysseus **yearning** to see if it were but the smoke leap upwards from his own land, hath a desire to die. As for thee, thine heart regardeth it not at all, Olympian! What! did not Odysseus by the ships of the Argives make thee free offering of sacrifice in the wide Trojan land? Wherefore wast thou then so **wroth** with him, O Zeus?"

And Zeus the cloud-gatherer answered her, and said, "My child, what word hath escaped the door of thy lips? Yea, how should I forget divine Odysseus, who in understanding is beyond mortals and beyond all men hath done sacrifice to the deathless gods, who keep the wide heaven? Nay, but it is Poseidon, the **girdler** of the earth, that hath been wroth continually with **quenchless** anger for the **Cyclops'** sake whom he blinded of his eye, even godlike Polyphemus whose power is mightiest amongst all the Cyclopes. . . .

Then the goddess, grey-eyed Athene, answered him, and said: "O father, our father Cronides, throned in the highest, if indeed this thing is now well pleasing to the blessed gods, that wise Odysseus should return to his own home, let us then speed Hermes the Messenger, the slayer of Argos, to the island of Ogygia. There with all speed let him declare to the lady of the braided tresses our **unerring** counsel, even the return of the patient Odysseus, that so he may come to his home. But as for me I will go to Ithaca that I may **rouse** his son yet the more, planting **might** in his heart, to call an assembly of the long-haired **Achaeans** and speak out to all the **wooers** who slaughter continually the sheep of his **thronging** flocks, and his **kine** with trailing feet and **shambling gait**. And I will guide him to Sparta and to sandy Pylos to seek tidings of his dear father's return, if **peradventure** he may hear thereof and that so he may be had in good report among men."

She spake and bound beneath her feet her lovely golden sandals that **wax** not old, and bare her alike over the wet sea and over the limitless land, **swifth** as the breath of the wind. And she seized her **doughty** spear, **shod** with sharp bronze, weighty and huge and strong, **wherewith** she **quells** the ranks of heroes with whomsoever she is wroth, the daughter of the mighty **sire**. Then from the heights of Olympus she came glancing down, and she stood in the land of Ithaca, at the entry of the gate of Odysseus, on the threshold of the courtyard, holding in her hand the spear of bronze, in the semblence of a stranger, Mentes the captain of the **Taphians**. And there she found the lordly wooers: now they were taking their pleasure at **draughts** in front of the doors, sitting on hides of oxen, which themselves had slain. And of the **henchmen** and the ready **squires,** some were mixing for them wine and water in bowls, and some again were washing the tables with porous sponges and were setting them forth, and others were carving flesh in plenty.

And godlike Telemachus was far the first to **descry** her, for he was sitting with a heavy heart among the wooers dreaming on his good father, if **haply** he might come **somewhence,** and make a scattering of the wooers there throughout the palace, and himself get honour and bear rule among his own possessions. Thinking **thereupon,** as he sat among wooers, he saw Athene—and he went straight to the outer porch, for he thought it blame in his heart that a stranger should stand long at the gates: and halting **nigh** her he clasped her right hand and took from her the spear of bronze, and uttered his voice and spake unto her **winged words:** "Hail, stranger, with us thou shalt be kindly **entreated,** and thereafter, when thou hast tasted meat, thou shalt tell us that **whereof** thou hast need." . . .

But Telemachus spake unto grey-eyed Athene, holding his head close to her that those others might not hear: "Dear stranger, wilt thou of a truth be wroth at the word I shall say? **Yonder** men **verily** care for such things as these, the **lyre** and song, lightly, as they that devour the livelihood of another without atonement, of that man whose white bones, it may be, lie wasting in the rain upon the mainland, or the **billow** rolls them in the **brine.** Were but these men to see him returned to Ithaca, they all would pray rather for greater speed of foot than for gain of gold and **rainment.** But now he hath perished, even so, an evil doom, and for us is no comfort, no, not though any of earthly men should say that he will come again. Gone is the day of his returning! . . .

"For all the noblest that are princes in the isles, in Dulichium and Same and wooded Zacynthus, and as many as lord it in rocky Ithaca, all these woo my mother and waste my house. But as for her she neither refuseth the hated bridal, nor hath the heart to make an end: so they devour and **minish** my house, and **ere** long will they make havoc likewise of myself."

Wax: Were.

Swifth: Swiftly; quickly.

Doughty: Fearless.

Shod: Made.

Wherewith: With which.

Quells: Calms.

Sire: Father.

Taphians: A division of Greeks.

Draughts: Drinks.

Henchmen: Grooms; people who take care of horses.

Squires: Young noble attendants.

Descry: Notice.

Haply: By good fortune.

Somewhence: From somewhere.

Thereupon: On that.

Nigh: Near.

Winged words: Beautiful language.

Entreated: Treated.

Whereof: Whatever.

Yonder: At a distance.

Verily: Truly.

Lyre: A musical instrument similar to a harp.

Billow: Waves.

Brine: Seawater.

Rainment: Fine clothes.

Minish: Diminish; use up all the supplies of.

Ere: Before.

This third century CE Roman mosaic shows Odysseus facing the Sirens, who tempt him to abandon his quest to return home after the Trojan War. © CHARLES & JOSETTE LENARS/CORBIS.

Thither: Though.

Nowise: No way.

Consort: Associate.

Howbeit: How would it be if.

Vengeance: Revenge.

Counsel: Care.

On the morrow: Tomorrow.

Then in heavy displeasure spake unto him Pallas Athene: "God help thee! thou art surely sore in need of Odysseus that is afar, to stretch forth his hands upon the shameless wooers. If he could but come now and stand at the entering in of the gate, with helmet and shield and lances twain, as mighty a man as when first I marked him in our house drinking and making merry what time he came up out of Ephyra from Ilus son of Mermerus! For even **thither** had Odysseus gone on his swift ship to seek a deadly drug, that he might have wherewithal to smear his bronze-shod arrows: but Ilus would in **nowise** give it to him, for he had in awe the ever-living gods. But my father gave it him, for he bare him wondrous love. O that Odysseus might in such strength **consort** with the wooers: so should they all have swift fate and bitter wedlock! **Howbeit** these things surely lie on the knees of the gods, whether he shall return or not, and take **vengeance** in his halls. But I charge thee to take **counsel** how thou mayest thrust forth the wooers from the hall. Come now, mark and take heed unto my words. **On the morrow** call the Achaean lords to the assembly, and declare thy saying to all, and take the gods to witness. As for the wooers bid them scatter them each one to his own, and for thy mother, if her heart is moved to marriage, let her go back to the hall of that mighty man her father, and her kinsfolk will furnish a wedding feast, and array the gifts of wooing exceeding many, all that should go back with a daughter dearly beloved. And to thyself I will give a word of wise counsel, if **perchance thou will harken.** Fit out a ship, the best thou hast, with twenty oarsmen, and go to inquire concerning thy father that is long afar, if perchance any man shall tell thee **aught,** or if thou mayest hear the voice from Zeus, which chiefly brings tidings to men. Get thee first to Pylos and inquire of goodly Nestor, and from thence to Sparta to Menelaus of the fair hair, for he came home the last of the mail-coated Achaeans. If thou shalt hear news of the life and the returning of thy father, then verily thou mayest endure the wasting for yet a year. But if thou shalt hear that he is dead and gone, return then to thine own dear country and pile his **mound,** and over it pay burial rites, full many as is due, and give thy mother to a husband. But when thou hast done this and made an end, thereafter take counsel in thy mind and heart, how thou mayest slay the wooers in thy halls, whether by **guile** or openly; for thou shouldst not carry childish thoughts, being no longer **of years thereto.** Or hast thou not heard what **renown** the goodly Orestes **gat** him among all men in that he slew the slayer of his father, guileful Aegisthus, who killed his famous sire? . . . "

Then wise Telemachus answered her, saying: "Sir, verily thou speakest these things out of a friendly heart, as a father to his son, and never will I forget them. But now I pray thee **abide** here, though eager to be gone, to the end that after thou hast bathed and had all thy heart's desire, thou mayest **wend** to the ship joyful in spirit, with a costly gift and very goodly, to be an heirloom of my giving, such as dear friends give to friends." . . .

Now the wooers **clamoured** throughout the shadowy halls, and each one uttered a prayer to be her **bedfellow.** And wise Telemachus first spake among them:

"Wooers of my mother, men **despiteful** out of measure, let us feast now and make merry and let there be no **brawling**; for, lo, it is a good thing to **list** to a minstrel such as him, like to the gods in voice. But in the morning let us all go to the assembly and sit us down, that I may declare my saying outright, to wit that ye leave these halls: and busy yourselves with other feasts, eating your own substance, going in turn from house to house. But if ye **deem** this a likelier and a better thing, that one man's goods should perish without atonement, then waste ye as ye will; and I will call upon the everlasting gods, if haply Zeus may grant that acts of **recompense** be made: so should ye hereafter perish within the halls without atonement."

Perchance thou will harken: By chance you will pay attention.

Aught: Of him.

Mound: Grave.

Guile: Deception.

Of years thereto: Of a childish age.

Renown: Famous.

Gat: Got.

abide: Stay.

Wend: Direct.

Clamoured or clamored: Made loud noises.

Bedfellow: One who shares the same bed.

Despiteful: Spiteful.

Brawling: Fighting.

List: Listen.

Deem: Consider.

Recompense: Compensation; payment.

Marvelled: Were amazed.

So spake he, and all that heard him bit their lips and **marvelled** at Telemachus, in that he spake boldly.

Then Antinous, son of Eupeithes, answered him: "Telemachus, in very truth the gods themselves instruct thee to be proud of speech and boldly to **harangue.** Never may Cronion [Zeus] make thee king in seagirt Ithaca, which thing is of inheritance thy right!"

Harangue: To make a ranting speech.

Then wise Telemachus answered him, and said: "Antinous, wilt thou indeed be wroth at the word that I shall say? Yea, at the hand of Zeus would I be **fain** to take even this thing upon me. Sayest thou that this is the worst hap that can **befal** a man? Nay, verily, it is no ill thing to be a king: the house of such an one quickly **waxeth** rich and himself is held in greater honour. Howsoever there are many other kings of the Achaeans in seagirt Ithaca, kings young and old; someone of them shall surely have this kingship since goodly Odysseus is dead. But as for me, I will be lord of our own house and **thralls,** that goodly Odysseus gat me with his spear." . . .

Fain: Unwilling.

Befal: Happen to.

Waxeth: Becomes.

Thralls: Possessions.

But Telemachus, where his chamber was built high up in the fair court, in a place with wide **prospect,** thither **betook** him to his bed, **pondering** many thoughts in his mind; and with him went trusty Eurycleia, and bare for him torches burning. She was the daughter of Ops, son of Peisenor, and Laertes bought her on a time with his wealth, while as yet she was in her first youth, and gave for her the worth of twenty oxen. And he honoured her even as he honoured his dear wife in the halls, but he never lay with her, for he shunned the wrath of his lady. She went with Telemachus and bare for him the burning torches: and of all the women of the household she loved him most, and she had nursed him when a little one. Then he opened the doors of the well-builded chamber and sat him on the bed and took off his soft **doublet,** and put it in the wise old woman's hands. So she folded the doublet and smoothed it, and hung it on a pin by the jointed **bedstead,** and went forth on her way from the room, and pulled to the door with the silver handle, and drew home the bar with the thong. There, all night through, wrapped in a fleece of wool, he meditated in his heart upon the journey that Athene had showed him.

Prospect: View.

Betook: Took.

Pondering: Thinking.

Doublet: Jacket.

Bedstead: Framework of a bed.

• • •

What happened next . . .

Books II through IV of *The Odyssey* depict the situation in Ithaca, where Penelope and Telemachus attempt to hold on to their authority in Odysseus's absence. In Book V, Zeus orders Calypso to release Odysseus, who sets out on a raft that is destroyed by his enemy, Poseidon. Odysseus washes ashore on the land of the Phaeacians, portrayed in Books VI through VIII. Books IX through XII contain Odysseus's account of his adventures since leaving Troy. These adventures include his stay in the land of the Lotus-Eaters; his blinding of Polyphemus; the loss of eleven of his twelve ships to a race of cannibals, or eaters of human flesh; his arrival at the island of the enchantress Circe; his visit to the Land of Departed Spirits; his encounter with the Sirens, partly human creatures who lure seamen to their deaths at sea; and his arrival at Calypso's island. In Books XIII through XVI, the Phaeacians return Odysseus to Ithaca. After Athena disguises him as a beggar, he reveals his true identity to Telemachus, and the two men plot to rid the kingdom of the king's rivals. In the final books (XVII through XXIV), Odysseus passes a test Penelope sets up to choose one of her suitors. Odysseus kills the suitors with the help of his son and resumes his place as Penelope's husband and king of Ithaca.

Did you know . . .

- While *The Iliad* and *The Odyssey* are the earliest works of literature that portray the Greek gods and goddesses, other works give further detail. Most important are two works by Hesiod, a poet who lived at almost the same time (c. 800 BCE) as Homer: *Theogony* and *Works and Days*. In these books, Hesiod provides accounts of the origins of the universe, the succession of gods and goddesses, the ages of the world, and the sources of human misfortune.

- Readers of (or listeners to) *The Odyssey* who knew *The Iliad,* the earlier epic, would have already been familiar with Athena and her skill and practicality in the art of warfare. This skill is shown near the end of *The Iliad* when she helps the Greek Epeius build a huge wooden horse, referred to as the Trojan horse. The Greeks leave the horse outside the walls of Troy. The Trojans take the horse inside as an offering to Athena—not knowing that the horse has been hollowed out and that inside are Greek soldiers under the command of Odysseus. At night, the soldiers emerge from the horse and unlock the gates of the city, allowing the Greeks to enter, sack the city, and end the Trojan War. The term *Trojan horse* is still used today to refer to any similar act of trickery; computer experts use the term to refer to a way of sneaking a virus into a computer system.

- The historical setting for *The Odyssey* is about the twelfth century BCE. Archeologists call this period of time the Bronze Age, named after the type of metal that was widely used. The Greeks believed that the Bronze Age was a time when their country was home to heroic people with superhuman characteristics and when gods moved freely about Earth. There are several mentions of bronze in the excerpted passage, for example, in reference to Athena, who is described as seizing "the rugged spear tipped with a bronze point." Odysseus is said to have sailed past Ephyra, "hunting deadly poison to smear on his arrows' bronze heads." The epic tries to capture the glorious spirit of the age by using a high poetic style rather than everyday language.

Consider the following...

- Explain how Homer establishes the importance of the story he is about to tell.

- Summarize ways in which the gods and goddesses portrayed in *The Odyssey* behave and think. Compare these behaviors and ways of thought to those of deities in other religions.

- Explain the relationship between Athena and Odysseus and between Athena and Telemachus. Summarize the role Athena plays in the affairs of these two human beings.

For More Information

BOOKS

Clay, Jenny Strauss. *The Wrath of Athena: Gods and Men in the "Odyssey."* Totowa, NJ: Littlefield Adams, 1996.

Osborne, Mary Pope, and Troy Howell. *Tales from The Odyssey.* New York: Hyperion, 2005.

Picard, Barbara Leonie. *The Odyssey of Homer.* New York: Oxford University Press, 2000.

WEB SITES

Arkwright, Tony, Justin Eichenlaub, and John Ramsey. *Homer's "Iliad" and "Odyssey."* http://library.thinkquest.org/19300/data/homer.htm (accessed on June 5, 2006).

Homer. *The Odyssey.* Samuel Henry Butcher and Andrew Lang, translators. *Ancient History Sourcebook.* http://www.fordham.edu/halsall/ancient/odysseyBL.html (June 5, 2006).

Mitchell-Boyask, Robin. "Study Guide for Homer's *Odyssey.*" *Classical Mythology.* http://www.temple.edu/classics/odysseyho.html (accessed on June 5, 2006).

Mythweb.com. http://www.mythweb.com/ (accessed on June 5, 2006).

Sri Guru Granth Sahib

"Jup," from the Sri Guru Granth Sahib, available online from the Internet Sacred Text Archive at http://www.sacred-texts.com/skh/granth/gr01.htm
Compiled by Guru Gobind Singh in the eighteenth century

"Endless are His Praises, endless are those who speak them.

Endless are His Actions, endless are His Gifts.

Endless is His Vision, endless is His Hearing."

Sikhism emerged in the Punjab region of what is now India and Pakistan in the fifteenth century. The founder of Sikhism was Sri Guru Nanak Dev Ji (1449–1538), who was born in an area of the Punjab that is now part of Pakistan. From an early age, he came to believe that external forms of worship were not as important as inner beliefs. He rejected many of the beliefs and practices of the Hindus who surrounded him, as well as that of Muslims. At one time Guru Nanak famously proclaimed, "There is no Hindu, there is no Muslim."

At the city of Sultanpur in India he had a revelation instructing him to preach about paths to enlightenment and to God. He opposed the caste system of Hindus (a hereditary system that defined and separated social classes) and any form of worship of idols, or substitutes for God. He also adopted the monotheism (belief in one supreme god) of Islam and placed a great deal of emphasis on the brotherhood of humankind.

The excerpt presents Guru Nanak's concept of God, a concept that all Sikhs adopt. It is taken from the Sikh sacred scripture, called the Sri Guru Granth Sahib. The section from which the excerpt is taken, titled "Jup," is an epic poem written by Guru Nanak. An epic poem is a work of poetry that may be as long as a book. The fundamental beliefs of Sikhs are reflected in the excerpt and are relatively simple. Sikhs believe that the purpose of religion is to create a close, loving relationship with

God. One way to do this is through prayer, which repeatedly emphasizes the attributes, or characteristics, of God. The God of the Sikhs is a single God with no form that could be represented in, for example, a painting or sculpture. This is a contrast to the beliefs of Hinduism, in which God can take on many forms and be present in many things. The Sikh God fills the universe ("Endless are His Actions, endless are His Gifts"). He can be known only through meditation ("The faithful have intuitive awareness and intelligence").

The "Jup" consists entirely of an ongoing list of the features and qualities of God. God is to be honored and worshipped because of his creative power, his gifts to humankind, his virtue, his greatness, his beauty, his watchfulness over people, and many other characteristics. He has many names, such as True One, Infinite Lord, Highest of the High, and Treasure of Excellence. People can create a loving relationship with God by listening to Him and by striving to be pleasing to Him. Repeatedly, the prayer says, "May I never forget Him." The goal of always remembering God is central to the Sikh faith.

Guru Nanak was the first in a succession of ten gurus of Sikhism. A guru is a spiritual and religious teacher and counselor. The nine that followed him were regarded as reincarnations of Nanak. That is, they were considered to be new bodies into which Nanak was reborn. These gurus were the leaders of the Sikh faith until the early eighteenth century. The fifth guru, Sri Arjan Dev Ji (1563–1606), assembled the Sikh holy text, the Sri Guru Granth Sahib, in 1603. The book consists of the hymns and writings of Sikhism's early gurus as well as those of various Hindu and Muslim saints. In later years, the Guru Granth was updated to include the writings of the some of the later gurus. In all it contains the work of six gurus: Nanak, Angad Dev, Amar Das, Ram Das, Arjan Dev, and Teg Bahadur.

Then, early in the eighteenth century, the last of the gurus, Gobind Singh Ji (1666–1708), compiled all of these writings into an updated version of the Sri Guru Granth Sahib. He proclaimed the text to be the eleventh and final guru of Sikhism. The Guru Granth Sahib is still personified in the early twenty-first century as the final guru, the living embodiment of the previous gurus, almost like a person. It remains the sacred scripture and spiritual guide of Sikhism.

The Guru Granth is the focus of worship in a Sikh temple, called a *gurdwara,* which literally means "residence of the Guru" or "door that

Sikhs hold an image of Guru Nanak, Sikhism's founder. Guru Nanak discussed his concept of God in the "Jup," an epic poem within the Sri Guru Granth Sahib. AFP/GETTY IMAGES.

leads to the Guru." Because Sikhs reject any form of idol worship (the worship of images that are not God) and believe that God has no physical form, there are no statues, pictures, incense, bells, or any other objects associated with religious ritual. Additionally, no copy of the Guru Granth is illustrated.

Any building that has a copy of the Guru Granth can be regarded as a Gurdwara. While a leader, called a Granthi, reads passages from the Guru Granth for the assembled worshippers, this person is not a priest. He is regarded simply as a reader and custodian of the Guru Granth, though he is expected to live an exemplary life. The Guru Granth is stored in a room by itself during the night. When Sikhs gather to worship, it is carried out in ceremonial fashion and placed on a raised platform or throne, where it is covered by a rich cloth when not being read. Sikhs regard the Guru Granth as an expression of God and a living embodiment of the gurus, so copies of it are treated respectfully.

The Gurdwara

The *gurdwara* is a Sikh temple. Each gurdwara has four doors that lead into it. They are called the Door of Livelihood, the Door of Peace, the Door of Grace, and the Door of Learning. The four doors have symbolic meaning. They suggest that anyone is welcome to enter from the four points of the compass. They also suggest that members of any of the four Hindu castes are welcome. A light is always kept burning in the gurdwara to show that the Guru Granth's visible light can be seen by anyone at any time. There are approximately two hundred gurdwaras in India and an equal number in the United States.

While Sikhism rejected certain elements of Hinduism, particularly what it saw as Hinduism's emphasis on rituals and outward forms of worship, Sikhs believe in several central Hindu concepts:

- *samsara,* or the endlessly repeated cycle of birth, life, and death;
- karma, or the concept that the sum of a person's good and bad actions determines how he or she lives a future life; and
- reincarnation, or rebirth following death.

In this respect Sikhism differs from many other religions in the world that teach that when a person dies, his or her soul goes either to heaven or hell forever. A person can become a Sikh by recognizing a single immortal God, by believing in the ten gurus as well as the Guru Granth Sahib, and by accepting the teachings of the gurus.

Things to remember while reading the excerpt from the Sri Guru Granth Sahib:

- The "Jup" differs from much of the rest of the Guru Granth in being more like an epic poem than a song, prayer, or hymn. The Guru Granth evolved from an earlier text called the Adi Granth. The Adi Granth consisted of poems, prayers, verses, and hymns that Nanak and later gurus wrote down.
- The excerpt repeatedly calls on Guru Nanak ("O Nanak") for spiritual wisdom. Because a guru to Sikhs embodies divine wisdom, calling on Nanak is akin to calling on God.
- At the time the Guru Granth was being compiled, religious texts in India were written largely in Sanskrit. This was a written language that the people did not speak. In contrast, the Granth was written largely in Punjabi, the language of the people. When asked why this was so, the third guru, Amar Das (1479–1574), replied (according to Sandeep Singh Brar, author of "The Third Master Guru Amar Das (1479–1574)"): "Sanskrit is like a well, deep, inaccessible [out of reach] and confined to the elite [a select few], but the language of the people is like rain water—ever fresh, abundant and accessible to all."

• • •

Excerpt from the Sri Guru Granth Sahib

Section 01—Jup—Part 001

One Universal Creator God. The Name Is Truth. Creative Being Personified. No Fear. No Hatred. Image Of The Undying,

Beyond Birth, Self-Existent. By Guru's Grace ~

Chant And Meditate:

True In The Primal Beginning. True Throughout The Ages.

True Here And Now. O Nanak, Forever And Ever True.

By thinking, He cannot be **reduced** to thought, even by thinking hundreds of thousands of times.

Reduced: Simplified or limited.

By remaining silent, inner silence is not **obtained,** even by remaining lovingly **absorbed** deep within.

Obtained: Acquired.

The hunger of the hungry is not **appeased,** even by piling up loads of worldly goods.

Absorbed: Occupied, having one's attention held.

Appeased: Satisfied.

Hundreds of thousands of clever tricks, but not even one of them will go along with you in the end.

So how can you become truthful? And how can the veil of **illusion** be torn away?

Illusion: A false idea.

O Nanak, it is written that you shall obey the **Hukam** of His Command, and walk in the Way of His Will.

Hukam: Divine will.

By His Command, bodies are created; His Command cannot be described.

By His Command, souls come into being; by His Command, glory and greatness are obtained.

By His Command, some are high and some are low; by His Written Command, pain and pleasure are obtained.

Some, by His Command, are blessed and forgiven; others, by His Command, wander aimlessly forever.

Everyone is subject to His Command; no one is beyond His Command.

O Nanak, one who understands His Command, does not speak in ego.

Some sing of His Power—who has that Power?

Some sing of His Gifts, and know His Sign and **Insignia.**

Insignia: Symbol of authority, like a badge.

Some sing of His Glorious Virtues, Greatness and Beauty.

Some sing of knowledge obtained of Him, through difficult philosophical studies.

Some sing that He fashions the body, and then again reduces it to dust.

Some sing that He takes life away, and then again restores it.

Some sing that He seems so very far away.

Section 01—Jup—Part 002

Some sing that He watches over us, face to face, ever-present.

There is no shortage of those who preach and teach.

Millions upon millions offer millions of sermons and stories.

The Great Giver keeps on giving, while those who receive grow weary of receiving.

Throughout the ages, consumers consume.

The Commander, by His Command, leads us to walk on the Path.

O Nanak, He blossoms forth, Carefree and Untroubled.

True is the Master, True is His Name—speak it with infinite love.

People beg and pray, "Give to us, give to us," and the Great Giver gives His Gifts.

So what offering can we place before Him, by which we might see the **Darbaar** of His Court?

What words can we speak to **evoke** His Love?

In the Amrit Vaylaa, the **ambrosial** hours before dawn, chant the True Name, and contemplate His Glorious Greatness.

By the karma of past actions, the robe of this physical body is obtained. By His Grace, the Gate of Liberation is found.

O Nanak, know this well: the True One Himself is All.

He cannot be established, He cannot be created.

He Himself is **Immaculate** and Pure.

Those who serve Him are honored.

O Nanak, sing of the Lord, the Treasure of Excellence.

Sing, and listen, and let your mind be filled with love.

Your pain shall be sent far away, and peace shall come to your home.

The Guru's Word is the Sound-current of the **Naad;** the Guru's Word is the Wisdom of the **Vedas;** the Guru's Word is **all-pervading.**

The Guru is **Shiva,** the Guru is **Vishnu** and **Brahma;** the Guru is **Paarvati** and **Lakhshmi.**

Even knowing God, I cannot describe Him; He cannot be described in words.

The Guru has given me this one understanding:

there is only the One, the Giver of all souls. May I never forget Him!

If I am pleasing to Him, then that is my **pilgrimage** and cleansing bath. Without pleasing Him, what good are ritual cleansings?

I gaze upon all the created beings: without the karma of good actions, what are they given to receive?

Darbaar: The court of a king.

Evoke: To bring forth.

Ambrosial: Very pleasing.

Immaculate: Without fault.

Naad: The essence of all sounds.

Vedas: Hindu sacred texts.

All-pervading: Present everywhere.

Shiva: Hindu god of destruction and transformation; one of the trinity of gods that includes Brahma the Creator and Vishnu the Preserver.

Vishnu: Hindu god of preservation; the second member of the trinity that includes Brahma the Creator and Shiva the Destroyer.

Brahma: Hindu god of creation and also of knowledge; the third member of the trinity that includes Vishnu the Preserver and Shiva the Destroyer.

Paarvati: The consort, or wife, of Shiva.

Lakhshmi: The consort, or wife, of Vishnu.

Pilgrimage: Trip to a sacred place, taken for a religious reason.

A Sikh priest reads from the Sri Guru Granth Sahib, the Sikh holy book. The writings contained in it were compiled in the eighteenth century by Guru Gobind Singh. © CHRIS LISLE/CORBIS.

Within the mind are gems, jewels and rubies, if you listen to the Guru's
Teachings, even once.

The Guru has given me this one understanding:

there is only the One, the Giver of all souls. May I never forget Him!

Even if you could live throughout the four ages, or even ten times more,

and even if you were known throughout the nine continents and followed by all,

with a good name and reputation, with praise and fame throughout the
world

still, if the Lord does not bless you with His Glance of Grace, then who
cares? What is the use?

Among worms, you would be considered a lowly worm, and even
contemptible sinners would hold you in contempt.

O Nanak, God blesses the unworthy with virtue, and **bestows** virtue on
the virtuous.

Contemptible: Looked
upon with disgust.

Bestows: Gives as a gift.

Siddhas: Human beings who have reached perfection.

Yogic: Having to do with yoga, the Hindu discipline aimed at gaining a state of perfect spiritual understanding.

Akaashic: In Hinduism, relating to one of the five great elements that make up the world.

Nether: Located below or in a lower position.

Indra: In the Hindu Vedas, a warrior god, ruler of the sky and weather.

No one can even imagine anyone who can bestow virtue upon Him.

Listening—the **Siddhas,** the spiritual teachers, the heroic warriors, the **yogic** masters.

Listening—the earth, its support and the **Akaashic** ethers.

Listening—the oceans, the lands of the world and the **nether** regions of the underworld.

Listening—Death cannot even touch you.

O Nanak, the devotees are forever in bliss.

Listening—pain and sin are erased.

Listening—Shiva, Brahma and **Indra.**

Listening—even foul-mouthed people praise Him.

Listening—the technology of Yoga and the secrets of the body.

. . .

O Nanak, the devotees are forever in bliss.

Section 01—Jup—Part 003

Listening—pain and sin are erased.

Listening—truth, contentment and spiritual wisdom.

Listening—take your cleansing bath at the sixty-eight places of pilgrimage.

Listening—reading and reciting, honor is obtained.

Listening—**intuitively** grasp the **essence** of meditation.

O Nanak, the **devotees** are forever in bliss.

Listening—pain and sin are erased.

Listening—dive deep into the ocean of virtue.

Listening—the Shaykhs, religious scholars, spiritual teachers and emperors.

Listening—even the blind find the Path.

Listening—the Unreachable comes within your grasp.

O Nanak, the devotees are forever in bliss.

Listening—pain and sin are erased.

The state of the faithful cannot be described.

One who tries to describe this shall regret the attempt.

No paper, no pen, no **scribe**

can record the state of the faithful.

Such is the Name of the Immaculate Lord.

Only one who has faith comes to know such a state of mind.

The faithful have intuitive awareness and intelligence.

Intuitively: Instinctively, without needing explanation.

Essence: The most important quality or feature.

Devotees: Dedicated followers.

Scribe: One who copies down documents or religious texts.

The faithful know about all worlds and realms.

The faithful shall never be struck across the face.

The faithful do not have to go with the Messenger of Death.

Such is the Name of the Immaculate Lord.

Only one who has faith comes to know such a state of mind.

The path of the faithful shall never be blocked.

The faithful shall depart with honor and fame.

The faithful do not follow empty religious rituals.

The faithful are firmly bound to the **Dharma.**

Such is the Name of the Immaculate Lord.

Only one who has faith comes to know such a state of mind.

The faithful find the Door of Liberation.

The faithful uplift and **redeem** their family and relations.

The faithful are saved, and carried across with the Sikhs of the Guru.

The faithful, O Nanak, do not wander around begging.

Such is the Name of the Immaculate Lord.

Only one who has faith comes to know such a state of mind.

The chosen ones, the self-elect, are accepted and approved.

The chosen ones are honored in the Court of the Lord.

The chosen ones look beautiful in the courts of kings.

The chosen ones meditate single-mindedly on the Guru.

No matter how much anyone tries to explain and describe them,

the actions of the Creator cannot be counted.

The mythical bull is Dharma, the son of **compassion;**

this is what patiently holds the earth in its place.

One who understands this becomes truthful.

What a great load there is on the bull!

So many worlds beyond this world—so very many!

What power holds them, and supports their weight?

The names and the colors of the assorted species of beings

were all **inscribed** by the Ever-flowing Pen of God.

Who knows how to write this account?

Just imagine what a huge scroll it would take!

What power! What fascinating beauty!

And what gifts! Who can know their extent?

You created the vast expanse of the Universe with One Word!

Hundreds of thousands of rivers began to flow.

Dharma: Divine law as a source of happiness and contentment.

Redeem: Restore the reputation of or pay for the sins of.

Compassion: Sympathy for the suffering of others.

Inscribed: Written down.

Potency: Strength.

How can Your Creative **Potency** be described?
I cannot even once be a sacrifice to You.
Whatever pleases You is the only good done,
You, Eternal and Formless One!
Countless meditations, countless loves.

Austere: Strict.

Countless worship services, countless **austere** disciplines.
Countless scriptures, and ritual recitations of the Vedas.
Countless Yogis, whose minds remain detached from the world.

• • •

What happened next . . .

The Sikhs have a political as well as a religious history. After the death of the tenth guru in 1708, leadership of the Sikhs fell to his follower, Banda Singh Bahadur (1670–1716). His goal was to create a Sikh homeland in the Punjab. At the time, though, the Persian army was repeatedly invading India, carrying back captured riches and slaves. On their expeditions, they had to pass through the Punjab region, where they encountered ferocious resistance from the Sikhs. Using the tactics of guerrilla warfare, Sikh warriors harassed the Persians, reclaiming the booty and freeing the slaves. When the Persians pursued them, the Sikhs would suddenly turn and assault them, usually killing most of their pursuers. By the middle of the eighteenth century, Sikhs were largely in control of the Punjab region.

Through the early 1600s, the Sikhs lived in relative peace with Muslims in the region. That changed, though, under the Muslim emperor Jahan-gir, who opposed Sikhism. He was determined to convert its followers, including Guru Arjan Dev, to Islam. In the following decades, Sikhs took up arms and conducted military training to defend their faith. Violent battles between Sikh and Muslim armies erupted. The Sikhs were determined to defend the principle of religious toleration, not just of Sikhs but of Hindus as well.

Did you know . . .

• Strict Sikhs continue to exhibit the five emblems of Sikhism, sometimes called the "five K's." The first emblem is *Kesh,* or uncut hair, which is seen as a gift from God. Male Sikhs can typically be recognized by the turban that is wound tightly around the head to contain the hair. The second emblem is *Kungha,* or a wooden comb to keep the hair neat. The third is *Kasha,* or an undergarment, like shorts, that was worn by Sikh soldiers and suggests chastity and cleanliness. The fourth, *Kara,* is a steel bracelet that symbolizes a connection with God, and the last, *Kirpan,* is a saber carried in readiness to defend the weak or uphold the right.

- Sikhism's baptism and naming ritual began in 1699, when the first five Sikhs were baptized with *amrit,* a mixture of water and sugar that they drank from the same bowl. The five Sikhs were all members of different castes, and until that time it would have been unheard of for members of different castes to drink from the same bowl. With the use of *amrit,* this ceremony makes clear that anyone can be a Sikh, regardless of his or her background, family, social class, or other factor. As part of the ritual, each man's last name is replaced with the name Singh, meaning "lion." When women are baptized, their last names are replaced with Kaur, meaning "princess."

Consider the following . . .

- Throughout the poem, God is frequently referred to just as "He" or "Him." Give a possible explanation for why much of the text avoids mentioning God by name.
- Summarize the role that God plays in people's lives, as that role is developed in the "Jup."
- The "Jup" is regarded as a morning prayer by Sikhs. Explain why the poem seems suitable for this purpose, focusing especially on the repeated line "May I never forget Him."

For More Information

BOOKS

Kalsi, Sewa Singh. *Simple Guide to Sikhism.* Folkestone, UK: Global Press, 1999.

Mann, Gurinder Singh. *Sikhism.* Upper Saddle River, NJ: Prentice Hall, 2003.

Singh, Pashaura. *The Guru Granth Sahib: Canon, Meaning and Authority.* New York: Oxford University Press, 2003.

WEB SITES

Brar, Sandeep Singh. "The Third Master Guru Amar Das (1479–1574)." *Sikhism.* http://www.sikhs.org/guru3.htm (accessed on June 5, 2006).

"Religion and Ethics: Sikhism." *bbc.co.uk*. http://www.bbc.co.uk/religion/religions/sikhism/index.shtml (accessed on June 5, 2006).

"Shri Guru Granth Sahib: Jup." *The Internet Sacred Text Archive.* http://www.sacred-texts.com/skh/granth/gr01.htm (accessed on June 5, 2006).

The Sikh Home Page. http://www.sikhs.org/topics.htm (accessed on June 6, 2006).

"Sikhism: History, Beliefs, Practices." *Religious Tolerance.org*. http://www.religioustolerance.org/sikhism.htm (accessed on June 5, 2006).

Wicca: A Guide for the Solitary Practitioner

"The Deities," from Wicca: A Guide for the Solitary Practitioner
By Scott Cunningham
Published in 1988 by Llewellyn Publications

"The sight of a perfect blossom in a field of bare earth can instill feelings rivaling those of the most powerful formal rite. Living in nature makes every moment a ritual."

Scott Cunningham is a leading authority on Wicca, a modern religious movement that falls under the broader heading of neo-paganism (*neo* meaning "new"). Neo-paganism encompasses a number of modern groups that find religious truth in ancient practices and beliefs. Some neo-pagans, for example, identify themselves specifically as followers of Asatru, a god from ancient Norse (Scandinavian) mythology. Others call themselves Druids, whose religion is based on ancient Celtic practices. (The Celts were an early ethnic group found primarily in western Europe and the British Isles.) Other groups include shamans (priests or priestesses who use magic rituals to cure the sick or foretell the future), members of such movements as Goddess Spirituality or Sacred Ecology, and Wicca. Many of these terms tend to overlap in meaning because neo-paganism has no formal theology (a system of beliefs and teachings) or organization.

Wicca is a form of modern witchcraft, but the word *witchcraft* causes considerable confusion. In the Judeo-Christian tradition, witchcraft usually refers to those who have made a religious error of belief or practice. However, it more popularly refers to worship of Satan, or the devil. Witchcraft has often been mistakenly associated with bizarre rituals that may involve blood, animal sacrifices, unconventional sexual practices, and the like. Throughout the history of Christianity, many women and men have faced the wrath of the Christian church

The Salem Witch Trials, carried out in Salem, Massachusetts, in 1692, punished men and women suspected of witchcraft, which at the time was mistakenly thought to be connected with "black arts" and the devil. THE LIBRARY OF CONGRESS.

for supposed Satan worship and witchcraft. In 1692, for example, nineteen people, mostly women, were executed after the infamous witch trials in the town of Salem, Massachusetts. The church and the community believed that these people had been practicing black arts as witches. The accused, however, were innocent victims of unfortunate events.

Modern practitioners of witchcraft strongly deny that they worship evil or engage in strange practices. They maintain that witchcraft, as practiced by Wiccans and other groups, is an Earth-centered religion that sees the divine in the natural world, including, for example, the cycle of the seasons and the phases of the Moon. Most such groups have a strict code of behavior based on not doing harm to others.

While various neo-pagan groups, including Wiccans, follow different traditions and practices, they do have characteristics in common. Many are either solitary practitioners (reflected in the title of Scott

Cunningham's book) or practice in very small groups, variously referred to as covens, circles, groves, kindreds, garths, hearths, and other terms. These groups have little if any official ruling structure; that is, no ruling body has authority over members. Most believers prefer to practice their rituals outdoors when they can, which is consistent with their emphasis on nature. Many practice in secret, largely because many people associate neo-paganism with Satan worship and may discriminate against them, avoiding them or treating them unfairly in other ways.

Another characteristic that neo-pagan religions share is that they are generally reconstructed from ancient Western pre-Christian religions that have all but disappeared. In the case of Wicca, several theories have been offered about its origins, but a well-regarded theory is that Wicca evolved from ancient Celtic worship of the goddess of fertility and the god of the hunt. As Celtic society spread across northern Europe and the British Isles, the Celts carried Wiccan practices with them. The religion largely died out as a result of persecution (treating people unfairly, and often with violence, because of extreme differences) by the Romans, the Saxons, and the Norman French. Later, the Christian Church tried to forcefully eliminate Wicca during "the Burning Times," when accused witches were handed over to local authorities who saw to their deaths by hanging, drowning, or, though less common, burning at the stake. This took place roughly between the fifteenth through the eighteenth centuries.

Neo-pagan groups, including Wicca, tend to have similar teachings. They follow a belief system that is either duotheistic (believing in two deities, typically a god and a goddess) or polytheistic (believing in many deities). Neo-pagans feel close to the cycles of nature. Holy days tend to fall on the first day of each of the four seasons, that is the summer and winter solstices (respectively, the longest and shortest days of the year) and the spring and autumnal equinoxes (the first day of spring and autumn).

The emergence of Wicca as a modern religious movement can be traced to the 1950s in England and the efforts of a British civil servant named Gerald Gardner, who wrote extensively on witchcraft. Later, in 1974, a number of Wiccans gathered in Minneapolis, Minnesota, where they drafted a statement containing the principles of Wiccan belief. The following list summarizes some of the most important principles, along with ways they are reflected in Cunningham's book.

- Wiccans practice rites attuned to, or in step with, the "natural rhythm of life forces," Cunningham notes, referring to rituals that follow "the course of the Sun through its astronomical year . . . as well as the monthly waxing and waning of the Moon." A waxing moon means the moon is appearing larger, and is one where the side of the moon facing east is dark. A waning moon is one where the side of the moon facing west is dark. This gives the appearance that the moon is getting smaller.

- Wiccans encourage and support responsibility toward the environment. Cunningham points out that "many of us are involved in ecology—saving the Earth from utter destruction by our own hands."

- Wiccans "acknowledge a depth of power far greater than that apparent to the average person," as stated at the 1974 meeting. They find power and divine awe in seemingly ordinary aspects of nature, such as flowers and trees.

- The creative power of the universe is both masculine and feminine and contained within each person: "Wicca," writes Cunningham, "reveres [respects and honors] these twin deities [called the God and Goddess] because of its links with nature."

- Wiccans seek the interaction of the outer and inner (psychological) worlds and, as Cunningham writes, "can contact and communicate with [the God and Goddess] because a part of us is in them and they are within us."

- Wiccans do not have an organized structure of authority to oversee their religious beliefs. Throughout his book, Cunningham makes clear that every practitioner can be his or her own priest or priestess, performing rituals without the assistance of a class of specialists, a class that other religions would describe as priests (in Christianity) or rabbis (in Judaism) or imams (in Islam).

- Wisdom, religion, and "magick" (a spelling sometimes used in religious contexts to distinguish it from tricks and entertainment) are united in a way of living, or a life philosophy. As Cunningham notes elsewhere in the book, "magic plays a special role in Wicca. It allows us to improve our lives and return energy to our ravaged [damaged] planet."

- Wicca opposes Christianity and other religions only to the extent that they deny spiritual freedom to others.

- Meaning in the universe comes from fulfilling and affirming life: "Wiccans emphasize the bright aspects of the deities because this gives us purpose to grow and evolve to the highest realm of existence."

- Wiccans do not worship Satan, the devil, or evil. Cunningham makes clear throughout his book that worship of the God and Goddess is worship of the creative, life-affirming powers of the universe, those powers that sustain and support the universe.

Things to remember while reading *Wicca: A Guide for the Solitary Practitioner:*

- Wicca is regarded as a form of paganism. The modern word *pagan* has negative associations, suggesting that a person is backward and ignorant. The word comes from a Latin word, *paganus,* meaning "country dweller." The word was used by the ancient Romans after the empire converted to Christianity. People in rural areas tended to hold on to ancient religious beliefs rather than to adopt Christianity. People in cities who did become Christians thought of people outside of the cities as backward.

- Scholars debate the origins of Wicca. While most practitioners and religious scholars trace Wicca to the 1950s and the books of Gerald Gardner, others disagree about the nature of his role. They believe that Gardner adapted his claims about Wicca from various other authors, religious historians, and even a prominent witch named Dorothy Clutterbuck, who was well know in England at the time.

- Many neo-pagans, including Wiccans, have adopted the pentagram as a symbol. This symbol consists of a circle with a five-pointed star inside, with the tips of the points touching the circle. It is widely believed that the pentagram is a satanic symbol, but it

Do Witches Carry Brooms?

A common image of witches, and one that is reflected every year by children in Halloween costumes, is that they ride on broomsticks. While this is a stereotype, it is one based on an element of truth. Wiccans commonly use brooms as sacred tools, typically starting rituals by sweeping a sacred place where an altar is set up. This sweeping is not just for cleanliness. As part of the ritual, it symbolizes the act of purifying, or making holy, the sacred space for worship.

In fact, witches in many cultural traditions were believed to have been associated with brooms. In Mexico before the arrival of Christopher Columbus in the fifteenth century, the witch deity Tlazelteotl was often pictured naked, riding on a broom. The ancient Chinese worshipped a broom goddess they called on to bring good weather. In Europe, witches were believed to ride in the air on brooms, which some at the time believed "proved" that they were allied with the dark powers of Satan.

is not. The circle represents the magic circle used for rituals, and the five points of the star represent the five elements of earth, air, water, fire, and spirit.

• • •

Excerpt from the *Wicca: A Guide for the Solitary Practitioner*

"The Deities"

Reverence: Respect, devotion for.

All religions are structures built upon **reverence** of Deity. Wicca is no exception. The Wicca acknowledge a supreme divine power, unknowable, ultimate, from which the entire universe sprang.

Comprehension: Understanding.

The concept of this power, far beyond our **comprehension,** has nearly been lost in Wicca because of our difficulty in relating to it. However, Wiccans link with this force through their deities. In accordance with the principles of nature, the supreme power was **personified** into two basic beings: the Goddess and the God.

Personified: Represented as a being, given a concrete form.

Every deity that has received worship upon this planet exists with the **archetypal** God and Goddess. The complex **pantheons** of deities which arose in many parts of the world are simply *aspects* of the two. Every Goddess is resident within the concept of the Goddess; every God in the God.

Archetypal: Ideal.

Pantheons: Official groups.

Wicca reveres these twin deities because of its links with nature. Since most (but certainly not all) nature is divided into gender, the deities **embodying** it are similarly **conceived.**

Embodying: Representing.

Conceived: Formed an idea of.

In the past, when the Goddess and God were as real as the Moon and Sun, rites of worship and adoration were unstructured—spontaneous, joyous union with the divine. Later, rituals followed the course of the Sun through its astronomical year (and thusly the seasons) as well as the monthly waxing and waning of the Moon.

Today similar rites are observed by the Wicca, and their regular performance creates a truly magical closeness with these deities and the powers behind them.

Instill: Impart, produce.

Rivaling: Competing with.

Rite: An established ceremony, particularly in a religion.

Primeval: Original, ancient.

Fortunately, we needn't wait for ritual occasions to be reminded of the Gods' presence. The sight of a perfect blossom in a field of bare earth can **instill** feelings **rivaling** those of the most powerful formal **rite.** Living in nature makes every moment a ritual. The Wiccans are comfortable in communicating with animals, plants and trees. They feel energies within stones and sand, and cause fossils to speak of their **primeval** beginnings. For some Wiccans, watching the Sun or Moon rise and set each day is a ritual unto itself, for these are the heavenly symbols of the God and Goddess.

Because the Wicca see Deity **inherent** in nature, many of us are involved in ecology—saving the Earth from utter destruction by our own hands. The Goddess and God still exist, as they have always existed, and to honor them we honor and preserve our precious planet.

In Wiccan thought, the Deities didn't exist before our spiritual ancestor's acknowledgement of them. However, the *energies* behind them did; they created us. Early worshippers recognized these forces as the Goddess and God, personifying them in an attempt to understand them.

The Old Ones didn't die when the ancient Pagan religions fell to **upstart** Christianity in Europe. Most of the rites vanished, but they weren't the only effective ones. Wicca is alive and well and the Deities respond to our calls and **invocations.**

When **envisioning** the Goddess and God, many of the Wicca see Them as well-known deities from ancient religions. Diana, Pan, Isis, Hermes, Hina, Tammuz, Hecate, Ishtar, Cerridwen, Thoth, Tara, Aradia, Artemis, Pele, Apollo, Kanaloa, Bridget, Helios, Bran, Lugh, Hera, Cybele, Inanna, Maui, Ea, Athena, Lono, Marduk—the list is virtually endless. Many of these deities, with their corresponding histories, rites and mythic information, **furnish** the concept of deity for Wiccans.

Some feel comfortable associating such names and forms with the Goddess and God, feeling that they can't possibly revere nameless divine beings. Others find a lack of names and costumes a comforting lack of limitations.

As stated earlier, the Wicca as outlined in this book is "new," although built upon established rituals and myths, firmly rooted within the earliest religious feelings which nature aroused within our species. In these rituals I've used the words "the God" and "the Goddess" rather than specific names such as Diana and Pan. [. . .]

They have been given so many names they have been called the Nameless Ones. In appearance they look exactly as we wish them to, for they're all the Deities that ever were. The Goddess and God are all-powerful because they are the creators of all **manifest** and unmanifest existence. We can contact and communicate with them because a part of us is in them and they are within us.

The Goddess and God are equal; neither is higher or more deserving of respect. Though some Wiccans focus their rituals toward the Goddess and seem to forget the God entirely, this is a reaction to centuries of stifling **patriarchal** religion, and the loss of acknowledgement of the feminine aspect of Divinity. Religion based entirely on feminine energy, however, is as unbalanced and unnatural as one totally masculine in focus. The ideal is a perfect balance of the two. The Goddess and God are equal, complementary.

Inherent: Part of the inner nature or essence of something.

Upstart: Newly powerful.

Invocations: Acts of prayer or calling upon a spirit or god.

Envisioning: Forming a picture of.

Furnish: Supply.

Manifest: Clear to see, obvious to the senses.

Patriarchal: Characteristic of rule by men, not women.

Wiccans purify a wand in salt water during a ceremony. Neo-pagan religions such as Wicca are often very focused on nature and try to live in harmony with it. © REBECCA MEENTEE/CORBIS SYGMA.

Crone: An old woman, often one who is ugly.

Dormant: In a state of rest or inactivity, usually when growth and development have stopped.

Oblivion: The state of nothingness.

Incarnations: Lifetimes, the times spent in a particular human body.

Temptress: A woman who is considered extremely appealing.

The Goddess The Goddess is the universal mother. She is the source of fertility, endless wisdom and loving caresses. As the Wicca know Her, She is often of three aspects: the Maiden, the Mother and the **Crone,** symbolized in the waxing, full and waning of the Moon. She is at once the unplowed field, the full harvest and the **dormant,** frost-covered Earth. She gives birth to abundance. But as life is Her gift, She lends it with the promise of death. This is not darkness and **oblivion,** but rest from the toils of physical existence. It is human existence between **incarnations.**

Since the Goddess is nature, all nature, She is both the **Temptress** and the Crone; the tornado and the fresh spring rain; the cradle and the grave.

But though She is possessed of both natures, the Wicca revere Her as the giver of fertility, love and abundance, though they acknowledge Her darker side as well. We see Her in the Moon, the soundless, ever-moving sea, and in the green growth of the first spring. She is the embodiment of fertility and love. [. . .]

The God The God has been revered for **eons.** He is neither the stern, all-powerful deity of Christianity and Judaism, nor is He simply the **consort** of the Goddess. God or Goddess, they are equal, one.

We see the God in the Sun, brilliantly shining overhead during the day, rising and setting in the endless cycle which governs our lives. Without the Sun we could not exist; therefore it has been revered as the source of all life, the warmth that bursts the dormant seeds into life and hastens the greening of the Earth after the cold snows of winter.

The God is also tender of the wild animals. As the Horned God He is sometimes seen wearing horns on His head, symbolizing His connection with these beasts. In earlier times, hunting was one of the activities thought to be ruled by the God, while the domestication of animals was seen to be Goddess-oriented.

The God's domains include forests untouched by human hands, burning deserts and towering mountains. The stars, since they are but distant suns, are sometimes thought to be under His domain.

The yearly cycle of greening, maturation and harvest has long been associated with the Sun, hence the solar festivals of Europe [...] which are still observed in Wicca.

The God is the fully ripened harvest, **intoxicating** wine pressed from grapes, golden grain waving in a lone field, shimmering apples hanging from **verdant** boughs on October afternoons.

With the Goddess He also celebrates and rules sex. The Wicca don't avoid sex or speak of it in hushed words. It's a part of nature and is accepted as such. Since it brings pleasure, shifts our awareness away from the everyday world and **perpetuates** our species, it is thought to be sacred. The God **lustily imbues** us with the urge that ensures our species' biological future.

Symbols often used to depict or to worship the God include the sword, horns, spear, candle, gold, brass, diamond, the **sickle,** arrow, magical wand, **trident,** knife and others. Creatures sacred to Him include the bull, dog, snake, fish, stag, dragon, wolf, boar, eagle, falcon, shark, lizard and many others.

Eons: Long periods of time, ones that are too long to measure.

Consort: Husband, companion.

Intoxicating: Capable of making drunk.

Verdant: Lush or flourishing with vegetation.

Perpetuates: Continues.

Lustily: With energy and enthusiasm.

Imbues: Fills.

Sickle: A tool with a semicircular blade on a handle, used for cutting tall grass.

Trident: A spear with three prongs.

• • •

What happened next . . .

In *Wicca: A Guide for the Solitary Practitioner,* Cunningham goes on to explain both the theory and the practice of Wicca. He explains the roles of numerous sacred objects used in Wiccan worship, including the broom, the wand, the cauldron, the magic knife, the crystal sphere, and others. He draws on the Book of Shadows, a handbook of Wiccan rituals that discusses music, dance, construction of altars, and many other symbolic practices and items. The Book of Shadows has no particular author or publisher. It has been handed down, usually in handwritten form (though versions are available widely on the Internet), by generations of Wiccans.

Did you know...

- Wiccans estimate their numbers to be about 750,000 in the United States, which would make Wicca the fifth-largest religion in the country. For many years, Wiccans faced persecution, physical attacks, and discrimination. This could affect their ability to get and hold jobs and run businesses. For this reason, many tended to keep their beliefs private. Wiccans acknowledge that in the twenty-first century non-Wiccans have become more tolerant because of growing public awareness that Wiccans are not worshipers of Satan or of evil.

- Wiccans believe that the ideal number of persons in a coven is thirteen. When the number grows larger than thirteen, the coven splits, or "hives," into two or more covens. The covens remain associated as a larger unit called a grove.

- Wiccan wedding ceremonies are referred to most commonly as "handfastings." Some Wiccans adhere to an ancient Celtic practice of a "trial marriage" for a year and a day.

Consider the following...

- Some people, including government officials and the court system, have not regarded Wicca as a "religion" but more as a philosophy or a way of life. Respond to this point of view.

- Most mainstream religions that recognize a deity, such as Judaism, Christianity, and Islam, think of the deity as masculine. Explain how and why Wicca recognizes a female as well as a male deity.

- Define the word "witchcraft" as a Wiccan might use it. Explain how the Wiccan use of the term differs from the popular use of the term.

For More Information

BOOKS

Buckland, Raymond. *Wicca for One: The Path of Solitary Witchcraft.* Secaucus, NJ: Citadel Press, 2004.

Cunningham, Scott. *Wicca: A Guide for the Solitary Practitioner.* Saint Paul, MN.: Llewellyn Publications, 1988.

Grimassi, Raven. *Encyclopedia of Wicca and Witchcraft.* Saint Paul, MN.: Llewellyn Publications, 2000.

Holland, Eileen. *The Wicca Handbook.* Boston: Weiser Books, 2000.

WEB SITES

Herne. "What Is Wicca." *The Celtic Connection.* http://www.wicca.com/celtic/wicca/wicca.htm (accessed on June 5, 2006).

"Wicca: A Neopagan, Earth-Centered Religion." *Religious Tolerance.org.* http://www.religioustolerance.org/witchcra.htm (accessed on June 5, 2006).

"Paper on Hinduism"

"Paper on Hinduism," available online from the Universal Wisdom
at http://www.theuniversalwisdom.org/hinduism/paper-on-hinduism-vivekananda/
Speech delivered by Swami Vivekananda
Given at the World Parliament of Religions in Chicago on September 19, 1893

> "I am in every religion as the thread through a string of pearls. Wherever thou seest extraordinary...power raising and purifying humanity, know thou that I am there."

Swami Vivekananda delivered the "Paper on Hinduism," at the World Parliament of Religions on September 19, 1893. His speech became an important document in the history of modern religious tolerance. In this speech, and others that Vivekananda delivered to the parliament that September, he introduced Hinduism to the Western world.

For many centuries, knowledge of Hinduism had been confined largely to people in Southeast Asia and was mostly unknown to people in the West. After September 1893, however, the spiritual message of Hinduism gained attention in the Western world. Over the next century many westerners began to explore that message. More important, the "Paper on Hinduism" strengthened modern recognition that religious truths come in a variety of forms. While different cultures may have differing views of the nature and characteristics of God, each of the world's religions reflects the culture and history of the people who practice the religion. All provide spiritual nourishment to people throughout the world.

As part of his message of religious tolerance, Vivekananda discusses in his speech the nature of God. He notes that throughout the world, different peoples have varying concepts of God. Christians worship God, Muslims worship Allah, Hindus worship Brahma, and so on. Vivekananda, though, says that each of these gods, and many others, are all expressions

109

of the same fundamental truth: that God is eternal and unchanging and the creative force and power throughout the universe. Differing ideas of the nature and being of God are simply the result of different cultural needs. God is multifaceted, meaning that He has many characteristics. Just as Hindus worship numerous gods that are facets, or aspects, of Brahma, so the world community can worship numerous gods that are aspects of a single, unchanging supreme deity. Each religion, then, has its own "light of truth." The differences among them represent "glasses of different colors" through which that light of truth passes.

The paper presents a number of views that were new to most westerners at the time. Vivekananda says, for example, that the universe was not created but that it is eternal; it has always existed. He explained reincarnation (the idea that people die and are born again into the physical world in different bodies and life circumstances) and why people are unable to remember their past lives. He states that the goal of human life is to realize the divinity that lies within and to express that divinity through concern for the welfare of others. Perhaps most important, he rejects the concept, prominent in Christianity, that all people are sinners.

Vivekananda's chief goal, however, was to encourage religious tolerance. In his address, he quotes from the Bhagavad Gita, a prominent Hindu scripture: "As the different streams having their sources in different places all mingle their water in the sea, so, O Lord, the different paths which men take through different tendencies [preferences], various though they appear, crooked or straight, all lead to Thee." In other words, despite differences in religions, they all lead to the same God. Vivekananda's address was a call for open-mindedness and acceptance and an end to religious extremism and prejudice. Religious extremism is when violence is carried out in the name of a religion. Prejudice is when individuals, or specific groups of people, are singled out for unfair treatment due to the characteristics of that particular person or group.

Swami Vivekananda was one of Hinduism's great modern teachers. He was born into an educated, well-to-do family in Calcutta, India, on January 12, 1863. He grew up in a home that encouraged learning. From an early age he had a great capacity for absorbing and remembering what he read, including the entire contents of the *Encyclopaedia Britannica*. As a young man, Vivikananda attended the University of Calcutta. There, he acquired a broad-based education in science, philosophy, and religion and learned to speak several languages, including

English. He was also an accomplished musician and singer. During his college days Vivikananda began to discover that many of the principles and beliefs of Western science and philosophy were similar to beliefs found in Hindu sacred scriptures written thousands of years earlier. In time, he came to see little conflict between the teachings of Hinduism and the findings of modern science.

A turning point in Vivekananda's life came in 1881, when he began to study under Sri Ramakrishna, another great nineteenth-century Hindu teacher. At this point, Vivekananda was still somewhat of a religious skeptic; that is, he was not prepared to accept Ramakrishna as a spiritual guru, or spiritual leader, or to believe that the guru was truly able to directly experience the divine. The divine refers to realizations and understandings of God and the teachings of God. Yet by his second meeting with Ramakrishna, Vivekananda began to see the world in a new way.

Over the next five years, Vivekananda studied under Ramakrishna. During these years he explored the basics of Hindu thought. Among them were:

Brahma is the one supreme god of Hinduism. The many gods and goddesses of the Hindu religion are merely different representations of this one God. © LINDSAY HEBBERD/CORBIS.

- Brahma;
- the nature of the soul;
- meditation, the practice of focusing on one thought or image to quiet the mind and gain greater understanding of the divine;
- yoga, a physical and spiritual practice aimed at focusing the mind to achieve greater understanding of the divine;
- karma, a person's good or bad actions throughout life, which determine the nature of his or her next life; and
- reincarnation

Vivekananda also studied the Hindu sacred scriptures, particularly the Vedas and the Upanishads. When Ramakrishna died in 1886, Vivekananda inherited his role as a spiritual master. For two years he went on a pilgrimage throughout India, journeying to sacred places.

During this time he became exposed to the poverty and hunger that troubled many of his countrymen. From these experiences he became determined not only to help improve the condition of Indians but also to preach the message of the divine unity of humankind. He carried out these intentions until his death on July 4, 1902.

Vivekananda made his first trip to the United States in 1893. When he arrived in Chicago, he did not even know the dates when the World Parliament of Religions was to be held, nor did he have any credentials that entitled him to speak. Nonetheless, as a highly respected guru, he was able to address the seven thousand people in attendance on three occasions, bringing the audience to its feet in applause. The most important occasion was September 19, when he presented the "Paper on Hinduism."

Things to remember while reading the "Paper on Hinduism":

- Vivekananda earned the title *swami*, which comes from a word in Hindi (the language of northern India) meaning "owner" or "lord." A swami is a spiritual teacher and philosopher. Typically, a swami is the head of a school of thought or the head of a social or educational institution.

- Swami Vivekananda's significance is that he, more than any other person of his time, introduced Hinduism to the Western world. In the century that followed, more and more westerners began to study Hinduism. Although many came to regard themselves as Hindus (one can be a Hindu simply by accepting the teachings of Hindu scripture, especially the Vedas), others were interested in Hinduism more as a life philosophy or as a way of achieving inner peace.

- The 1893 World Parliament of Religions was the first-ever meeting of this worldwide body. Its goal was to bring together people from different religions to encourage relationships with one another, peace, and justice. It was held in conjunction with the Columbian Exposition in Chicago, a world's fair that celebrated modern scientific and technological innovations. It also identified Chicago as a major world city. This gathering of religious leaders provided a spiritual dimension for the hundreds of thousands of people who visited the exposition.

A Primer on Hindu Sacred Scripture

Hindus recognize a number of documents as scripture, or holy writings. The chief documents are the Vedas (from a word meaning "vision," "knowledge," or "wisdom"), which were written sometime between 1500 to 1200 BCE. There are four Vedas: the Rig Veda, the Sama Veda, the Yajur Veda, and the Atharva Veda. Each Veda consists of four elements: *Samhitas,* or hymns; *Brahmanas,* or rituals, encompassing religious duties of all Hindus; *Aranyakas,* or religious principles, usually studied by Hindu monks; and the Upanishads.

While the Upanishads are part of the Vedas, they generally are treated as if they were separate from them. Hindus typically do not read the other portions of the Vedas, primarily because they are complex. They are more likely to focus their study on the Upanishads. There are 108 surviving Upanishads; among them, 13 are regarded as the most important, in that they contain the essential teachings of Hinduism. Because they come at the end of the Vedas, they are referred to as the Vedanta, or "end of the Vedas."

Although numerous other texts are sacred to Hindus, one that is central is the Bhagavad Gita. Many Hindus, and westerners as well, find the Bhagavad Gita to be one of the most beautiful Hindu scriptures. It is part of Book VI of an epic poem called the Mahabharata, which means "Great Epic of the Bharata Dynasty" and was probably written in the first or second century CE. It is written as a dialogue between a warrior prince, Arjuna, and his companion and chariot driver, Krishna, who is an incarnation of the Hindu god Vishnu. The dialogue occurs on the battlefield: Krishna tells the prince that he is required to perform his duty and to maintain his faith in God, despite his self-doubts and questions about the nature of the universe. The Bhagavad Gita goes on to examine the nature of God and to explore the ways in which human beings can come to know Him.

• • •

Excerpt from the "Paper on Hinduism"

The Hindus have received their religion through **revelation,** the Vedas. They hold that the Vedas are without beginning and without end. It may sound **ludicrous** to this audience, how a book can be without beginning or end. But by the Vedas no books are meant. They mean the accumulated treasury of spiritual laws discovered by different persons in different times. Just as the law of gravitation existed before its discovery, and would exist if all humanity forgot it, so is it with the laws that govern the spiritual relations between soul and soul and between individual spirits and the Father of all spirits [that they] were there before their discovery, and would remain even if we forgot them.

The discoverers of these laws are called Rishis, and we honor them as perfected beings. I am glad to tell this audience that some of the very greatest of them were women.

Revelation: Communication through divine means.

Ludicrous: Ridiculous.

Manifested: Obvious, realized.

Potential: Existing in possibility but not in reality.

Kinetic: Characterized by motion or action.

Mutable: Capable of changing in form or substance.

Simile: A figure of speech that makes a comparison between two different things.

Providence: Divine guidance.

Aptitude: Natural ability.

Configuration: The way in which parts are arranged or fitted together.

Peculiar: Unique, distinct.

Affinity: Natural attraction or feeling of belonging together.

Immortal: Undying, lasting forever.

Infinite: Unlimited, without boundaries.

Chasm: Gap.

Here it may be said that these laws as laws may be without end, but they must have had a beginning. The Vedas teach us that creation is without beginning or end. Science is said to have proved that the sum total of cosmic energy is always the same. Then, if there was a time when nothing existed, where was all this **manifested** energy? Some say it was in a **potential** form in God. In that case God is sometimes potential and sometimes **kinetic,** which would make Him **mutable.** Everything mutable is a compound and everything compound must undergo that change which is called destruction. So God would die, which is absurd—Therefore, there never was a time when there was no creation.

If I may be allowed to use a **simile,** creation and creator are two lines, without beginning and without end, zoning parallel to each other. God is the ever-active **providence,** by whose power systems after systems are being evolved out of chaos, made to run for a time, and again destroyed. . . .

Are not all the tendencies of the mind and the body accounted for by inherited **aptitude**? Here are two parallel lines of existence—one of the mind, the other of matter. If matter and its transformations answer for all that we have, there is no necessity for supposing the existence of a soul. . . .

We cannot deny that bodies acquire certain tendencies from heredity, but those tendencies only mean the physical **configuration** through which a **peculiar** mind alone can act in a peculiar way. There are other tendencies peculiar to a soul caused by his past actions. And a soul with a certain tendency would, by the laws of **affinity,** take birth in a body which is the fittest instrument for the display of that tendency. This is in accord with science, for science wants to explain everything by habit, and habit is got through repetitions. So repetitions are necessary to explain the natural habits of a new born soul. And since they were not obtained in this present life, they must have come down from past lives. . . .

So then the Hindu believes that he is a spirit. Him the sword cannot pierce—him the fire cannot burn—him the water cannot melt—him the air cannot dry. The Hindu believes that every soul is a circle whose circumference is nowhere but whose center is located in the body, and that death means the change of the center from holy to body. Nor is the soul bound by the conditions of matter. . . .

Well, then, the human soul is eternal and **immortal,** perfect and **infinite,** and death means only a change of center from one body to another. The present is determined by our past actions, and the future by the present. The soul will go on evolving up or reverting back from birth to birth and death to death. But here is another question: Is man a tiny boat in a tempest, raised one moment on the foamy crest of a billow and dashed down into a yawning **chasm** the next, rolling to and from at the mercy of good and bad actions—a powerless, helpless wreck in an ever-raging, ever-rushing, **uncompromising** current of cause and effect—a little moth placed under the wheel of **causation**, which rolls on crushing everything in its way and waits not for the widow's tears or the orphan's cry? The heart sinks at the idea, yet this is the law of nature. Is there no hope? Is there no escape?—was the cry that went up from the bottom of the heart of despair. It reached the throne of mercy, and words of hope and consolation came down.... We are the Children of God, the sharers of immortal bliss, holy and perfect beings, divinities on earth....

Thus it is that the Vedas **proclaim,** not a dreadful combination of unforgiving laws, not an endless prison of cause and effect, but that at the head of all these laws, in and through every particle of matter and force, stands One, "by whose command the wind blows, the fire burns, the clouds rain and death stalks upon the earth."

And what is His nature?

He is everywhere, the pure and formless One, the Almighty and the All-merciful. "Thou art our father, Thou art our mother, Thou art our beloved friend, Thou art the source of all strength; give us strength. Thou art He that beareth the burdens of the universe; help me bear the little burden of this life." Thus sang the Rishis of the Veda. And how to worship Him? Through love He is to be worshiped as the one beloved, dearer than everything in this and the next life."...

The Vedas teach that the soul is divine, only held in the **bondage** of matter; perfection will be reached when this bond will burst, and the word they use for it is, therefore, Mukti—*freedom, freedom from the bonds of imperfection, freedom from death and misery*—And this bondage can only fall off through the mercy of God.... Purity is the condition of His mercy. How does that mercy act? He reveals Himself to the pure heart; the pure and the stainless see God, ... even in this life; then and then only all the crookedness of the heart is made straight.... So the best proof a Hindu **sage** gives about the soul, about God, is: "I have seen the soul; I have seen God." And that is the only condition of perfection. The Hindu religion does not consist in struggles and attempts to believe a certain doctrine or **dogma,** but in realizing—not in believing, but in being and becoming....

Descend we now from the **aspirations** of philosophy to the religion of the ignorant. At the very outset, I may tell you that there is no **polytheism** in India. In every temple, if one stands by and listens, one will find the worshipers applying all the attributes of God, including **omnipresence,** to the images. It is not polytheism....

"The rose, called by any other name, would smell as sweet." Names are not explanations....

Uncompromising: Showing no willingness to find a middle ground or negotiate.

Causation: The process of causing an effect.

Proclaim: Announce.

Bondage: Slavery.

Sage: Holy man.

Dogma: Code of belief.

Aspirations: Ambitions, goals.

Polytheism: Belief in more than one god.

Omnipresence: Presence everywhere, throughout all of creation.

Superstition: Belief not founded on reality, often a belief in the magical power of objects or the magical effects of certain actions.

Bigotry: Prejudice, narrow-mindedness.

Brethren: Members of the same community or family.

Constitution: Makeup, combined parts.

Mosque: Place of worship in the religion of Islam.

Idol: A physical object that is worshipped as if it were a god.

Assent: Voicing of agreement.

Doctrines: Bodies of ideas taught as truths in religion.

Fetishism: Worship of an object thought to have magical powers.

Absolutism: Belief in a being who is without limits and beyond human control.

Compulsory: Required.

Superstition is a great enemy of man, but **bigotry** is worse. Why does a Christian go to church? Why is the cross holy? Why is the face turned toward the sky in prayer? Why are there so many images in the Catholic Church? Why are there so many images in the minds of Protestants when they pray? My **brethren,** we can no more think about anything without a mental image than we can live without breathing—By the law of association the material image calls up the mental idea and vice versa. This is why the Hindu uses an external symbol when he worships. He will tell you, it helps to keep his mind fixed on the Being to whom he prays. . . .

As we find that somehow or other, by the laws of our mental **constitution,** we have to associate our ideas of infinity with the image of the blue sky, or of the sea, so we naturally connect our idea of holiness with the image of a church, a **mosque,** or a cross. The Hindus have associated the ideas of holiness, purity, truth, omnipresence, and such other ideas with different images and forms. But with this difference that while some people devote their whole lives to their **idol** of a church and never rise higher, because with them religion means an intellectual **assent** to certain **doctrines** and doing good to their fellows, the whole religion of the Hindu is centered in realization. Man is to become divine by realizing the divine. Idols or temples or churches or books are only the supports, the helps, of his spiritual childhood; but on and on he must progress. . . .

To the Hindu, man is not traveling from error to truth, but from truth to truth, from lower to higher truth. To him all the religions from the lowest **fetishism** to the highest **absolutism,** mean so many attempts of the human soul to grasp and realize the Infinite, each determined by the conditions of its birth and association, and each of these marks a stage of progress; and every soul is a young eagle soaring higher and higher, gathering more and more strength till it reaches the Glorious Sun.

Unity in variety is the plan of nature, and the Hindu has recognized it. Every other religion lays down certain fixed dogmas and tries to force society to adopt them. It places before society only one coat which must fit Jack and John and Henry, all alike. If it does not fit John or Henry he must go without a coat to cover his body. The Hindus have discovered that the absolute can only be realized, or thought of, or stated through the relative, and the images, crosses, and crescents are simply so many symbols—so many pegs to hang spiritual ideas on. It is not that this help is necessary for everyone, but those that do not need it have no right to say that it is wrong. Nor is it **compulsory** in Hinduism. . . .

To the Hindu, then, the whole world of religions is only a traveling, a coming up, of different men and women, through various conditions and circumstances, to the same goal. Every religion is only evolving a God out

Hindu followers of Krishna parade through the street during a religious festival. God spoke through Krishna and said, "I am in every religion as the thread through a string of pearls." © MARKO GEORGIEV/STAR LEDGER/CORBIS.

of the material man, and the same God is the inspirer of all of them. Why, then, are there so many **contradictions?** They are only apparent, says the Hindu. The contradictions come from the same truth adapting itself to the varying circumstances of different natures.

It is the same light coming through glasses of different colors—And these little variations are necessary for purposes of adaptation. But in the heart of everything the same truth reigns. The Lord has declared to the Hindu in His incarnation as Krishna: "I am in every religion as the thread through a string of pearls. Wherever thou seest extraordinary holiness and extraordinary power raising and purifying humanity, know thou that I am there." And what has been the result? I challenge the world to find, throughout the whole system of Sanskrit philosophy, any such expression as that the Hindu alone will be saved and not others. Says Vyasa, "we find perfect men even beyond the pale of our **caste** and creed." One thing more. How, then, can the Hindu, whose whole fabric of thought centers in God, believe in Buddhism which is **agnostic,** or in Jainism which is **atheistic?**

Contradictions: Opposition between two ideas.

Caste: A hereditary class into which Hindu society was divided and which governs such things as one's profession.

Agnostic: Believing that God is unknown and probably unknowable.

Atheistic: Believing that there is no god.

The Buddhists or the Jains do not depend upon God; but the whole force of their religion is directed to the great central truth in every religion, to evolve a God out of man. They have not seen the Father, but they have seen the Son. And he that hath seen the Son hath seen the Father also.

This, brethren, is a short sketch of the religious ideas of the Hindus. The Hindu may have failed to carry out all his plans, but if there is ever to be a universal religion, it must be one which will have no location in place or time; which will be infinite like the God it will preach, and whose sun will shine upon the followers of Krishna and of Christ, on saints and sinners alike; which will not be Brahminic or Buddhistic, Christian or Mohammedan, but the sum total of all these, and still have infinite space for development; which in its **catholicity** will embrace in infinite arms, and find a place for, every human being from the lowest **grovelling savage,** not far removed from the **brute,** to the highest man towering by the virtues of his head and heart almost above humanity, making society stand in awe of him and doubt his human nature. It will be a religion which will have no place for persecution or intolerance in its **polity,** which will recognize divinity in every man and woman, and whose whole scope, whose whole force, will be centered in aiding humanity to realize its own true, divine nature. . . .

May He who is the Brahman of the Hindus, the Ahura-Mazda of the Zoroastrians, the Buddha of the Buddhists, the Jehovah of the Jews, the Father in Heaven of the Christians, give strength to you to carry out your noble idea! . . .

Catholicity: Universality, the quality of including everyone.

Grovelling, or groveling: Crawling or lying on the ground as a mark of meekness or obedience.

Savage: An uncivilized person.

Brute: A lower animal, a beast.

Polity: Society, institution.

• • •

What happened next . . .

During the 1880s and 1890s, Swami Vivekananda actively tried to improve the material lives of Indians. One way he achieved this aim was through the Ramakrishna mission in India, which, among other accomplishments, provided care for Indians during an outbreak of the plague and was credited with saving many lives. During the twentieth century, the work of the mission continued worldwide. Under the name Vivekananda Vedanta Society, it maintains 135 missions throughout the world, 12 of them in the United States. In Chicago, a branch of the society was founded in 1930, with the twin goals of helping people find the God within and of serving others.

Hinduism in the early twenty-first century is the third largest religion in the world. People in the West, the nations of the Americas and

Europe, became interested in Hinduism after Swami Vivekananda's presentation. More than 900,000 people in the United States are Hindu. There are more than 400,000 Hindus in the United Kingdom. The largest concentration of Hindu followers remains in South Asia.

The World Parliament of Religions changed its name to the Council for a Parliament of the World's Religions. It continues to pursue harmony between religions and encourages religious communities to become involved with the world. The Parliament has met in various locations around the world, including Cape Town, South Africa, in 1999, and Barcelona, Spain, in 2004. Nearly eight thousand religious leaders attended the 2004 meeting.

Did you know...

- Hindus worship many gods and goddesses. Many Hindus worship a particular god or goddess or a group of them based on personal identification with that deity. This means that they have a strong feeling of connection with a particular god. Hindus, however, believe in a supreme god, called Brahma. Brahma is the creator-god and is thought of as being in harmony with the universe. All other gods are considered to be forms or aspects of Brahma. Other major deities in Hinduism are Vishnu (or Krishna), the preserver-god, and Shiva (or Siva), the destroyer-god.

- Hindus conduct their personal lives according to a variety of principles, but two of the most important are *dharma* and *karma*. Dharma means something like "righteousness." Because of dharma, for example, most Hindus are vegetarians, believing that all creatures belong to God and that killing them would violate, or go against, dharma. The other principle, karma, is based on the Hindu belief in an eternal cycle of birth, death, and reincarnation. Karma determines how a person will live his or her next life. In this life a person who stores up good karma will lead a future life on a higher plane, while one who builds up bad karma will be reincarnated on a lower plane.

- Yoga is an ancient form of Hindu meditation. Although in modern Western life yoga is practiced as a form of exercise or as a relaxation technique, yoga for Hindus has a higher purpose, which is to become one with the universal god.

Consider the following . . .

- Explain why, according to Swami Vivekananda, the universe was not created.
- Explain the basis for the Hindu rejection of the belief that all humans are sinners.
- Summarize Hinduism's explanation for the major differences in the world's religions.

For More Information

BOOKS

Cole, Owen, and Hemant Kanitkar. *Teach Yourself Hinduism.* New York: McGraw-Hill, 2003.

Flood, Gavin D. *An Introduction to Hinduism.* Cambridge, UK: Cambridge University Press, 1996.

Knott, Kim. *Hinduism: A Very Short Introduction.* New York: Oxford University Press, 2000.

Vivekananda, Swami. *Complete Works of Swami Vivekananda,* 8th ed. West Bengal, India: Advaita Ashrama, 1999.

WEB SITES

"Swami Vivekananda." *Ramakrishna–Vivekananda Center of New York.* http://www.ramakrishna.org/sv.htm (accessed June 5, 2006).

Vivekananda, Swami. "Paper on Hinduism." *Universal Wisdom.* http://www.theuniversalwisdom.org/hinduism/paper-on-hinduism-vivekananda/ (accessed on June 5, 2006).

3

Religion as a Guide to Living

Belief in religion has a central role in many people's lives. The existence of a god who may approve or disapprove of their actions may motivate people in their decisions. Belief in God can give people comfort that life has meaning and purpose. Religious figures, both historical and contemporary, can inspire people to find the courage to handle their difficulties and overcome hardship. People may wish to live lives modeled after the teachings of their religion so that they can achieve the rewards that religion offers. For some, that reward is the promise of heaven. For others, it is the possibility of ending the cycle of existence and their achieving Salvation. Each religion makes clear that the way to achieve its promises is to follow its teachings. This requires more than attending worship services at a temple or church. A religion's teachings as they apply to everyday life may have the greatest impact on one's behavior and attitudes.

All religions provide for their followers a moral code, or guideline, that establishes what behavior is acceptable and what is not. They may approach the issue differently, but they all have a common theme of respect for life and upright (honest and respectable) living. Confucianism is a religion built not around a god, but around proper behavior. **The Analects of Confucius** instruct Confucian followers to have filial piety, or respect for parents, as well as respect for other elders. Among its central teachings is that a person is responsible for his or her own behavior and should act humbly and with moderation.

Like Confucianism, Jainism advises respect for other people and also for all living beings. The Akaranga Sutra in the **Gaina Sutras,** states that one should honor and respect all life by following the five Great Vows. These vows include not harming any living thing, not lying or stealing, and not becoming too involved with worldly, or material, concerns. The Akaranga Sutra relays the causes of sin so that Jains can avoid it and live a moral (honorable and decent) life.

Moral living is also central to Daoism, where following "the way" leads to an honorable life and spiritual understanding. Daoism's main religious text, the **Dao De Jing,** emphasizes that all things, living and non-living, are connected, and that a moral person should live in harmony with them. One of the best ways to do this is to not be too materialistic or aggressive. To be materialistic is to desire objects, such as cars, money, and success, in hopes of having a fulfilling life. A person is aggressive when he or she responds angrily or tries to force things to happen a certain way. This is not harmonious behavior. By following the Dao De Jing's advice on living a good life, a person will gain greater spiritual understanding and become closer to the spiritual center of Daoism, the *Dao.*

One of Buddhism's major and most referenced sacred texts is the **The Dhammapada.** This text consists solely of sayings from the Buddha instructing followers on how to live their lives. As with the previously mentioned religions, proper behavior is very important in Buddhism. A Buddhist who lives according to the words of the Buddha will follow the Eightfold Path to enlightenment and achieve *nirvana,* or the end of suffering. Such a life includes respect for living beings, non-attachment (as in Daoism and Jainism, not being attached to material objects), honesty, and moderation in all things.

Zoroastrianism's **Avesta,** which contains the Gathas, offers its followers instructions that are quite similar to those of Buddhists, Daoists, and others. The central message of the Gathas is "good thoughts, good words, good deeds." Zoroastrians believe that each person is capable of understanding the differences between good and evil and should strive to do no harm. To live a good life, one must exercise truth, order, tolerance, and discipline. Violence, such as anger, is discouraged as being very harmful.

The founder of Christianity, Jesus Christ, believed that following a standard of behavior was not enough. In his Sermon of the Mount from the **Bible,** Jesus explained that acting honestly and refraining from judging others were important. Equally important, however, were showing love, compassion (sympathy and kindness), and forgiveness to others. According to Jesus, these emotional and spiritual expressions bring one closer to God in a way that simply behaving properly cannot achieve.

The Baháʾí religion also states that there is more to being close to God than living a moral life. The Kalimat-i-Maknunih, or **The Hidden Words of Baháʾuʾlláh,** tells Baháʾís to be humble and love all of creation, but it also urges them to show their devotion to God by serving others. An example of this type of service is work supporting peace efforts or the elimination of poverty. Efforts to achieve positive results such as peace, education for those who have none, and job training for those who are unskilled are called social justice. This is a central element of the Baháʔí faith.

Social justice is the driving force behind Emma Goldman's atheism. Atheism is the belief that there is no god. In her essay **"The Philosophy of Atheism,"** Goldman states that humankind can only rely on itself. She wrote that the existence of a kind and concerned God was impossible given the injustice and suffering in the world. She urged people to take responsibility and action through social justice to make the changes that would improve the world.

Whether a person chooses to believe the message of atheism or of a different belief system, each offers a message that one must take responsibility for one's life. Respect, honesty, and compassion are key elements in all faiths. Concern with acquiring possessions or winning a certain status are not fulfilling. People seeking guidance in their daily lives can consult with one of these moral codes or those from another religion. The fact that most of these codes have existed for hundreds of years and continue to be followed shows that there is value and inspiration in their messages.

The Analects of Confucius

Books 1 and 2 of the The Analects of Confucius,
available online from Exploring Ancient World Cultures Anthology
at http://eawc.evansville.edu/anthology/analects.htm
Attributed to Confucius or his followers
Completed around 475 BCE
Translator unknown

"The Master said, 'A youth, when at home, should be filial, and, abroad, respectful to his elders. He should be earnest and truthful. He should overflow in love to all, and cultivate the friendship of the good. When he has time and opportunity, after the performance of these things, he should employ them in polite studies'."

The Lun Yu, also known as the Analects, is one of the most influential books that survives from the ancient Chinese world. An analect is any collection of assorted writings. It has been said that all later Chinese philosophy (thought or study on the arts and sciences) is in some way rooted in the Analects. This slim, twenty-chapter book is thought to have been written by Confucius (551–479 BCE), a philosopher, educator, politician, and public servant. In the centuries following his death, Confucius came to be regarded as an almost mythic figure, a "sage-king" whose name remains readily identifiable with practical wisdom, or wisdom that can be applied to life.

The Analects record Confucius's teachings as dialogues, or conversations, with students. In Books 1 and 2, the "Master" is Confucius, and other names refer to students who ask him questions. In these dialogues, he presented his thoughts not as new but as wisdom that had been handed down over the course of hundreds of years. The core of his belief was that while people live their lives subject to the rules and commandments both of heaven and of the cycle of natural forces, they are also responsible for their own behavior, particularly their treatment of others. This concept, which he called *ren,* meaning "loving others" or "compassion," remains central to Confucian belief. Confucius believed that the best way to love others was to maintain humility and to avoid being clever or trying to gain favor with others. He also supported what in the West is called the Golden Rule, an ethical principle that can be found in some form in the scriptures of at least eight world religions. As Confucius put it, "perfect virtue" meant "not to do to others as you would not wish done to yourself" (Book 12). An important part of compassion, or sympathy and understanding of others, is devotion to one's brothers and sisters and parents.

For generations Chinese diplomats and other government officials turned to Confucius for guidance on behavior, as reflected in these passages from Book 10:

Confucius, in his village, looked simple and sincere, and as if he were not able to speak.

When he was in the prince's ancestral temple, or in the court, he spoke minutely [thoroughly] on every point, but cautiously.

When he was waiting at court, in speaking with the great officers of the lower grade, he spoke freely, but in a straightforward manner; in speaking with those of the higher grade, he did so blandly "mildly," but precisely.

When the ruler was present, his manner displayed respectful uneasiness; it was grave, but self-possessed.

In other words, Confucius urged his followers to be humble and moderate in their behavior. This is the kind of simple, almost homespun wisdom that runs throughout the Analects. Repeatedly, Confucius emphasizes such virtues as being upright and courteous, kind and proper, faithful and sincere.

The historical Confucius Little is known about Confucius's life. Historians regard much that is known about him as legend rather than fact. The chief source of information about his life comes from a second-century BCE biography by a court historian, Sima Qian (145–c. 85 BCE), the author of *Records of the Grand Historian.* Sima Qian's book claims that Confucius was a descendant of royal ancestors. He was born in the town of Lu, near

Students dressed in ancient clothing stand before a statue of Confucius, the founder of Confucianism. His teachings are recorded in the Lun Yu, or the Analects. CHINA PHOTOS/GETTY IMAGES.

the present-day city of Qufu in China's southeastern Shandong province, in answer to prayers his parents had offered at the nearby sacred hill of Ni.

His original family name was Kong (K'ung), and the name Confucius is a Latinized (written using the Latin alphabet) version of "Kong Fuzi" (K'ung Fu-tzu), a name that means "the Master Kong." "Confucius" was the name used by early Catholic missionaries, priests who tried to convert the Chinese people to Christianity, in China. Nothing is known about Confucius's education, but part of the legend is that he studied the religion of Daoism (Taoism) and music. In his early years he took jobs that he considered undignified, such as caring for livestock. By the time he reached middle age he had gathered around himself a number of disciples, or followers, to whom he taught his philosophy. This philosophy grew into the religion of Confucianism. The major beliefs of Confucianism are contained in the Analects.

When he was about fifty years old, Confucius entered public service. He was appointed Minister of Public Works and Minister of Crime by the duke of Lu. He was forced into exile when he offended members of the court, and he spent the following years traveling about China, facing danger and hardship. He returned to Lu in 484 BCE and spent his remaining years collecting classic works of literature and putting together the court chronicle, or record, of Lu. During these years, he earned a reputation for good manners and courtesy. It was for this reason that people began to follow the teachings of the Analects as a guide for everyday living.

Confucianism as a guide for politics One theme that runs through the Analects, and specifically the excerpts from Books 1 and 2, has to do with government and the characteristics best suited to leaders. For example, Confucius refers to agreements within and between governments. He points out that agreements should be based on what is right. Leaders should show respect to others and follow through with what they say they are going to do. Diplomats and leaders would consult Confucius's words and model their actions after his advice. Even into the twenty-first century, leaders in East Asian countries such as China, Japan, and South Korea quote Confucius to support their policies. They believe that the Confucian values of loyalty, thrift, and hard work contribute to the economic success of their countries.

Confucius believed that the political institutions of his time had collapsed. China was in a state of turmoil because of the claims to power of competing warlords. Rulers often did not live up to their responsibilities, and their assistants frequently were given their jobs not because of merit but because they had flattered their superiors or otherwise won favor. Confucius's view was that good government was the result of self-discipline by leaders. He also urged that leaders govern by keeping in mind the principle of *de,* or virtue. In Book 2, he wrote: "He who exercises government by means of his virtue may be compared to the north polar star, which keeps its place and all the stars turn towards it." Similarly, he wrote in Book 2 that rulers should be kind and firm in their decisions, that they should strive to keep goodness in their work and their lives. Many of these principles also applied to everyday people. They, too, in their dealings with others and with their government, have to show similar virtues.

The Literary Style of The Analects

The effect of many of the sayings in the Analects relies on a type of figure of speech called *chiasmus* (kee-AZ-muhs). This refers to a reversal of parallel, or corresponding, elements in a sentence or saying. A good example is found in Book 2: "Learning without thought is labor lost; thought without learning is perilous [dangerous]." The chiasmus is the reversal of the words "learning without thought" to form "thought without learning." Another good example, also from Book 2, is advice for leaders: "Advance the upright and set aside the crooked [dishonest, corrupt], then the people will submit. Advance the crooked and set aside the upright, then the people will not submit."

A major reason that Confucius used this and other figures of speech was to make the sayings in the Analects more memorable. If the Analects were to serve as a guide to everyday living, people had to remember them so that they could apply them in their dealings with others. Rather than writing in an abstract, philosophical style that people would find hard to understand, Confucius wrote in a way that enabled people to remember his teachings. In this respect, the Analects are similar to the Ten Commandments, which are also written in a language and style that can be easily remembered. Leaders, such as politicians and business executives, often quote from Confucius for the same reason: these figures of speech provide practical wisdom in pithy phrases, or phrases that are brief and full of meaning. Perhaps the best example of this style of phrasing in modern times comes from U.S. president John F. Kennedy's 1960 inaugural speech: "Ask not what your country can do for you. Ask what you can do for your country."

Translating ancient Chinese texts into modern English (or any other language) is difficult. Chinese characters may not have close English equivalents, ancient Chinese has no punctuation marks, and the language is often open to wide interpretation by translators. For example, the sentence about learning from Book 2 has been translated in many different ways, among them, "Study without thought is vain [useless]; thought without study is dangerous"; "Study without thinking, and you are blind; think without studying, and you are in danger"; and "He who learns but does not think is lost. He who thinks but does not learn is in great danger." These difficulties with translation in their own way add to the appeal of the Analects. If the Analects are to serve as a guide for living, they have to apply in many different situations. Because their language is general and can take on different meanings, their wisdom is not forever fixed but is subject to interpretation as the circumstances of everyday life change.

Things to remember while reading the excerpt from The Analects of Confucius:

- Confucius was born into a social class of people called *shi*. The shi were people, like Confucius's parents, who could say that they had royal ancestors. They themselves, though, had little wealth and usually held low-level military and government jobs. Confucius's social class would likely have contributed to his frame of mind in composing the Analects, for its teachings provided Confucius and others of his status with a way to succeed among more powerful people.

- A Chinese education such as that which Confucius received as a child focused on the Six Arts: military skills, arithmetic, the appreciation of music, calligraphy (artistic writing), learning to play a musical instrument, and *li,* or etiquette and rituals. Being a gentleman required a youngster to master the complex principles of li. One of the primary purposes of the Analects, then, was to serve as a text that would provide Confucius's followers with a more detailed understanding of etiquette and proper behavior.

- The Analects were written in part as a response to the political turmoil and corrupt governments of the day. In fact, the turmoil was so great that the Chinese refer to the period from about the fifth century through 221 BCE as the Warring States Period. This was a time when Chinese warlords were gaining power by taking over neighboring regions. The Analects attempted to provide an antidote, or remedy, to these problems by defining the qualities of kind and just leadership.

• • •

Excerpt from The Analects of Confucius

Book 1

The Master said, "Is it not pleasant to learn with a constant **perseverance** and application?

"Is it not delightful to have friends coming from distant quarters?

"Is he not a man of complete virtue, who feels no **discomposure** though men may take no note of him?"

The philosopher Yu said, "They are few who, being **filial** and **fraternal,** are fond of offending against their superiors. There have been none, who, not liking to offend against their superiors, have been fond of stirring up confusion.

"The superior man bends his attention to what is **radical.** That being established, all practical courses naturally grow up. Filial **piety** and fraternal submission,—are they not the root of all benevolent actions?"

The Master said, "Fine words and an **insinuating** appearance are seldom associated with true virtue."

The philosopher Tsang said, "I daily examine myself on three points:— whether, in **transacting** business for others, I may have been not

Perseverance: Determination.

Discomposure: Uneasiness.

Filial: Relating to a child's feelings for his or her parents.

Fraternal: Showing friendship or brotherly feeling.

Radical: Essential or far-reaching in scope.

Piety: Devotion, loyalty.

Insinuating: Gaining favor through effort, often sly and underhanded.

Transacting: Doing, carrying out.

People parade through the street during the Confucius Culture Festival in Yunnan province, China, as they honor Confucianism's founder. Confucius valued education and proper behavior. CHINA PHOTOS/ GETTY IMAGES.

faithful;—whether, in **intercourse** with friends, I may have been not sincere;—whether I may have not mastered and practiced the instructions of my teacher."

The Master said, "To rule a country of a thousand chariots, there must be reverent attention to business, and sincerity; **economy** in expenditure, and love for men; and the employment of the people at the proper seasons."

The Master said, "A youth, when at home, should be filial, and, abroad, respectful to his elders. He should be earnest and truthful. He should overflow in love to all, and cultivate the friendship of the good. When he has time and opportunity, after the performance of these things, he should employ them in polite studies."

Tsze-hsia said, "If a man withdraws his mind from the love of beauty, and applies it as sincerely to the love of the virtuous; if, in serving his parents, he can exert his **utmost** strength; if, in serving his prince, he can devote his life; if, in his intercourse with his friends, his words are sincere:—although men say that he has not learned, I will certainly say that he has.

The Master said, "If the scholar be not grave, he will not call forth any **veneration**, and his learning will not be solid.

"Hold faithfulness and sincerity as first principles.

Intercourse: Communication or interaction.

Economy: Thrift or saving, careful use of finances or resources.

Utmost: Greatest.

Veneration: Respect, admiration.

"Have no friends not equal to yourself.

"When you have faults, do not fear to abandon them."

The philosopher Tsang said, "Let there be a careful attention to perform the funeral rites to parents, and let them be followed when long gone with the ceremonies of sacrifice;—then the virtue of the people will resume its proper excellence."

Tsze-ch'in asked Tsze-kung saying, "When our master comes to any country, he does not fail to learn all about its government. Does he ask his information? or is it given to him?"

Benign: Kind and caring.

Temperate: Mild-mannered, calm, self-controlled.

Complaisant: Unworried.

Bent: Direction.

Tsze-kung said, "Our master is **benign,** upright, courteous, **temperate,** and **complaisant** and thus he gets his information. The master's mode of asking information,—is it not different from that of other men?"

The Master said, "While a man's father is alive, look at the **bent** of his will; when his father is dead, look at his conduct. If for three years he does not alter from the way of his father, he may be called filial."

Propriety: Good manners, decency.

The philosopher Yu said, "In practicing the rules of **propriety,** a natural ease is to be prized. In the ways prescribed by the ancient kings, this is the excellent quality, and in things small and great we follow them.

Manifests: Shows.

"Yet it is not to be observed in all cases. If one, knowing how such ease should be prized, **manifests** it, without regulating it by the rules of propriety, this likewise is not to be done."

The philosopher Yu said, "When agreements are made according to what is right, what is spoken can be made good. When respect is shown according to what is proper, one keeps far from shame and disgrace. When the parties upon whom a man leans are proper persons to be **intimate** with, he can make them his guides and masters."

Intimate: Friendly, close.

Gratify: Satisfy.

Appliances: Things that make tasks easier.

Ease: Comfort.

Rectified: Corrected, put right.

The Master said, "He who aims to be a man of complete virtue in his food does not seek to **gratify** his appetite, nor in his dwelling place does he seek the **appliances** of **ease;** he is earnest in what he is doing, and careful in his speech; he frequents the company of men of principle that he may be **rectified:**—such a person may be said indeed to love to learn."

Pronounce: Say.

Tsze-kung said, "What do you **pronounce** concerning the poor man who yet does not flatter, and the rich man who is not proud?" The Master replied, "They will do; but they are not equal to him, who, though poor, is yet cheerful, and to him, who, though rich, loves the rules of propriety."

Apprehend: Understand.

Tsze-kung replied, "It is said in the Book of Poetry, 'As you cut and then file, as you carve and then polish.'—The meaning is the same, I **apprehend,** as that which you have just expressed."

The Master said, "With one like Ts'ze, I can begin to talk about the **odes.** I told him one point, and he knew its proper sequence."

The Master said, "I will not be **afflicted** at men's not knowing me; I will be afflicted that I do not know men."

Odes: Lyric poems marked by high feeling.

Afflicted: Upset, distressed.

Book 2

The Master said, "He who exercises government by means of his virtue may be compared to the north polar star, which keeps its place and all the stars turn towards it."

The Master said, "In the Book of Poetry are three hundred pieces, but the design of them all may be embraced in one sentence 'Having no **depraved** thoughts.'"

Depraved: Evil, wicked.

The Master said, "If the people be led by laws, and uniformity sought to be given them by punishments, they will try to avoid the punishment, but have no sense of shame.

"If they be led by virtue, and uniformity sought to be given them by the rules of propriety, they will have the sense of shame, and moreover will become good."

The Master said, "At fifteen, I had my mind bent on learning.

"At thirty, I stood firm.

"At forty, I had no doubts.

"At fifty, I knew the **decrees of Heaven.**

"At sixty, my ear was an obedient organ for the reception of truth.

"At seventy, I could follow what my heart desired, without **transgressing** what was right."

Decrees of Heaven: Destinies.

Transgressing: Violating; going against.

Mang I asked what filial piety was. The Master said, "It is not being disobedient."

Soon after, as Fan Ch'ih was driving him, the Master told him, saying, "Mang-sun asked me what filial piety was, and I answered him,—'not being disobedient.'"

Fan Ch'ih said, "What did you mean?" The Master replied, "That parents, when alive, be served according to **propriety;** that, when dead, they should be buried according to propriety; and that they should be sacrificed to according to propriety."

Propriety: Good behavior, correctness.

Mang Wu asked what filial piety was. The Master said, "Parents are anxious lest their children should be sick."

Tsze-yu asked what filial piety was. The Master said, "The filial piety nowadays means the support of one's parents. But dogs and horses likewise are able to do something in the way of support;—without **reverence,** what is there to distinguish the one support given from the other?"

Tsze-hsia asked what filial piety was. The Master said, "The difficulty is with the **countenance**. If, when their elders have any troublesome

Reverence: Respect.

Countenance: Look, appearance.

affairs, the young take the toil of them, and if, when the young have wine and food, they set them before their elders, is THIS to be considered filial piety?"

The Master said, "I have talked with Hui for a whole day, and he has not made any objection to anything I said;—as if he were stupid. He has retired, and I have examined his conduct when away from me, and found him able to illustrate my teachings. Hui!—He is not stupid."

The Master said, "See what a man does.

"Mark his motives.

"Examine in what things he rests.

"How can a man conceal his character? How can a man conceal his character?"

Cherishing: Valuing, appreciating.

The Master said, "If a man keeps **cherishing** his old knowledge, so as continually to be acquiring new, he may be a teacher of others."

The Master said, "The accomplished scholar is not a utensil."

Constituted: Made up, represented.

Tsze-kung asked what **constituted** the superior man. The Master said, "He acts before he speaks, and afterwards speaks according to his actions."

Catholic: All-embracing, wide-reaching.

The Master said, "The superior man is **catholic** and not **partisan.** The mean man is partisan and not catholic."

Partisan: Biased, taking sides.

The Master said, "Learning without thought is labor lost; thought without learning is **perilous.**"

Perilous: Dangerous.

The Master said, "The study of strange **doctrines** is **injurious** indeed!"

Doctrines: Policies, practices.

The Master said, "Yu, shall I teach you what knowledge is? When you know a thing, to hold that you know it; and when you do not know a thing, to allow that you do not know it;—this is knowledge."

Injurious: Harmful.

Emolument: Compensation, in the form of payment, benefits, or privileges, for services or employment.

Tsze-chang was learning with a view to official **emolument.**

The Master said, "Hear much and put aside the points of which you stand in doubt, while you speak cautiously at the same time of the others:—then you will **afford** few occasions for blame. See much and put aside the things which seem perilous, while you are cautious at the same time in carrying the others into practice: then you will have few occasions for **repentance.** When one gives few occasions for blame in his words, and few occasions for repentance in his conduct, he is in the way to get emolument."

Afford: Provide.

Repentance: Guilt or regret.

The Duke Ai asked, saying, "What should be done in order to secure the submission of the people?" Confucius replied, "Advance the upright and set aside the crooked, then the people will submit. Advance the crooked and set aside the upright, then the people will not submit."

Nerve: Encourage.

Chi K'ang asked how to cause the people to reverence their ruler, to be faithful to him, and to go on to **nerve** themselves to virtue. The Master said,

"Let him **preside over** them with gravity;—then they will reverence him. Let him be final and kind to all;—then they will be faithful to him. Let him advance the good and teach the **incompetent**;—then they will eagerly seek to be virtuous."

Preside over: Supervise, be in charge of.

Incompetent: People who lack ability or skills.

Some one addressed Confucius, saying, "Sir, why are you not engaged in the government?"

The Master said, "What does the Shu-ching say of filial piety?—'You are final, you **discharge** your brotherly duties. These qualities are displayed in government.' This then also constitutes the exercise of government. Why must there be THAT—making one be in the government?"

Discharge: Carry out, fulfill.

The Master said, "I do not know how a man without truthfulness is to get on. How can a large carriage be made to go without the crossbar for yoking the oxen to, or a small carriage without the arrangement for yoking the horses?" ...

The Master said, "For a man to sacrifice to a spirit which does not belong to him is flattery.

"To see what is right and not to do it is **want** of courage."

Want: Lack.

• • •

What happened next ...

Confucianism came about partly as a response to self-seeking, corrupt rulers, so in the early centuries it was not very popular among the ruling classes. In 213 BCE the Zhou (Chou) Dynasty issued a decree ordering all Confucian books to be destroyed, under pain of death. Many Confucian scholars refused to obey the ruling, and they were buried alive. In 191 BCE, however, the Han Dynasty lifted the ban on Confucianism, and many of the ancient Confucian texts were again published and read.

Did you know ...

- Many Asian countries celebrate the date of Confucius's birth on September 28, though it is not certain that he was born on this date. In Taiwan the holiday is called Teachers' Day, because Confucius was one of the first great teachers.

- Confucianism and Daoism, which took root at roughly the same time in ancient China, were regarded at the time as sharply differing forms of religion. Daoism was "otherworldly" and urged its followers to withdraw from earthly concerns. In contrast, Confucianism was "this worldly," providing advice about how to behave in the physical world.

- The Analects are not the only Confucian texts. In addition, there are two more groups of texts that are important to Confucianism. One group is called the Five Classics, and the other is called the Four Books. Most of these works were written before Confucius was born, but they gained authority because he approved of them. The Five Classics include the Record of Rites, the Classic of Odes, the Classic of Documents, the Book of Changes, and the Spring and Autumn Annals. The Four Books include Doctrine of the Mean and Great Learning. In the eleventh century Books 1 and 2 of the Analects were incorporated into the Four Books.

Consider the following...

- Based on your reading of Books 1 and 2 of the Analects, explain why some people would not regard Confucianism as a religion but rather as a life philosophy. Explain on what basis others might disagree with that view.

- Explain how some of the events of Confucius's life may have contributed to the development of his philosophical-religious views.

- Summarize Confucius's view of "filial piety" and say why this virtue was so important to him.

For More Information

BOOKS

Fingarette, Herbert. *Confucius: The Secular as Sacred.* Long Grove, IL: Waveland Press, 1998.

Ivanhoe, Philip J. *Confucian Moral Self Cultivation,* 2nd ed. Cambridge, MA: Hackett, 2000.

Weiming, Tu, and Mary Evelyn Tucker. *Confucian Spirituality,* vol. 1. New York: Herder and Herder, 2003.

WEB SITES

"The Analects of Confucius." *Exploring Ancient World Cultures Anthology,* University of Evansville. http://eawc.evansville.edu/anthology/analects.htm (accessed June 5, 2006).

Riegel, Jeffery. "Confucius." *Stanford Encyclopedia of Philosophy.* http://plato.stanford.edu/entries/confucius/ (accessed on June 5, 2006).

Ross, Kelley L. "Confucius." *The Proceedings of the Friesian School.* http://www.friesian.com/confuci.htm (accessed on June 5, 2006).

Gaina Sutras

"Knowledge of the Weapon," from "Akaranga Sutra" in the Gaina Sutras,
available online from the Internet Sacred Text Archive at
http://www.sacred-texts.com/jai/akaranga.htm
Compiled around the fifth century CE
Translated by Hermann Jacobi
Published in Sacred Books of the East *(Clarendon Press, 1884)*

> "He who has the true knowledge about all things, will commit no sinful act, nor cause others to do so."

"K nowledge of the Weapon" consists of seven lessons that make up the first of twenty-four books, or chapters, contained in the Akaranga Sutra, which is found in the Gaina Sutras. It is a *sutra,* or a collection of religious teachings. This sutra is a holy text of Jainism. Jainism is an ancient religion practiced primarily in India, and it shares many beliefs with Hinduism. The Akaranga Sutra is one of twelve central Jain religious texts, collectively referred to as the Twelve Limbs. Like many Jain holy texts, it developed over a long period of time and was passed down orally until it was recorded in Sanskrit roughly a thousand years after it was first composed.

The Akaranga Sutra, including "Knowledge of the Weapon," was created by one of the central figures in the history of Jainism, Mahavira. During his lifetime, Mahavira made and lived by five vows, called the Great Vows. These vows, or promises, still form the central belief system of Jainism, and all Jain ascetics (monks) continue to fulfill them. Ordinary people fulfill these vows to the extent that the circumstances of their lives allow. The Great Vows are as follows:

Ahimsa: not killing or injuring humans or any other living thing;
Satya: speaking only the truth;
Asteya: not stealing or being greedy;

Brahmacharya: chastity (for a monk, this means remaining celibate, or not married and refraining from sexual relations; for laypeople, it means remaining faithful to one's spouse);

Asparigrah: not being overly concerned with the cares of the world.

These practices grew out of Jain viewpoints about the nature of life in the universe. Jains do not believe in a creator-god (a god who created the world and living beings); instead, they consider the universe to be eternal and unchanging. Jains see the world as composed of six categories, and two of these are *jiva,* or soul, and non-jiva, or non-soul. Non-jiva is further divided into matter, space, time, and motion, and nonmotion. Jiva, reveals itself in six forms: earth-bodied, fire-bodied, air-bodied, water-bodied, stationary (unmoving, for example, plants and trees, and moving (including humans, insects, animals, gods, and "hell-beings"). These six forms are discussed in the excerpts from the Akaranga Sutra in the context of not doing harm to living creatures.

Jains use the concept of *karma* to explain the differences among living things. Karma is the built-up effect of a person's good or bad actions on his or her future lives. The basic notion is that all forms of jiva attract karma. Some of this karma does no harm; it determines such things as a person's gender and length of life. Other types of karma, however, are harmful. They lead to a loss of faith, knowledge, and energy. A person who lives a life of self-discipline is able to ward off and wear away these damaging forms of karma and eventually, perhaps, reach a state of omniscience (all-knowingness or universal understanding) and liberation, or freedom. At death, such a person moves to the roof of the universe and lives there in a state of pure knowledge, bliss, and energy. This state, however, can be achieved only through the fire of self-denial.

This is the teaching of the Akaranga Sutra. In "Knowledge of the Weapon," the speaker, who is passing along the teachings of Mahavira, outlines the way in which people can lead a moral, sin-free life of denial. He explains the presence of life, like insects, small animals and plants, in fire, wind, water, earth, and so on. For example, small life-forms can be found swimming in water, so one has to be careful not to destroy those life-forms when using water. In this way Mahavira expresses the fundamental Jain doctrine, or set of guidelines, that opposes injuring or harming living creatures. Knowing the causes of sin gives people "knowledge of the weapon" being used to keep them from a virtuous life, and knowledge is power to help them avoid sin.

Sculptures of Jain tirthankaras *adorn the wall of a cave in Ellora, India. Jains believe in 24 tirthankaras, or respected teachers, with Mahavira being the final one.* © LINDSAY HEBBERD/CORBIS.

The dates of Mahavira's life are uncertain, but evidence shows that he lived at the same time as the Buddha, the founder of Buddhism. This means that he was probably born in about 490 BCE and died in about 410 BCE, though many sources give dates in the sixth century BCE. Mahavira, whose name means "Great Hero," was born Nataputta Vardhamana and grew up surrounded by luxury as the son of a local king. After his parents died when he was about thirty years old, however, he left his home, gave up all of his possessions, and eventually became one of the great teachers of Jainism. As a teacher, he provided his students and followers with guidelines for living a holy life. Jain tradition regards Mahavira as the last of twenty-four respected teachers called *Jina,* a word meaning "conqueror" and referring to conquering one's inner enemies, such as greed, dishonesty, pride, and anger. The word *tirthankara* means "makers of the ford" and is also used to refer to these teachers. The term signifies the construction of ways to cross the

Jainism and Vegetarianism

Some people think of Jainism as almost identical with strict vegetarianism. Vegetarians do not eat meat. Strict vegetarians also will not consume animal-based products, such as milk and eggs. The two are thought of in relation to each other because of the Jain concept of *ahimsa*, or nonviolence, and many vegetarians' wish not to harm living beings, even for food. While this view oversimplifies the religion, the emphasis on vegetarianism in Jain life has led to the development of what is called a "Jain menu," which defines suitable dishes to be served both in the home and at restaurants.

Some Jains are more strict than others when it comes to their diet. Many, for example, refuse to eat root vegetables (vegetables that grow in the earth, such as onions, garlic, potatoes, and carrots) because they are likely to hide other life-forms. Others fast (refrain from eating) extensively during the monsoon season, which is the growing season; they are likely to avoid roots during this time, so that they do not risk injuring living things that are growing. Jains typically avoid eating after dark because of the possibility of accidentally harming a living being that cannot be seen.

Nonetheless, Jains still enjoy many meals common in everyday life, such as burgers. Instead of beef, however, the chief ingredients in a Jain burger are bananas, peas, and chilies, pressure-cooked with tomato sauce, vinegar, sugar, and oil and served with tomatoes, cucumbers, and spicy condiments.

"ocean" of rebirth. The Akaranga Sutra includes Mahavira's teachings, which were recorded by a group of his followers.

Mahavira was an ascetic, meaning that he gave up worldly activities and interests and lived a life of self-denial, poverty, and contemplation, or deep thought, in a monastery. A monastery is the residence of a group of people who have taken religious vows. At first, his only possession was a single robe, but eventually he gave up even that and went naked. For years he wandered throughout India, never staying in one village for more than a day at a time and refusing to shelter himself from either cold or heat. When he walked or sat, he was careful never to cause hurt to any life-form. For this reason, he would remain in one place for long periods of time during the rainy season, when the paths he walked would have been covered with life-forms he did not want to injure. Because of this refusal to do harm, Mahavira was a strict vegetarian, meaning he did not eat meat or any food that came from an animal. He was so strict that he even strained his drinking water to ensure that no creature was living in it. In these ways, Mahavira was setting an example for his followers about how to live.

Things to remember while reading the excerpt from the Gaina Sutras:

- A defining doctrine of Jainism is *ahimsa*, not killing or harming other living creatures. In the modern world, Jains pledge to follow this doctrine by means of pacifism, or opposition to violence (especially the refusal to fight in a war); vegetarianism; and concern with not harming or polluting the environment.

- According to Jain belief, "sin" and "acting sinfully" means in large part to do any kind of harm to other living creatures, not just humans but even the smallest living things. This type of sin can occur through any type of daily activity, or what the excerpt calls "through his doing acts relating to earth." People who "pretend to be houseless" commit sin by pretending to adhere to Jain practices but are insincere in their beliefs.

- The text uses the term *Bauddha* to refer to those who object to the teachings of Jainism. The word *Bauddha* comes from the word *buddha,* referring to the founder of Buddhism. In Jain contexts, it refers to intellectuals, to thinkers who examine and question Jain doctrines.

• • •

Excerpt from the Gaina Sutras

"Knowledge of the Weapon"

Second Lesson The (living) world is **afflicted**, miserable, difficult to instruct, and without **discrimination**. In this world full of pain, suffering by their different acts, see the **benighted** ones cause great pain. See! there are beings individually **embodied** (in earth; not one all-soul). See! there are men who control themselves, whilst others only) pretend to be houseless (i.e. monks, such as the **Bauddhas,** whose conduct differs not from that of householders), because one destroys this (earth-body) by bad and **injurious** doings, and many other beings, besides, which he hurts by means of earth, through his doing acts relating to earth. About this the **Revered** One has taught the truth: for the sake of the splendour, honour, and glory of this life, for the sake of birth, death, and final **liberation,** for the removal of pain, man acts sinfully towards earth, or causes others to act so, or allows others to act so. This **deprives** him of happiness and perfect wisdom. About this he is informed when he has understood or heard, either from the Revered One or from the monks, the faith to be **coveted**. There are some who, of a truth, know this (i.e. injuring) to be the **bondage**, the **delusion,** the death, the hell. For this a man is longing when he destroys this (earth-body) by bad, injurious doings, and many other beings, besides, which he hurts by means of earth, through his doing acts relating to earth. Thus I say. . . .

Third Lesson ... See! there are men who control themselves; others pretend only to be houseless; for one destroys this (water-body) by bad, injurious doings, and many other beings, besides, which he hurts by means of water, through his doing acts relating to water. About this the Revered One

Afflicted: Troubled.

Discrimination: Common sense, judgment.

Benighted: Living in a state without knowledge or morals, unenlightened.

Embodied: Alive, having physical form.

Bauddhas: Buddhists.

Injurious: Harmful.

Revered: Respected, honored.

Liberation: Release, freedom.

Deprives: Takes away, leaves without.

Coveted: Desired.

Bondage: Slavery.

Delusion: False impression.

has taught the truth: for the sake of the splendour, honour, and glory of this life, for the sake of birth, death, and final liberation, for the removal of pain, man acts sinfully towards water, or causes others to act so, or allows others to act so. This deprives him of happiness and perfect wisdom. About this he is informed when he has understood and heard from the Revered One, or from the monks, the faith to be coveted. There are some who, of a truth, know this (i.e. injuring) to be the bondage, the delusion, the death, the hell. For this a man is longing when he destroys this (water-body) by bad and injurious doings, and many other beings, besides, which he hurts by means of water, through his doing acts relating to water. Thus I say.

Distinctly Clearly.

Declared: Stated.

Object: Disagree.

There are beings living in water, many lives; of a truth, to the monks water has been declared to be living matter. See! considering the injuries (done to water-bodies), those acts (which are injuries, but must be done before the use of water, e.g. straining) have been **distinctly declared.** Moreover he (who uses water which is not strained) takes away what has not been given (i.e. the bodies of water-lives). (A Bauddha will **object:** "We have permission, we have permission to drink it, or (to take it) for toilet purposes." Thus they destroy by various injuries (the water-bodies). But in this their doctrine is of no authority.

Comprehend: Understand.

Renounce: Give up, reject.

He who injures these (water-bodies) does not **comprehend** and **renounce** the sinful acts; he who does not injure these, comprehends and renounces the sinful acts. Knowing them, a wise man should not act sinfully towards water, nor cause others to act so, nor allow others to act so. He who knows these causes of sin relating to water, is called a reward-knowing sage. Thus I say.

Accord: Free will.

Deny: Refuse to let have.

Fourth Lesson (Thus I say): A man should not, of his own **accord, deny** the world (of fire-bodies), nor should he deny the self. He who denies the world (of fire-bodies), denies the self; and he who denies the self, denies the world (of fire-bodies). He who knows that (viz. [namely] fire) through which injury is done to the long-living bodies (i.e. plants), knows also that which does no injury (i.e. control); and he who knows that which does no injury, knows also that through which no injury is done to the long-living bodies. This has been seen by the heroes (of faith) who conquered ignorance; for they control themselves, always **exert** themselves, always mind their duty. He who is **unmindful** of duty, and desiring of the qualities (i.e. of the pleasure and profit which may be **derived** from the elements) is called the **torment** (of living beings). Knowing this, a wise man (**resolves**): "Now (I shall do) no more what I used to do . . . before." See! there are men who control themselves; others pretend only to be houseless; for one destroys this (fire-body) by bad and injurious doings, and many other

Exert: Make an effort.

Unmindful: Careless or unaware.

Derived: Obtained, gotten.

Torment: Suffering.

Resolves: Makes a firm decision.

beings, besides, which he hurts by means of fire, through his doing acts relating to fire. About this the Revered One has taught the truth: for the sake of the splendour, honour, and glory of this life, for the sake of birth, death, and final liberation, for the removal of pain, man acts sinfully towards fire, or causes others to act so, or allows others to act so. This deprives him of happiness and perfect wisdom. About this he is informed when he has understood, or heard from the Revered One or from the monks, the faith to be coveted. There are some who, of a truth, know this (i.e. injuring) to be the bondage, the delusion, the death, the hell. For this a man is longing, when he destroys this (fire-body) by bad and injurious doings, and many other beings, besides, which he hurts by means of fire, through his doing acts relating to fire. Thus I say.

There are beings living in the earth, living in grass, living on leaves, living in wood, living in cowdung, living in dust-heaps, jumping beings which coming near (fire) fall into it. Some, certainly, touched by fire, shrivel up; those which shrivel up there, lose their sense there; those which lose their sense there, die there.

He who injures these (fire-bodies) does not comprehend and renounce the sinful acts; he who does not injure these, comprehends and renounces the sinful acts. Knowing them, a wise man should not act sinfully towards fire, nor cause others to act so, nor allow others to act so. He who knows the causes of sin relating to fire, is called a reward knowing sage. Thus I say.

Fifth Lesson I shall not do (acts relating to plants) after having entered the order [having become a Jainist], having recognised (the truth about these acts), and having conceived that which is free from danger (i.e. control). . . .

See! there are men who control themselves; others pretend only to be houseless, for one destroys this (body of a plant) by bad and injurious doings, and many other beings, besides, which he hurts by means of plants, through his doing acts relating to plants. About this the Revered One has taught the truth: for the sake of the splendour, honour, and glory of this life, for the sake of birth, death, and final liberation, for the removal of pain, man acts sinfully towards plants, or causes others to act so, or allows others to act so. This deprives him of happiness and perfect wisdom. About this he is informed when he has understood, or heard from the Revered One, or from the monks, the faith to be coveted. There are some who, of a truth, know this (i.e. injuring) to be the bondage, the delusion, the death, the hell. For this a man is longing when he destroys this (body of a plant) by bad and injurious doings, and many other beings, besides, which he hurts by means of plants, through his doing acts relating to plants. Thus I say.

As the nature of this (i.e. men) is to be born and to grow old, so is the nature of that (i.e. plants) to be born and to grow old; as this has reason, so that has reason; as this falls sick when cut, so that falls sick when cut; as this needs food, so that needs food; as this will **decay,** so that will decay; as this is not eternal, so that is not eternal; as this **takes increment,** so that takes increment; as this is changing, so that is changing. He who injures these (plants) does not comprehend and renounce the sinful acts; he who does not injure these, comprehends and renounces the sinful acts. Knowing them, a wise man should not act sinfully towards plants, nor cause others to act so, nor allow others to act so. He who knows these causes of sin relating to plants, is called a reward-knowing sage. Thus I say. . . .

Seventh Lesson . . . There are jumping beings which, coming near wind, fall into it. Some, certainly, touched by wind, shrivel up; those which shrivel up there, lose their sense there; those which lose their sense there, die there.

He who injures these (wind-bodies) does not comprehend and renounce the sinful acts; he who does not injure these, comprehends and

Decay: Rot.

Takes increment: Proceeds one step at a time.

renounces the sinful acts. Knowing them, a wise man should not act sinfully towards wind, nor cause others to act so, nor allow others to act so. He who knows these causes of sin relating to wind, is called a reward-knowing sage. Thus I say.

Be aware that about this (wind-body) too those are involved in sin who **delight** not in the right conduct, and, though doing acts, talk about religious discipline, who **conducting** themselves according to their own will, pursuing **sensual** pleasures, and **engaging** in acts, are **addicted** to worldliness. He who has the true knowledge about all things, will commit no sinful act, nor cause others to do so, &c [etc.]. Knowing them, a wise man should not act sinfully towards the aggregate of six (kinds of) lives, nor cause others to act so, nor allow others to act so. He who knows these causes of sin relating to the aggregate of the six (kinds of) lives, is called a reward-knowing sage. Thus I say.

Delight: Find pleasure or enjoyment.

Conducting: Behaving, acting.

Sensual: Relating to the five senses.

Engaging: Taking part, involving oneself.

Addicted: Dependent on, regularly occupied with.

• • •

What happened next...

The "Knowledge of the Weapon" is a portion of a description of the life of an ascetic. The five Great Vows taken by Mahavira are also taken by modern-day ascetics, such as monks and nuns. For most Jains, however, renunciation, or self-denial, is not the major focus of their lives. Nonetheless, they follow what are called the Small Vows, which they find a way to incorporate into their daily lives.

These vows include avoiding a job or profession that is likely to involve violence to other life-forms (for example, agriculture), being honest in business dealings, not stealing, not showing off material possessions, and donating excess wealth to charity. Jains also try to live by three Subsidiary Vows (additional vows), which are to avoid unnecessary movement, excessive enjoyment, and self-indulgent brooding, or feeling sorry for one's self.

Did you know...

- Jains do not worship a god, nor do they believe that the world was formed by a creator-god. Jainism, in this sense, is as much a philosophy of life as it is a religion. Its core belief is that people can achieve knowledge and understanding about their role in the world, as well as freedom from rebirth, by leading a life of renunciation and withdrawal from sensory experiences. Sensory experiences are those that a person comprehends through sight, sound, taste, and touch.

- The number of Jains in the world can only be estimated, but most experts think that about 3.3 to 3.6 million people follow the religion. Nearly all of them live in India. Approximately 100,000 Jains live abroad in other countries.

- Some scholars believe that Jainism gave rise to Buddhism. They point out, for example, that just as the Jains identify twenty-four Jina, Buddhism speaks of twenty-four Buddhas before Siddhartha Gautama (563–483 BCE), the founder of Buddhism, who is referred to as the Buddha. They see a connection between Jainism and Buddhism based on the possibility that the Jina and the Buddhas are the same. They believe that the Buddhist doctrine of the Middle Way, a philosophy of moderation, may have been a reaction against the strict and active self-denial of the Jains.

- Jains hold many beliefs in common with Hindus. In fact, Jainism can be regarded as a sect, or subgroup, of Hinduism. However, the two religions are different enough that Jains think of theirs as a separate religion, one that is culturally distinct from Hinduism. Good examples of beliefs that the two religions hold in common are karma, or the belief that a person's deeds determine the nature of his or her future; reincarnation, or rebirth in another body and time; and *moksha,* or the belief that a person can escape from the eternal cycle of birth, death, and rebirth and achieve salvation.

- For Jains, karma is not an abstract idea. Rather, they view karma as an actual physical substance, like dust, that weighs down a person's soul.

Consider the following...

- Describe the one principle above others that defines Jainism.
- Define ahimsa and explain its importance for Jains.
- If someone were to state that "Jains do not believe in God," explain how a Jain might respond.

For More Information

BOOKS

Dundas, Paul. "Jainism." *Encyclopedia of Religion,* edited by Lindsay Jones, 2nd ed., vol. 7. Detroit, MI: Macmillan Reference USA, 2005.

Dundas, Paul. *The Jains,* 2nd ed. London and New York: Routledge, 2002.

Jaini, Padmanabh S. *The Jaina Path of Purification,* rev. ed. New Delhi, India: Motilal Banarsidass, 2001.

"Knowledge of the Weapon." In *Gaina Sutra,* translated by Hermann Jacobi. Vol. 22 of *The Sacred Books of the East.* Oxford, UK: Clarendon Press, 1884. This excerpt can also be found online at http://www.sacred-texts.com/jai/akaranga.htm.

Singh, Nagendra. *Encyclopaedia of Jainism,* 30 vols. New Delhi, India: Anmol, 2001.

WEB SITES

Jainism: Jain Principles, Tradition and Practices. http://www.cs.colostate.edu/~malaiya/jainhlinks.html (accessed on June 5, 2006).

Jayaram, V. "The Jain Canonical Literature." *Hindu Website.* http://hinduwebsite.com/jainism/jaincanon.htm (accessed on June 5, 2006).

Dao De Jing

Selections from Tao Te Ching, *available online from Chinese Cultural Studies at*
http://academic.brooklyn.cuny.edu/core9/phalsall/texts/taote-v3.html
Compiled around the third century BCE
Translated by Stephen Mitchell
Published in 1988 by Harper Collins

"The Tao is like a well:

used but never used up.

It is like the eternal void:

filled with infinite possibilities."

The Dao De Jing (also known as Tao Te Ching) is a religious text of Daoism (Taoism, pronounced DOW-ism). The text is short, made up of 81 brief chapters. Its shortness, however, does not reflect its importance in the history of Chinese philosophy. Philosophy is a branch of study that looks for a general understanding of values and reality. Traditionally, the Dao De Jing was thought to have been written by the Chinese sage, or wise man, Laozi (also spelled Lao-tzu; 604–531 BCE). Laozi, a name that means "Old Master," is believed to have been a record keeper and librarian in the court of the Zhou Dynasty (also called the Chou Dynasty, c. 1100–256 BCE). The details of the authorship of the Dao De Jing, however, are still questioned. Little is known, for example, about the life of Laozi, primarily because no records about him survive from that time. The earliest mentions of him date to about 400 BCE, and it was not until about 100 BCE that a biography of him was written. Some scholars believe that the author of the Dao De Jing may, in fact, have been several men who composed the book over the years.

The title of the Dao De Jing can be translated in many ways, but it is usually given as something like "The Book of the Way and Its Virtue."

Chinese written words are referred to as "characters." The first character in the Dao De Jing, *dao,* means "the way ahead" or "the way." *De* means "righteousness" or "virtue." Virtue here refers to both the values of proper, honest living and to power, as in the healing virtue, or power, of medicine. The third character, *jing,* is often translated as "doctrine," which is a set of guidelines.

The center of the Dao The views expressed in the Dao De Jing are similar to views that have been voiced in other religions and philosophies, both Eastern and Western. The core of the book is the dao, or the way, suggesting a path to virtue (*de*). Virtue is the condition of being morally good. The path also leads one toward a state of spiritual understanding. What distinguishes Daoism from most other world religions is its emphasis on nothingness or detachment. It promotes acceptance and openness to achieve harmony with all things. To do this, one should be detached, not involved in worldly matters or desiring material goods and instead focused on improving virtue and improving one's understanding of the Dao. One should also practice nonaction, known as *wu wei.* A person can do this by being detached and not responding to things in an aggressive manner. Wu wei was seen as a balance to the social turmoil that troubled China at a time when local rulers were competing for power and influence in the various regions of the country.

Daoism emphasizes a belief that all things, living and not living, are connected. The tradition says that the differences between physical objects are an illusion, or false impression, and that the universe exists independently of this illusion. All creation is part of the dao, and this will never change. Because the dao is infinite, or never-ending, and all of creation; it is beyond our understanding.

In this respect, Daoism as reflected in the Dao De Jing is different from many other religions, particularly Western religions. Islam, Judaism, and Christianity, for example, do not believe that the physical world is an illusion. They believe that it is real and that it was created by the will of God. Additionally, these and other religions, including Baháʾí, with its emphasis on social justice and service, have different guides for living. Rather than teaching detachment, they teach involvement with the world in an effort to make it a better place. They believe that in carrying out the commandments, or instructions, of God in their daily lives, they are fulfilling God's will and helping God to perfect His creation.

A man visits a Daoist temple on Mount Qingcheng, near Guanxian, China. Daoists believe that by following the natural order, which is eternal, social stability can be obtained. © JOHN T. YOUNG/CORBIS.

Other themes of the Dao Other themes run through the Dao De Jing. One is an emphasis on the value of the feminine principle, with its qualities of fluidness and softness, like water (as opposed to the male principle of solidity, represented by the mountain). In this way, the Dao De Jing challenges its readers to reject such "male" traits as action, force, command, and ruling in favor of such "female" traits as dependence, intuition (the ability to know instinctively, without having to discover something) and recognizing the mysterious and obscure, or unclear, aspects of creation.

Another theme has to do with return. On the face of it, this has been simply interpreted to mean something like a return to nature, or to a simpler, more natural state of existence before the beginning of civilization. In Daoism, though, the concept is more complex. Returning to an earlier time of existence is really a kind of stripping away, or shrinking, of one's existence and retreating into the core of one's being. The goal is to lessen ego, or the emphasis on the self and its concerns, which is glorified by action in the world, and instead seeking enlightenment and salvation (saving from sin).

The Dao De Jing develops a number of other themes as well:

that force gives rise to force;

that beauty, power, and wealth bring about envy, shame, and crime;

that exerting effort creates resistance;

that the simpler a person's needs are, the more they will be fulfilled; and

that achievement comes from acting in harmony with the universe, especially the female principle of flexibility.

Each of these themes is reflected in the excerpts given here, and each provides followers of Daoism with a set of principles that they apply in their daily lives. Still, these principles are not always entirely clear. For example, the Dao De Jing says, "When people see some things as good, other things become bad." This sentence tells readers that they cannot know evil unless they know the good. The question is how a person might apply this principle in everyday life. One possibility among many is that good and evil are both part of the same scale used to measure the value of things. People cannot know either good or evil, or any opposite, without thinking deeply about both. In doing so, they are likely to better understand them and follow the good, whatever that may be in a particular circumstance.

Although little is known about the circumstances surrounding how the Dao De Jing was written, the text itself has survived with few of the kinds of changes and additions that were often made by scribes (people who copy manuscripts or documents by hand) who passed down ancient texts. The earliest form of the Dao De Jing that exists, as far as is known in the early twenty-first century, was written on stone tablets that date to about 300 BCE. In 1973 silk scrolls were discovered with two versions of the text, one dating to about 200 BCE. The oldest known version was discovered in 1993 and is believed to be from roughly the same time period as the other two, only slightly earlier. It, too, was written down, but on strips of bamboo.

One challenge that runs throughout the entire Dao De Jing is that of how to translate it. There are many translations, at least one hundred in English, and all differ from one another in ways that are both large and small. The problem is made worse by a number of factors. One is that the Chinese characters make indirect references to other Chinese texts that were widely read at the time but that are lost in modern times. A second is the absence of punctuation marks in ancient Chinese texts, making division of the lines into phrases and sentences a matter of the translator's own choice. The most important factor, though, is that the language of the text, both in the original and in translation, tends to be abstract, meaning that it refers not to objects but to ideas, feelings, or qualities. As a result, the text is open to different ways of reading and understanding. This abstractness has turned out to be an advantage. Both Daoism and the Dao De Jing have survived for centuries, providing people with a guide for living. Interpretations of the Dao De Jing can change and adapt as people's circumstances and the nature of the world change. In this way, the book can continue to serve as a guide for living over the course of long periods of time without seeming outdated.

The Dao De Jing is written in two sections and is probably a combination of two different texts. The Dao section includes chapters 1 through 37; the De section consists of chapters 38 through 81. Many of the chapters are quite short, as few as a handful of lines. The language of the book is simple, consisting of only about five thousand different Chinese characters. There are tens of thousands of Chinese characters, but only a few thousand are commonly used. This simplicity has made the Dao De Jing a book with wide appeal. Over the centuries it has been a source of inspiration to artists, military leaders, poets, corporate executives, and even gardeners, because of its practical wisdom. It is an important text in China not only to Daoists but to Chinese Buddhists as well, for many of the ideas in Daoism are similar to those found in Buddhism. Both, for example, believe in some form of reincarnation, or the belief that people are reborn into a new existence. Some early scholars have seen Daoism and Chinese Buddhism as similar religions, though most modern scholars see them as distinct.

Translation from Chinese

A major challenge for the English-speaking world is changing Chinese characters into English using the Latin alphabet. Two systems are used. Under the older one, called the Wade-Giles system, the title of the work would be written "Tao Te Ching," its author's name would be written "Lao Tzu," and the religion would be written "Taoism." The more modern system, called Pinyin, produces "Dao De Jing" (or Daodejing), "Laozi," and "Daoism," respectively. These differences are largely caused by the differences in the sound systems of the English and Chinese, which make it difficult for translators to find exact English equivalents for Chinese pronunciations. A great many Western translations of the book continue to use the form Tao Te Ching, because that was the form commonly used during the nineteenth and early twentieth centuries. Contemporary standards of translation, however, are more often adopting the Pinyin system, which is the system used by the People's Republic of China.

Things to remember while reading the excerpt from the Dao De Jing:

- Dao De Jing brings together the basic and most important points of ancient Chinese wisdom. It was designed to promote a stable social order at a time of great political and social unrest, primarily because warlords were competing with one another. These warlords were military rulers who controlled the people in their local region by force. They often battled with neighboring warlords for power and influence. The basic message of the book is that the natural order, the boundlessness of the universe, is more stable and enduring than any political order. Human learning, in contrast to rest and meditation, is an uncertain path to salvation and enlightenment.

- Dao is sometimes seen as a feminine principle, a mother that is the source of all things. This distinction between masculine and feminine is often seen as a stereotype in modern times, but at the time the Dao De Jing was written, masculinity was associated with action, purpose, drive, aggressiveness, and the like. Femininity, in contrast, was associated with feelings, emotion, thought, and especially being passive and nonaggressive. Daoism valued feminine principles over masculine ones.

• • •

Excerpts from the Dao De Jing

1 The tao [dao] that can be told
is not the eternal Tao.
The name that can be named
is not the eternal Name.

The unnamable is the eternally real.
Naming is the origin
of all particular things.

Free from desire, you realize the mystery.
Caught in desire, you see only the manifestations.

Manifestations: Outward examples or appearances.

Yet mystery and **manifestations**
arise from the same source.
This source is called darkness.

Darkness within darkness.
The gateway to all understanding.

2 When people see some things as beautiful,
other things become ugly.
When people see some things as good,
other things become bad.

Being and non-being create each other.
Difficult and easy support each other.
Long and short define each other.
High and low depend on each other.
Before and after follow each other.

Therefore the Master
acts without doing anything
and teaches without saying anything.
Things arise and she lets them come;
things disappear and she lets them go.
She has but doesn't possess,
acts but doesn't expect.
When her work is done, she forgets it.
That is why it lasts forever.

4 The Tao is like a well:
used but never used up.
It is like the eternal **void:**
filled with infinite possibilities.

Void: Empty space.

It is hidden but always present.
I don't know who gave birth to it.
It is older than God.

5 The Tao doesn't take sides;
it gives birth to both good and evil.
The Master doesn't take sides;
she welcomes both saints and sinners.

The Tao is like a **bellows:**
it is empty yet infinitely capable.
The more you use it, the more it produces;
the more you talk of it, the less you understand.

Bellows: A device that
draws in air and blows it
back out.

Hold on to the center.

7 The Tao is infinite, eternal.
Why is it eternal?
It was never born;
thus it can never die.
Why is it infinite?
It has no desires for itself;
thus it is present for all beings.

A Daoist priest prays during a ceremony. Daoists strive to live in harmony with all things, living and not living, which they believe are connected to one another. © REUTERS/ CORBIS.

Subtle: Difficult to understand.

Conception: Forming of an idea.

The Master stays behind;
that is why she is ahead.
She is detached from all things;
that is why she is one with them.
Because she has let go of herself,
she is perfectly fulfilled.

12 Colors blind the eye.
Sounds deafen the ear.
Flavors numb the taste.
Thoughts weaken the mind.
Desires wither the heart.

The Master observes the world
but trusts his inner vision.
He allows things to come and go.
His heart is open as the sky.

14 Look, and it can't be seen.
Listen, and it can't be heard.
Reach, and it can't be grasped.

Above, it isn't bright.
Below, it isn't dark.
Seamless, unnamable,
it returns to the realm of nothing.
Form that includes all forms,
image without an image,
subtle, beyond all **conception.**

Approach it and there is no beginning;
follow it and there is no end.
You can't know it, but you can be it,
at ease in your own life.
Just realize where you come from:
this is the essence of wisdom.

16 Empty your mind of all thoughts.
Let your heart be at peace.
Watch the turmoil of beings,
but contemplate their return.

Each separate being in the universe
returns to the common source.
Returning to the source is serenity.

If you don't realize the source,
you stumble in confusion and sorrow.
When you realize where you come from,

you naturally become tolerant,
disinterested, amused,
kindhearted as a grandmother,
dignified as a king.
Immersed in the wonder of the Tao,
you can deal with whatever life brings you,
and when death comes, you are ready.

Immersed: Wrapped up, absorbed.

17 When the Master governs, the people
are hardly aware that he exists.
Next best is a leader who is loved.
Next, one who is feared.
The worst is one who is despised.

If you don't trust the people,
you make them untrustworthy.

The Master doesn't talk, he acts.
When his work is done,
the people say, "Amazing:
we did it, all by ourselves!"

25 There was something formless and perfect
before the universe was born.
It is serene. Empty.
Solitary. Unchanging.
Infinite. Eternally present.
It is the mother of the universe.
For lack of a better name,
I call it the Tao.

It flows through all things,
inside and outside, and returns
to the origin of all things.

The Tao is great.
The universe is great.
Earth is great.
Man is great.
These are the four great powers.

Man follows the earth.
Earth follows the universe.
The universe follows the Tao.
The Tao follows only itself.

28 Know the male,
yet keep to the female:
receive the world in your arms.

If you receive the world,
the Tao will never leave you
and you will be like a little child.

Know the white,
yet keep to the black:
be a pattern for the world.
If you are a pattern for the world,
the Tao will be strong inside you
and there will be nothing you can't do.

Know the personal,
yet keep to the impersonal:
accept the world as it is.
If you accept the world,
Luminous: Bright, radiant,
glowing.
the Tao will be **luminous** inside you
and you will return to your primal self.

The world is formed from the void,
like utensils from a block of wood.
The Master knows the utensils,
yet keeps to the block:
thus she can use all things.

33 Knowing others is intelligence;
knowing yourself is true wisdom.
Mastering others is strength;
mastering yourself is true power.

If you realize that you have enough,
you are truly rich.
If you stay in the center
and embrace death with your whole heart,
you will endure forever.

34 The great Tao flows everywhere.
All things are born from it,
yet it doesn't create them.
It pours itself into its work,
yet it makes no claim.
It nourishes infinite worlds,
yet it doesn't hold on to them.
Since it is merged with all things
and hidden in their hearts,
it can be called humble.
Since all things vanish into it
and it alone endures,
it can be called great.

It isn't aware of its greatness;
thus it is truly great.

38 The Master doesn't try to be powerful;
thus he is truly powerful.
The ordinary man keeps reaching for power;
thus he never has enough.

The Master does nothing,
yet he leaves nothing undone.
The ordinary man is always doing things,
yet many more are left to be done.

The kind man does something,
yet something remains undone.
The just man does something,
and leaves many things to be done.
The moral man does something,
and when no one responds
he rolls up his sleeves and uses force.

When the Tao is lost, there is goodness.
When goodness is lost, there is morality.
When morality is lost, there is ritual.
Ritual is the husk of true faith,
the beginning of chaos.

Therefore the Master concerns himself
with the depths and not the surface,
with the fruit and not the flower.
He has no will of his own.
He dwells in reality,
and lets all illusions go.

51 Every being in the universe
is an expression of the Tao.
It springs into existence,
unconscious, perfect, free,
takes on a physical body,
lets circumstances complete it.
That is why every being
spontaneously honors the Tao.

The Tao gives birth to all beings,
nourishes them, maintains them,
cares for them, comforts them, protects them,
takes them back to itself,
creating without possessing,

acting without expecting,
guiding without interfering.
That is why love of the Tao
is in the very nature of things.

60 Governing a large country
is like frying a small fish.
You spoil it with too much poking.

Center your country in the Tao
and evil will have no power.
Not that it isn't there,
but you'll be able to step out of its way.

Give evil nothing to oppose
and it will disappear by itself.

78 Nothing in the world
is as soft and yielding as water.
Yet for dissolving the hard and inflexible,
nothing can surpass it.

The soft overcomes the hard;
the gentle overcomes the rigid.
Everyone knows this is true,
but few can put it into practice.

Therefore the Master remains
serene in the midst of sorrow.
Evil cannot enter his heart.
Because he has given up helping,
he is people's greatest help.

True words seem paradoxical.

• • •

What happened next...

Daoism began originally as a combination of philosophy and psychology (the study of the human mind and behavior) and was seen as an alternative to Confucianism. It became a religion in 440 BCE, when it was adopted as the state religion of China. Along with Confucianism and Buddhism, it remained for centuries as one of the three major religious traditions of China. When the Qing (Ch'ing) Dynasty ended in 1911, support for Daoism began to decline. In the decades that followed much of the Daoist heritage was destroyed. The situation worsened after the communist takeover of China in 1949, when religious freedom was severely restricted. Communists are people who follow the political theory of a classless society where all people are equal, property is owned in common, and work is done for the benefit of the entire group. Communists believe that religion is not good for society. In the early twenty-first century about 20 million people practice Daoism, most of them living in Taiwan.

Did you know...

- Unlike religions such as Christianity, Judaism, and Islam, Daoism does not believe in a single God. Daoists do not worship God; their goal is to find harmony with the dao. The dao represents the sum of all that is right and harmonious. When people complicate their lives with selfishness, ambition, and the desire for fame, they lose harmony, fail to become enlightened, and are unhappy.

- Daoism has had a growing impact on the Western world. Many Westerners, for example, are turning to acupuncture (the treatment of certain disorders by inserting needles into the skin to release blocked energy) to cure disease, relieve pain, and even deal with such problems as alcoholism and smoking. Acupuncture developed from the Daoist belief that physical distress is the result of an imbalance in *qi* (*chi*), which literally means "air" or "breath" and represents a person's life force or energy. Similarly, *taijichuan,* also known as *tai chi,* is a form of exercise increasingly practiced in the West. It is based on rhythmic movements that bring about relaxation, lower blood pressure, and improve digestion and circulation.

- Daoists do not pray as Westerners probably understand the term. Westerners typically, but not always, address prayers to a single God, often to ask for forgiveness, a solution to a problem, or God's blessing. In contrast, Daoist prayer is more like meditation and reflection. Daoists see the universe as eternal and infinite, and they believe that meditation rather than prayer is the answer to life's problems.

- The People's Republic of China, or the Chinese mainland, prevented the spread of Daoism, particularly during the early decades of the nation's founding in the late 1940s and 1950s. The communist leadership that took power in 1949 believed that Daoism was passive, or lacking in will, and fatalistic, meaning that they have the belief that people are powerless against destiny. These views were at odds with the communist ideal of reconstructing society through labor. Some observers believed that by the end of the twentieth century, as the communist leadership in China was relaxing its grip on the people, it was becoming somewhat more tolerant of Daoism and the other religions practiced within the country's borders.

Consider the following...

- Respond to the point of view that Daoism does not believe in God.
- Using Daoism and the Dao De Jing as examples, explain why certain types of religious beliefs might arise as a response to social disorder and other historical circumstances. In ancient China during the period when the Dao De Jing was composed, many competing warlords were trying to build kingdoms. They tried to build economic and military power. To that end, they needed large numbers of literate teachers and civil servants. As a result, many new ideas and philosophies arose, leading historians to refer to the era as the Warring States period or the Hundred Schools of Thought period. Compare these types of events in ancient China with similar events in other cultures. For example, consider how Islam arose as a way of uniting the Arab peoples at a time when they were divided into competing clans and tribes.
- Choose one image from the Dao De Jing, such as the image of the bellows, and discuss what the image reveals about Daoist beliefs.

For More Information

BOOKS

Le Guin, Ursula K. *Lao Tzu: Tao Te Ching: A Book about the Way and the Power of the Way*. Boston, MA: Shambhala Publications, 1997.

Mitchell, Stephen, trans. *Tao Te Ching*. New York: HarperCollins, 1988. This extract can also be found online at http://academic.brooklyn.cuny.edu/core9/phalsall/texts/taote-v3.html.

Mitchell, Stephen, trans. *Tao Te Ching: An Illustrated Journey*. New York: HarperCollins, 1999.

Star, Jonathan. *Tao Te Ching*. New York: Tarcher, 2003.

PERIODICALS

Berling, Judith A. "Dao/Taoism: The Way." *Focus on Asian Studies*, vol. 2, no. 1 (Fall 1982): 9–11. This article can also be found online at http://www.askasia. org/frclasrm/readings/r000005.htm.

WEB SITES

Chan, Alan. "Laozi." *Stanford Encyclopedia of Philosophy.* http://setis.library.usyd. edu.au/stanford/entries/laozi/ (accessed on June 5, 2006).

Giri, Nirmalananda. "The Ineffable Tao." *Spiritual Writings.* http://www. atmajyoti.org/sw_Tao_Teh_King_1.asp (accessed on June 5, 2006).

The Dhammapada

"The Mind" and "The Path," from The Dhammapada:
Wisdom of the Buddha, *available online from the Theosophical Society at*
http://www.theosociety.org/pasadena/dhamma/dham-hp.htm#Contents
Compiled around the first century BCE
Translated by Harischandra Kaviratna
Published in 1980 by the Theosophical University Press

> "One should be watchful over his speech, well-restrained in mind, and commit no unwholesome deed with his body."

The Dhammapada is a Buddhist text that is believed to record the actual words of the founder of Buddhism, Siddhartha Gautama. Gautama, better known as the Buddha, lived between 563 and 483 BCE. His words were passed along orally until they were written down in about the first century BCE. The word *dhamma* means "the teachings of Buddhism." The title of the Dhammapada is often translated as "Words of the Doctrine." It consists of 423 aphorisms. These are short statements that contain a truth, principle, or sentiment, usually in memorable language. The verses are numbered sequentially and are divided into twenty-six *vaggas,* or sections, with such titles as "On Vigilance," "The Mind," "The Fool," and "The Wise." For more than two thousand years, Buddhists have used the Dhammapada and other sacred Buddhist texts as a reference to provide guidance in their lives.

The Buddha laid out the essence of the Dhammapada as a guide for living in one of his earliest sermons, which he delivered in a deer refuge in the town of Isipatana, India. For this reason, the sermon is often called the "Deer Park Sermon," but Buddhists also sometimes call it the "Setting in Motion the Wheel of the Doctrine" sermon. In this sermon, the Buddha outlined what he called the Four Noble Truths. These truths became the cornerstones of Buddhist teaching.

The Four Noble Truths The first of the Four Noble Truths is *duhka*. This refers to the Buddhist belief that life consists of pain and sorrow and that people are trapped in a cycle of birth, old age, death, and rebirth. This cycle is called *samsara*. This is a life that has no permanence and no lasting essence, or core nature. The second of the Four Nobel Truths refers to *avidya*, or "ignorance," and *trishan*, or the cravings of the senses. These words refer to the belief that people cannot escape the bonds of samsara if they remain ignorant of the nature of reality and if they crave the sensual (bodily) pleasures of earthly existence. At the time of death, *avidya* and *trishan* bind a person to the material world and rebirth into earth existence. The third of the Four Noble Truths is *nirvana,* a word that means "blowing out." It refers to the path to enlightenment (a state of pure spiritual understanding) the Buddha urged his believers to follow. He taught that only by breaking the chain of ignorance and worldly passions could a person be released from rebirth and from the physical world. This release is called nirvana. A person who has achieved nirvana can mystically escape the impermanent world and find a form of bliss that cannot be described.

The first three of the Four Noble Truths make clear that ignorance and earthly passions trap people in a life of suffering, pain, and death but that there is a way out of this cycle. The Buddha outlined this way out in the fourth of the Four Noble Truths, which he called the Eightfold Path. By following the Eightfold Path, a person can reach nirvana and enlightenment. The Eightfold Path might be considered similar to the Ten Commandments in the Western Judeo-Christian tradition because it consists of a series of specific guides for living.

The first two parts of the Eightfold Path, called Right Understanding and Right Thought, help a person achieve wisdom. (Sometimes different translations of the words are found; for example, Right Understanding is also translated as "Right View" and Right Thought is also translated as "Right Intention.") Both involve learning and thinking about the teachings of Buddhism and becoming motivated to apply them to everyday life. The next three parts of the Eightfold Path include Right Speech, Right Action, and Right Livelihood. These promote ethical, or moral, conduct in dealing with other people. A person who follows them avoids such things as lying, gossiping, cruelty, stealing, and overeating. Right Livelihood requires followers to earn their living in ways that do not harm the world. The final three parts of the Eightfold Path, Right Effort, Right Mindfulness, and Right Concentration, all encourage mental development. They require followers to avoid mental laziness, to meditate, and to seek enlightenment.

Taken together, the various elements of the Eightfold Path promote mental and physical discipline and release from earthly passions.

A key theme that runs through the Dhammapada, suggested in the excerpts included here, is the idea that the human mind is not somehow a by-product of the physical universe. Rather, according to the Buddha, mind comes before all that exists. The destruction of the body is not the end of existence; instead, the external world is a creation of the mind. But the Buddha also points out that the mind is unstable and flighty, or inconsistent. It is also fickle, meaning changeable and indecisive; sometimes it thrashes around like a fish taken out of the water. It is unstable and apt to wander. It is fearful and sometimes tempted to follow evil, represented in the excerpts here as Mara, who tried to tempt the Buddha away from the Eightfold Path. Because of these weaknesses, a person has to develop a well-guarded mind in order to follow the Eightfold Path. For this reason, Buddhists turn to the verses of the Dhammapada to provide them with truths they can apply to their daily lives.

Growth of Buddhism A major difficulty faced by modern students of Buddhism is that because it is an ancient religion, it is impossible to trace its history and development accurately through a universally accepted group of texts. While, for example, Christianity is based on the Bible and Islam is based on the Qur'an, Buddhism has produced an almost overwhelming number of texts that can be considered sacred writings. Many of these texts have not survived into the twenty-first century. Many are no longer in their original form, but exist only in translation. Others form the core scriptures (the sacred writings of a religion) of various sects of Buddhism. A sect is a smaller group within a larger religious body, which has beliefs that differ from the main body.

One of the major traditional sects of Buddhism is referred to as Theravada, a term that means "doctrine of the elders." A doctrine is a set of rules or principles. In the early twenty-first century, Theravada is the dominant form of Buddhism practiced in such countries as Cambodia, Laos, Burma (Myanmar), Sri Lanka, and Thailand. It is also practiced in Bangladesh, parts of China, and in Vietnam, and it has experienced a revival in southern India. Through missionary activity, in which believers seek to spread the religion to nonbelievers, Theravada has also spread throughout the world.

The only early Buddhist scriptural texts that exist in full in the early twenty-first century are those of Theravada Buddhists. These texts make

The Buddha is shown seated under a bodhi, *or fig, tree as he gives a sermon to his followers (left) and engages in meditation. Many of the Buddha's sayings are recorded in the Dhammapada and consulted by Buddhists for guidance in their daily lives.* © MICHAEL FREEMAN/CORBIS.

up what is called the Tipitaka, a term that translates as "Threefold Basket," with the word *basket* meaning a collection of texts. The second of the Threefold Baskets, called the Suttapitaka, or "Basket of the Discourses," contains the Khuddakanikaya, or "Group of Small Texts." The Dhammapada appears as the second text in the Group of Small Texts. Put simply, while most other religions have only one holy text or a small number of texts considered sacred, Buddhists have many, and all can provide Buddhists with principles to follow in their lives.

According to Buddhist tradition, a council of Buddhist elders met three weeks after the death of the Buddha. Their purpose was to remember the truths that the Buddha had taught and to implant these truths in the minds of the Buddha's followers. Because the Buddha's teachings had never been written down, the elders organized them and brought them together so that they could be more easily recited orally. Only later were they written down. To this day millions of Buddhists recite verses from the Dhammapada daily, regarding them, in effect, as prayers that keep them focused on the teachings of the Buddha and to guide them in their daily activities.

Things to remember while reading the excerpt from the Dhammapada:

- The Dhammapada is believed to contain statements the Buddha actually made in sermons that he delivered to a wide range of people, from kings and queens to cowherds. *Dhamma* means "the teachings of Buddhism." The Dhammapada was written to help people follow the teachings of Buddhism.

- The text refers to "Mara (the Evil One)." Mara is the lord of five desires. He and other demons threatened the Buddha with windstorms and darkness as he sat in meditation under a *bodhi,* or fig, tree. They were unsuccessful in their efforts to make him fearful and abandon his search for enlightenment. People must battle the temptations and fears presented by Mara on a daily basis. The Buddha's words in the Dhammapada provide guidance on how to do this.

- Having fought and beaten Mara, a person should protect what he has learned through the dhamma, or dharma, but do so without attachment. One of the central practices of Buddhism is nonattachment, or not desiring to have or keep something, because everything is changing and cannot be held onto.

- The excerpt refers to "the Eightfold Path" and "the Four Noble Truths." The Four Noble Truths are the foundations of Buddhism: that life is suffering; that desire causes suffering; that suffering can end; and that the end of suffering can be achieved by following the Eightfold Path. The Eightfold Path describes the proper behavior, or basic guidelines for living, that Buddhists should practice in order to end suffering.

• • •

Excerpt from the Dhammapada

The Mind—CANTO III

33. The **discerning** man straightens his mind, which is **fickle** and unsteady, difficult to guard and restrain as the skilled **fletcher** straightens the shaft (of the arrow).

34. As the fish, taken out of its watery home and thrown on land, thrashes around, so does the mind tremble, while freeing itself from the **dominion** of Mara (the Evil One).

Discerning: Showing good judgment.

Fickle: Likely to change.

Fletcher: Arrow maker.

Dominion: Control, authority.

Flighty: Changing constantly.

Incomprehensible: Beyond understanding.

Subtle: Complex, capable of understanding small differences.

Aspirant: Someone who wants to achieve something.

Incorporeal: Without a body.

Dhamma: The teachings of Buddhism.

Ruffled: Disturbed.

Defiled: Damaged, polluted.

Devoid: Missing, lacking in.

Dichotomy: Division into two widely different things.

Vigilant: Watchful, cautious, on one's guard.

Corporeal: Physical.

Citadel: Fortress, castle.

Attachment: A feeling of closeness, an emotional tie or bond.

Ere: Before.

Unheeded: Not given attention.

Kindred: Relative, family member.

Detachment: Lack of interest or involvement.

Foremost: Most important.

Insight: Ability to understand clearly.

Bewilders: Puzzles, confuses.

Fetters: Chains.

35. The mind is unstable and **flighty.** It wanders wherever it desires. Therefore it is good to control the mind. A disciplined mind brings happiness.

36. The mind is **incomprehensible** and exceedingly **subtle.** It wanders wherever it desires. Therefore, let the wise **aspirant** watch over the mind. A well-guarded mind brings happiness.

37. Those who control the mind which wanders afar, solitary, **incorporeal,** and which resides in the inner cavern (of the heart), will liberate themselves from the shackles of Mara.

38. He whose mind is not steady, who is ignorant of the true **Dhamma,** whose tranquility is **ruffled,** the wisdom of such a man does not come to fullness.

39. Fear has he none, whose mind is not **defiled** by passion, whose heart is **devoid** of hatred, who has surpassed (the **dichotomy** of) good and evil and who is **vigilant.**

40. Knowing the **corporeal** body to be fragile as an earthen jar, and fortifying the mind like a **citadel,** let the wise man fight Mara with the sword of wisdom. He should now protect what he has won, without **attachment.**

41. Alas! **ere** long, this corporeal body will lie flat upon the earth, **unheeded,** devoid of consciousness, like a useless log of wood.

42. An ill-directed mind does greater harm to the self than a hater does to another hater or an enemy to another enemy.

43. Neither father nor mother, nor any other **kindred,** can confer greater benefit than does the well-directed mind.

The Path—CANTO XX

273. Of paths the Eightfold is the best; of truths the Four Noble Truths are the best; of all states **Detachment** is the best; of men the Seeing One (Buddha) is the **foremost.**

274. This is the path; there is no other path that leads to purity of **insight.** Follow this path, for this path **bewilders** the Evil One (Mara).

275. Having entered upon the path you will come to an end of your suffering. Having myself recognized this, I proclaimed this path which removes all thorns.

276. You yourself must make the effort. The Tathagatas (Buddhas) can only point the way. Those who have entered the path and become meditative are freed from the **fetters** of Mara.

277. "**Transient** are all **composite** things"; he who **perceives** the truth of this gets disgusted with this world of suffering. This is the path to purity.

278. "Sorrowful are all composite things"; he who perceives the truth of this gets disgusted with this world of suffering. This is the path to purity.

279. "All forms of existence are unreal" (*an-atta*); he who perceives the truth of this gets disgusted with this world of suffering. This is the path to purity.

280. He who does not get up when it is time to do so; who, although youthful and strong, is yet given to **indolence** is weak in **resolution** and thought—such an idle and lazy person does not find the path to wisdom.

281. One should be watchful over his speech, well-restrained in mind, and commit no **unwholesome** deed with his body. Let him **purify** this threefold avenue of action (karma), and he will tread the path made known by the **sages.**

282. **Verily,** from devotion (*yoga*) arises wisdom, from nondevotion springs the loss of wisdom. Having become aware of this two-fold path that leads to progress and decline, let him place himself in such a way that his wisdom increases.

283. Cut down the whole forest (of desires), not just a tree. From the forest arises fear. Cut down the forest and its brushwood, O monks, and be **emancipated.**

284. As long as the brushwood of a man's **lust** towards women is not completely destroyed, even to the last seedling, so long is his mind fettered as a **suckling** calf is bound to its mother.

285. Cut off the love of self as one would pluck an **autumnal** white lotus. Proceed then upon that (Eightfold) path of peace—the **nirvana** as **expounded** by Sugata (Buddha).

286. "Here shall I dwell in the rainy season; here shall I dwell in winter and summer." Thus the fool **muses,** but never **reflects** on the dangers that might befall him.

287. As a great flood carries off a sleeping village, so death seizes and carries off a man who is distracted and overly attached to his children and cattle.

288. Sons are no protection, neither father nor **kinsfolk;** when one is **assailed** by death, there is no protection among one's kin.

289. Having perceived this significant fact, let the wise and self-restrained man quickly clear the path that leads to nirvana.

Transient: Lasting for a short time.

Composite: Made of different parts.

Perceives: Understands.

Indolence: Laziness.

Resolution: Firmness of purpose.

Unwholesome: Harmful, unhealthy.

Purify: Make clean, remove unclean parts.

Sages: Wise men.

Verily: In truth, surely.

Emancipated: Freed.

Lust: Desire, longing.

Suckling: A baby animal that still feeds on its mother's milk.

Autumnal: Having to do with autumn, or fall.

Nirvana: The end of suffering.

Expounded: Explained.

Muses: Thinks.

Reflects: Thinks carefully.

Kinsfolk: Family members.

Assailed: Attacked or overwhelmed.

A stone tablet engraved with part of the Tipitaka, a sacred Buddhist text, stands in Mandalay, Burma. The Dhammapada is one of the many texts within the Tipitaka. © CHRISTINE KOLISCH/CROBIS.

· · ·

What happened next ...

About a century after the first council of elders, or about a century after the death of the Buddha, another council was held to confirm the teaching of Buddhist doctrine. During this council, a major split emerged in Buddhism between two schools of thought. One school of thought, the Southern School, practiced a traditional form of Buddhism that emphasized finding personal enlightenment. Theravada is a part of this school of thought. The other major school of thought, the Northern School, was referred to by the term Mahayana. The goal of this school was collective, or group, enlightenment, meaning that its focus was less on the individual and more on helping everyone achieve enlightenment.

Did you know ...

- The Dhammapada, which was written in an Indian language called Pâli, was the first Pâli text ever translated into a Western language. It was translated and edited by the Danish scholar Viggo Fausböll (1821–1908) in 1855.

- Very early Buddhist texts, such as the Dhammapada, were not written down for a variety of reasons. One practical reason was the lack of convenient writing materials. But the emphasis on oral transmission, or retelling Buddhist texts and stories from person to person, came from deeper causes. Early Buddhist wise men believed that the way to achieve enlightenment and contact with a divine reality was through self-deprivation (going without or denying oneself something) and intuition (the state of being aware of or knowing something without having evidence). It was believed that contemplation, or the study of spiritual matters calmly and over a long period of time, of wisdom that was heard rather than read was a purer path to enlightenment and that writing actually took away from the value and wisdom of the words. Further, while historical events were typically written down, it was believed that spiritual and philosophical truths were best understood through oral poetry, which was more easily remembered.

- There is no "Indian" language. A principal language in India is Hindi, but this is a literary and official language used primarily in the north. It is estimated that India is home to about 428 languages. Of them, 415 are still spoken, while the rest are no longer used. Pâli is just one of these languages that no longer exists. The language spoken in one region in India generally cannot be understood by Indians living in another region, who do not speak it every day. Pâli was never a language spoken by a community of people. Rather, it was more like the Latin used by Christianity, an official language used in texts such as the Dhammapada.

- It is probable that the verses of the Dhammapada were altered over time. Verses were borrowed by other Buddhist texts, and it is likely that scribes (someone who copies documents or manuscripts by hand) and monks added material to the Dhammapada. The language of the verses, however, indicates that at least some of them date back to the early years of Buddhism.

Consider the following ...

- Explain how the verses from the Dhammapada use down-to-earth images to express their truths and why this type of language was used.

- Summarize the view of the relationship between the physical and spiritual worlds contained in the Dhammapada.

- Discuss ways in which the Eightfold Path is similar to guides for everyday life in another religion you are familiar with. Examples might be the Ten Commandments of Judaism and Christianity or the Pillars of Islam.

For More Information

BOOKS

Carter, John Ross, and Mahinda Paliwadana, eds. *The Dhammapada: A New English Translation*. New York: Oxford University Press, 1987.

Hinüber, Oskar von, and K. R. Norman, eds. *Dhammapada*. Oxford, UK: Pâli Text Society, 1994.

"The Mind" and "The Path," from *Dhammapada: Wisdom of the Buddha,* translated by Harischandra Kaviratna. Pasadena, CA: Theosophical University Press, 1980. This extract can also be found online at http://www.theosociety.org/pasadena/dhamma/dham-hp.htm#Contents.

Müller, F. Max. "Introduction to the Dhammapada." In *The Dhammapada.* Vol. 10 of *The Sacred Books of the East.* Oxford, UK: Clarendon Press, 1881. This introduction can also be found online at http://www.sacred-texts.com/bud/sbe10/sbe1002.htm.

Norman, K. R. *The Word of the Doctrine.* Oxford, UK: Pali Text Society, 2000.

WEB SITES

Buddha Dharma Education Association. *The Illustrated Dhammapada: Treasury of Truth. BuddhaNet.* http://www.buddhanet.net/dhammapada/index.htm (accessed on June 5, 2006).

Thanissaro Bhikkhu, trans. *Dhammapada: A Translation.* http://www.accesstoinsight.org/canon/sutta/khuddaka/dhp/tb0/ (accessed on June 5, 2006).

The Hidden Words of Bahá'u'lláh

Excerpt from Part I of The Hidden Words of Bahá'u'lláh
Available online from the Bahá'í Reference Library
at http://reference.bahai.org/en/t/b/HW/
By Bahá'u'lláh
Written around 1857
Published in 1985 by Bahá'í Publishing Trust

"There is no peace for thee save by renouncing thyself and turning unto Me."

The Bahá'í faith is one of the world's youngest religions, dating only to about the mid-nineteenth century. Its founder was Bahá'u'lláh (1817–1892), Arabic for "the glory of God." Bahá'u'lláh wrote a number of texts that are important to members of the faith. One of these texts is called Kalimat-i-Maknunih, or The Hidden Words. The text consists of seventy-one Arabic and eighty-two Persian sayings. The stated purpose of The Hidden Words is to take the most important elements from the teachings of all religions to find their inner essence, or true meaning. Members of the faith are urged to read the sayings every day and to apply their wisdom in their daily lives.

Bahá'u'lláh wrote The Hidden Words in the mid- to late 1800s. The word "hidden" in the title refers to the Bahá'í belief that people could not have a true understanding of the knowledge within the book before Bahá'u'lláh revealed it. It details the spiritual path a person can follow and provides moral guidelines for living. Following this path and behavior, a person can become closer to God.

The Bahá'í understanding of God

In all his writings, Bahá'u'lláh explained and discussed three connected "unities." The first is the oneness of God, making the Bahá'í faith a monotheistic religion, in the tradition of Judaism, Christianity, and Islam. This means that the religion recognized only one god instead of many gods. The second unity is the oneness of God's many prophets and messengers. These are the people who deliver God's words and intentions to others. This means that Baháʾí teaches that religion is not fixed forever by a single prophet but grows and develops over time with the revelations of each of God's historical messengers. A revelation is an enlightening or astonishing discovery or disclosure of something. The third unity is the oneness of humanity, with emphasis on globalism (worldwide concerns), equality, and social justice. Social justice is the idea that all people should have the same rights, securities, opportunities, and benefits. To work towards social justice, such as in educational programs or economic development programs, is to engage in activity that will help bring about this goal.

This excerpt from The Hidden Words places emphasis on the oneness of God. The words are written as commands from God to His people. The picture of God that emerges from these verses is that of a divinity who is interested in justice. He urges people to remain humble, to develop their abilities and talents, and not to vaunt themselves over the poor. This means that they should not brag about their wealth. God emphasizes his love for his creation, a love that humans should share. Based on this love, humans should pursue such goals as eliminating prejudice (preconceived judgment), promoting world peace, and ridding the world of poverty. Because God is one with all of His creation, bringing about these ends is a way of worshipping God. In fact, members of the faith place little emphasis on outward forms of worship, such as rituals. They believe that serving others is the best way to show devotion to God.

Baháʾuʾlláh led an exciting and eventful life. He was born as Mirza Husayn-Ali (1817–1892) in Tehran, Persia (present-day Iran). In his early years, he was a follower of the Bab, which was a sect, or branch, of Shiʾa Islam that believed that a messiah would soon appear. A messiah is an inspiring leader who claims to have a message from God and can show people the way to salvation, or deliverance from sin or evil. The Bab expressed this belief with references to "He whom God shall make manifest" (visible).

The Bab's leader, Siyyid ʾAli-Muhammad, had declared himself the leader of the movement only in 1844. Baháʾuʾlláh saw himself as this expected messiah. He believed that he would lay the spiritual foundations for a worldwide religion based on harmony and peace. He announced this publicly in 1866, which can be regarded as the year that the religion was founded.

The Shrine of Bahá'u'lláh in Akko, Israel, is a sacred site honoring the Bahá'í founder and his vision of peace and unity for humanity.
© EMILIO EREZA/ALAMY.

The Islamic government in Persia regarded both the Bab and Bahá'u'lláh as threats to its authority, so Bahá'u'lláh was exiled, or sent away, first to Baghdad in the Ottoman Empire (present-day Iraq), then to Constantinople in Turkey, and finally to Adrianople (modern Edirne, Turkey). Later he was arrested and held at the prison colony in Akka, in present-day Israel. In his final years, Bahá'u'lláh was allowed to live at home, although officially he remained a prisoner of the city. He died in 1892, and members of the Bahá'í faith turn in the direction of his gravesite, the Mansion of Bahji at Akka, in prayer each day.

The sources of Bahá'í wisdom

Throughout his life, Bahá'u'lláh produced a large number of writings. His primary works on religion include the Kitab-i-Aqdas (The Most Holy Book, containing the laws and rules of the faith) and the Kitab-i-Iqan (The Book of Certitude). Bahá'u'lláh believed that God can only be understood through direct knowledge. Thinking or reasoning will not give one an understanding of God. He wrote about these and other spiritual matters in the Haft-Vádí, or "Seven Valleys," and The Hidden Words, excerpted here.

Perhaps the best summary of Bahá'u'lláh's teachings comes from Shoghi Effendi (1897–1957), who was the successor to Bahá'u'lláh's son, Abdu'l-Baha. Shoghi Effendi was the first Guardian of the Bahá'í Faith. In this role, he translated Bahá'u'lláh's works and greatly expanded the size of the Bahá'í community. In his book *God Passes By*, Shoghi Effendi writes about some of the essential elements that stand out from what Bahá'u'lláh proclaimed, including world peace, education for everyone, and the oneness of humanity. He also called for such things as the creation of a world body to resolve disputes between nations. He said that the most important goal for the faith was "justice as the ruling principle in human society."

Elsewhere, Shoghi Effendi comments on the inclusiveness, or all-embracing nature, of Bahá'í and its tolerance and acceptance of other faiths. Bahá'í followers believe that all religions come from the same sacred source. They believe that the basic principles of all faiths are in harmony with one another and that their goals and purposes are the same. In this respect, the Bahá'í faith differs from some other religions, which historically have held that theirs is the only true faith. While many religions in modern life have become more accepting of other religious views, Bahá'í is unique in making this acceptance a central element of its beliefs.

One characteristic of Bahá'í is its emphasis on social action, which many members regard as a form of worship. For example, the last lines of the following excerpt encourage Bahá'ís to help others as an expression of their faith in God: "Deny not My servant should he ask anything from thee, for his face is My face; be then abashed before Me." Members actively promote social and economic development projects in their communities and around the world. It is not uncommon to see road signs indicating that the local Bahá'í community has "adopted" a stretch of highway to keep it free of litter. Because they encourage the idea of world government, they support the United Nations (U.N.) and have engaged in many development projects through U.N. agencies. The United Nations is an international organization where countries can go to negotiate an end to conflicts and work together on issues that affect them. This concern for social justice is clear in The Hidden Words, a text that repeatedly emphasizes the divine nature of justice, love, peace, kindness to others, and humbleness before God.

Things to remember while reading the excerpt from The Hidden Words of Bahá'u'lláh:

- As with many other religious texts, the verses in the Hidden Words are numbered. This is so that readers can easily locate and identify particular passages. The number of the verses can be distinguished between those written in Arabic and those in Persian with a reference such as Arabic no. 7.

- The excerpt repeats phrases such as "O SON OF MAN" and "O SON OF BEING." "Son" here refers to mankind. The Hidden Words repeatedly calls on mankind to express love and to provide guidance.
- Bahá᾿í believes in the oneness of God and the oneness of religion, meaning that although religions may seem to differ, they all worship the same God and are, in fact, unified through that worship. Verse 13 says, " Turn thy sight unto thyself, that thou mayest find Me standing within thee." This is similar to a statement made in the Christian Bible's book of John, 14:20, which says, "The Father is the Son, and the Son is in you." Both mean that God's spirit is reflected in each person.

• • •

Excerpt from The Hidden Words of Bahá᾿u᾿lláh

Part I.— From the Arabic

Preamble *HE IS THE GLORY OF GLORIES*

*This is that which hath descended from the **realm** of glory, uttered by the tongue of power and might, and revealed unto the Prophets of old. We have taken the inner **essence thereof** and clothed it in the garment of **brevity**, as a **token** of grace unto the **righteous**, that they may stand faithful unto the **Covenant** of God, may fulfill in their lives His trust, and in the realm of spirit obtain the gem of Divine virtue.*

1: O SON OF SPIRIT! My first **counsel** is this: Possess a pure, kindly and **radiant** heart, that thine may be a **sovereignty** ancient, **imperishable** and everlasting.

2: O SON OF SPIRIT! The best beloved of all things in My sight is Justice; turn not away **therefrom** if thou desirest Me, and neglect it not that I may **confide** in thee. By its aid thou shalt see with thine own eyes and not through the eyes of others, and shalt know of thine own knowledge and not through the knowledge of thy neighbor. **Ponder** this in thy heart; how it **behooveth** thee to be. **Verily** justice is My gift to thee and the sign of My loving-kindness. Set it then before thine eyes.

3: O SON OF MAN! **Veiled** in My **immemorial** being and in the ancient eternity of My essence, I knew My love for thee; therefore I

Realm: Kingdom.

Essence: Spirit or heart.

Thereof: Of it.

Brevity: The quality of being brief or short.

Token: A sign or hint.

Righteous: Moral, good, honest.

Covenant: A promise or contract.

Counsel: Advice, guidance.

Radiant: Happy, joyful.

Sovereignty: Rulership, seat of power or government.

Imperishable: Undying.

Therefrom: From that.

Confide: Tell a secret to or give something into someone's care.

Ponder: Think over.

Behooveth: Is right or necessary.

Verily: In truth, indeed.

Veiled: Hidden, disguised.

Immemorial: Very old, going back in time beyond memory.

Engraved: Carved or imprinted, left a lasting impression.

Hence: For this reason.

Wherefore: Why.

In no wise: In no way.

Therein: Into that place or condition.

Tarry: Delay, linger, hang back.

Destined: Intended.

Dominion: Territory over which someone rules.

Renouncing: Giving up.

Stronghold: Fortress, a place that can be defended.

Perish: Die.

Utterance: A statement, something spoken.

Abide: Live.

Radiance: Bright light; joy.

Bountifully: Richly, generously.

Favor: Goodwill, kindness.

Binding: Required, necessary.

Wherewith: By what means.

Abase: Lower oneself in rank or status, shame, dishonor.

Enlightenment: Spiritual understanding.

Self-subsisting: Living by one's own means, without others' help.

created thee, have **engraved** on thee Mine image and revealed to thee My beauty.

4: O SON OF MAN! I loved thy creation, **hence** I created thee. **Wherefore,** do thou love Me, that I may name thy name and fill thy soul with the spirit of life.

5: O SON OF BEING! Love Me, that I may love thee. If thou lovest Me not, My love can **in no wise** reach thee. Know this, O servant.

6: O SON OF BEING! Thy Paradise is My love; thy heavenly home, reunion with Me. Enter **therein** and **tarry** not. This is that which hath been **destined** for thee in Our kingdom above and Our exalted **dominion**.

7: O SON OF MAN! If thou lovest Me, turn away from thyself; and if thou seekest My pleasure, regard not thine own; that thou mayest die in Me and I may eternally live in thee.

8: O SON OF SPIRIT! There is no peace for thee save by **renouncing** thyself and turning unto Me; for it behooveth thee to glory in My name, not in thine own; to put thy trust in Me and not in thyself, since I desire to be loved alone and above all that is.

9: O SON OF BEING! My love is My **stronghold;** he that entereth therein is safe and secure, and he that turneth away shall surely stray and **perish**.

10: O SON OF **UTTERANCE**! Thou art My stronghold; enter therein that thou mayest **abide** in safety. My love is in thee, know it, that thou mayest find Me near unto thee.

11: O SON OF BEING! Thou art My lamp and My light is in thee. Get thou from it thy **radiance** and seek none other than Me. For I have created thee rich and have **bountifully** shed My **favor** upon thee.

12: O SON OF BEING! With the hands of power I made thee and with the fingers of strength I created thee; and within thee have I placed the essence of My light. Be thou content with it and seek naught else, for My work is perfect and My command is **binding**. Question it not, nor have a doubt thereof.

13: O SON OF SPIRIT! I created thee rich, why dost thou bring thyself down to poverty? Noble I made thee, **wherewith** dost thou **abase** thyself? Out of the essence of knowledge I gave thee being, why seekest thou **enlightenment** from anyone beside Me? Out of the clay of love I molded thee, how dost thou busy thyself with another? Turn thy sight unto thyself, that thou mayest find Me standing within thee, mighty, powerful and **self-subsisting**.

14: O SON OF MAN! Thou art My dominion and My dominion perisheth not; wherefore fearest thou thy perishing? Thou art My light and My light shall never be extinguished; why dost thou dread extinction? Thou art My glory and My glory fadeth not; thou art My robe and My robe shall never be **outworn**. Abide then in thy love for Me, that thou mayest find Me in the realm of glory.

15: O SON OF UTTERANCE! Turn thy face unto Mine and **renounce** all **save** Me; for My sovereignty endureth and My dominion perisheth not. If thou seekest another than Me, yea, if thou searchest the universe for evermore, thy quest will be in vain.

16: O SON OF LIGHT! Forget all save Me and **commune** with My spirit. This is of the essence of My command, therefore turn unto it.

17: O SON OF MAN! Be thou content with Me and seek no other helper. For none but Me can ever **suffice** thee.

18: O SON OF SPIRIT! Ask not of Me that which We desire not for thee, then be content with what We have **ordained** for thy sake, for this is that which profiteth thee, if **therewith** thou dost content thyself.

19: O SON OF THE WONDROUS VISION! I have breathed within thee a breath of My own Spirit, that thou mayest be My lover. Why hast thou **forsaken** Me and sought a beloved other than Me?

20: O SON OF SPIRIT! My claim on thee is great, it cannot be forgotten. My grace to thee is **plenteous,** it cannot be veiled. My love has made in thee its home, it cannot be concealed. My light is manifest to thee, it cannot be **obscured.**

21: O SON OF MAN! Upon the tree of **effulgent** glory I have hung for thee the **choicest** fruits, wherefore hast thou turned away and contented thyself with that which is less good? Return then unto that which is better for thee in the realm on high.

22: O SON OF SPIRIT! Noble have I created thee, yet thou hast **abased** thyself. Rise then unto that for which thou wast created.

23: O SON OF THE SUPREME! To the eternal I call thee, yet thou dost seek that which perisheth. What hath made thee turn away from Our desire and seek thine own?

24: O SON OF MAN! **Transgress** not thy limits, nor claim that which **beseemeth** thee not. **Prostrate** thyself before the **countenance** of thy God, the Lord of might and power.

25: O SON OF SPIRIT! **Vaunt** not thyself over the poor, for I lead him on his way and behold thee in thy evil **plight** and **confound** thee for evermore.

26: O SON OF BEING! How couldest thou forget thine own faults and busy thyself with the faults of others? **Whoso** doeth this is accursed of Me.

Outworn: Worn out.

Renounce: Give up, reject.

Save: Except.

Commune: Communicate with, feel connected to

Suffice: Be enough.

Ordained: Commanded, established by law or decree.

Therewith: With that.

Forsaken: Deserted, abandoned.

Plenteous: Plentiful, present in great quantity.

Obscured: Made dark or dim or difficult to understand.

Effulgent: Radiating or spreading out brightly.

Choicest: Best.

Abased: Lowered, humiliated.

Transgress: Go beyond.

Beseemeth: Suits or is proper.

Prostrate: Bow or lie face down.

Countenance: Face.

Vaunt: Boast, brag.

Plight: Trouble, difficulty.

Confound: Confuse or make matters worse.

Whoso: Whoever.

An interior view of the Shrine of the Bab. The Bahá'í faith grew out of the Babi religion, which was itself an offshoot of Islam. The shrine houses the remains of the Bab, founder of the Babi movement, and of Abdu'l-Baha, son of Bahá'u'lláh. © TOMI JUNGER/ ALAMY.

Bear witness: Testify to.

Biddeth: Orders.

Just: Honest, moral.

Iniquity: Evil, wickedness.

Ascribe: Assign.

Abashed: Ashamed.

27: O SON OF MAN! Breathe not the sins of others so long as thou art thyself a sinner. Shouldst thou transgress this command, accursed wouldst thou be, and to this I **bear witness.**

28: O SON OF SPIRIT! Know thou of a truth: He that **biddeth** men be **just** and himself committeth **iniquity** is not of Me, even though he bear My name.

29: O SON OF BEING! **Ascribe** not to any soul that which thou wouldst not have ascribed to thee, and say not that which thou doest not. This is My command unto thee, do thou observe it.

30: O SON OF MAN! Deny not My servant should he ask anything from thee, for his face is My face; be then **abashed** before Me.

• • •

What happened next...

When Bahá'u'lláh died in 1892, he was succeeded by his eldest son, Abdu'l-Baha. In his will, Bahá'u'lláh named his son the Center of the Covenant, Head of the Faith, and the sole interpreter of his writings. Like his father, Abdu'l-Baha spent a great deal of time in prison for his beliefs, though he was released in 1908. Afterward, he spent the rest of his life traveling, speaking, and corresponding with Bahá'í communities throughout the world, until his death in 1921. In his will, Abdu'l-Baha included an outline of the Bahá'í organization. He established the post of guardianship of the faith and of the Universal House of Justice. He appointed his grandson, Shoghi Effendi, as the first Guardian. After Effendi's death in 1957, no clear candidate for the guardianship emerged. In the early twenty-first century, the faith is led by the nine-member board of the Universal House of Justice, headquartered in Haifa, Israel.

Did you know...

- The Hidden Words is based on a Shi'a Muslim tradition that comes from the Book of Fatima. Fatima was the daughter of

Muhammad, the founder of Islam. According to tradition, when Muhammad died, the archangel Gabriel appeared to Fatima to comfort her and reveal to her prophecies (predictions of the future) that she recorded in a book. The book did not survive, but Bahá'í followers believe that the prophecies will be revealed again at a later date. Bahá'ís believe that The Hidden Words may be a fulfillment of this tradition.

- Bahá'ís continue to face persecution (discrimination or mistreatment) in the Muslim world, particularly in Iran. From 1978 to 1998, at least two hundred Bahá'ís were put to death in Iran, and many more were imprisoned. Bahá'ís are not allowed to hold government jobs or attend universities, and their sacred sites have been repeatedly desecrated (violated or damaged) or destroyed.

- Some scholars see strong similarities between The Hidden Words and scriptural passages, or passages from sacred writings, in other religious traditions, including the Psalms in the Hebrew Bible, the Beatitudes in the Christian New Testament, and the *hadiths* in Islam, or the sayings and teachings of Islam's founder, Muhammad.

Consider the following...

- Explain the image of God that comes out of the excerpts from The Hidden Words.

- Explain why the word hidden is used in the title. In what sense are the words of this text hidden?

- The Bahá'í faith continues to grow in popularity, not just in the Middle East but around the world among people of widely different heritages, or traditions. Explain why the Bahá'í view of God might make the religion popular in the modern world.

For More Information

BOOKS

Bahá'u'lláh. *The Hidden Words of Bahá'u'lláh*. New Delhi, India: Bahá'í Publishing Trust, 1985. This excerpt can also be found online at http://reference.bahai.org/en/t/b/HW/hw-1.html.

Bowers, Kenneth E. *God Speaks Again: An Introduction to the Bahá'í Faith.* Wilmette, IL: Bahá'í Publishing, 2004.

Matthews, Gary I. *The Challenge of Bahá'u'lláh*. Wilmette, IL: Bahá'í Publishing Trust, 2005.

Smith, Peter. *A Concise Encyclopedia of the Bahá'í Faith.* Oxford, UK: Oneworld Publications, 1999.

WEB SITES

"Religion and Ethics: Bahá'í." *bbc.co.uk.* http://www.bbc.co.uk/religion/religions/bahai/ (accessed on June 5, 2006).

Universal House of Justice. http://www.uhj.net (accessed on June 5, 2006).

Avesta, as reproduced in *The Divine Songs of Zarathushtra*

In The Divine Songs of Zarathushtra,
available online from the Internet Sacred Text Archive at
http://www.sacred-texts.com/zor/sbe31/yasnae.htm
Compiled between 1700 BCE and 400 CE
Translated by Irach J. S. Taraporewala
Published in 1951 by D. S. Taraporevala Sons

"Violence must be put down! against cruelty make a stand,
ye who would make sure of the reward of Good Thought through
Right...."

The collection of Zoroastrianism's sacred texts is called the Avesta. It is sometimes referred to as the Zend-Avesta, but this term is inaccurate and is the result of a historical mistake in translation. *Avesta* is thought to come from an Iranian word that means "shelter" or "support." *Zend* refers to interpretations of the text. The Avesta contains twenty-one volumes of various documents that were written over a long period of time, ranging from 1700 BCE to 400 CE.

One of the documents within the Avesta is the Yasna, which means reverence or veneration. The Yasna describes rituals and other observances within the religion. The oldest part of the Avesta appears in the Yasna. This section is called the Gathas, or the Hymns of Zarathushtra. It is comprised of hymns, or songs, said to contain the original words of the religion's founder, Zarathushtra (also called Zoroaster). For this reason the Gathas are considered to be the core of the Avesta. These religious songs total about 6,000 words and 241 verses arranged in 17 chapters.

The Gathas are thought to have been composed by Zarathushtra around 1200 BCE. They are arranged into five different groups based

Zarathushtra speaks to followers about the religion he founded, Zoroastrianism. His writings, which are the religion's holy texts, were written for Ahura Mazda, not to provide specific instruction to the religion's followers. THE ART ARCHIVE.

on their meter, or rhythm or pattern in verse. These are: Ahunavaiti Gatha; Ustavaiti Gatha; Spenta Mainyu Gatha; Vohu Khshathra Gatha; and Vahisto Ishti Gatha. The Gathas can be difficult to understand because the songs are not accompanied by any commentary that explains their meaning. The songs have been used as a meditative tool, meaning that Zoroastrians meditate on the words to try to gain greater understanding. Zarathushtra did not write the Gathas to teach new followers about the religion. He wrote that Gathas in praise of the Zoroastrian god, Ahura Mazda (Wise Lord).

The message of the Gathas Zarathushtra wrote in the Gathas that there is one god, Ahura Mazda, and that everyone is able to receive God's message. Zarathushtra also provided details on how people should behave. These included acquiring knowledge, being righteous (honest and respectable), and protecting nature. The Amesha Spentas, or Bounteous Immortals (also called Holy Immortals), help guide Zoroastrians in life. The Amesha Spentas provide a channel of communication between humans and Ahura Mazda. They are thought by some to be actual beings and by others to be merely concepts, or ideas, to aid people. There are six immortal concepts that make up the Amesha Spentas:

Vohu Manah, good mind and purpose;

Asha Vahishta, truth and justice;

Spenta Ameraiti, devotion, serenity, and kindness;

Khashathra Vairya, power and just (fair) rule;

Hauravatat, wholeness and health; and

Ameretat, long life and immortality.

Based on the teachings of Zarathushtra, Zoroastrians follow the will of the Amesha Spentas. They dedicate themselves to a "threefold path," which is stated simply in the Zoroastrian motto, "Good thoughts, good words, good deeds." This goal is expressed by the term *asha*. Asha is a form of righteousness that comes from the natural order of things and includes truth, order, discipline, and progress. Zoroastrianism is a religion that is free of fixed teachings (required lessons to learn) and commandments (orders). Zarathushtra, who believed in the power of human reason, taught that each person was capable of knowing the difference between good and evil and of following the good. A person who has Vohu Manah, or good mind and purpose, will follow the path of righteousness in agreement with the law of asha.

Because the words of the Gathas are believed to come directly from Zarathushtra, members of the faith read and follow them as a guide in their daily lives. The passages of the Gathas excerpted here all have a single theme, usually translated as violence or fury. Violence, which includes not only anger but also destructive force (as in the fury of a storm), is seen as something that is damaging to the civilized world. One who does not have a good mind (Vohu Manah) acts in fury and with violence and harms others. Rulers can act in fury, bringing violence and unhappiness upon their people. As Zarathushtra says, "Violence must be put down! against cruelty make a stand, ye who would make sure of the reward of Good Thought through Right, to whose company the holy man belongs."

A person who can control his or her anger and violent behavior is a supporter of humankind. Those who find it hard to control their anger have to change their ways to acquire a good mind. If they do not, their fury will turn back on them and they will be harmed. If they do change their ways, they can eliminate violence from the mind, which will lead to good words and good deeds. This examination of the dangers of anger and violence reflects the tolerance, peacefulness, and emphasis on good works and service to others that characterize Zoroastrianism even in modern life. A person who can avoid fury is rational, logical, successful, happy, and peaceful.

History of the Gathas Zoroastrianism is one of the oldest religions still in existence and may be the oldest surviving monotheistic religion. This means that, like Islam, Judaism, and Christianity, its followers believe in a single god. Zarathushtra lived in Persia (modern-day Iran). Scholars are not entirely certain when he lived, but most think that it was between 1500 and 1000 BCE, probably around 1200 BCE. These dates are uncertain because throughout the religion's history, many of its texts were destroyed, first by the Greek conqueror Alexander the Great in 330 BCE and then by Arab and Mongol invaders beginning in 650 CE. Some of the earliest Zoroastrian texts were about such topics as medicine, law, science, and

Zoroastrianism: The First Ecological Religion?

At the time that Zoroastrianism was founded in northwestern Persia, the people believed in a polytheistic religion, which is a religion that recognizes many gods. Zarathushtra, perhaps for the first time in human history, taught his followers that there was only one God, Ahura Mazda. This god was omniscient (knowing everything), omnipresent (present everywhere), and omnipotent (all-powerful). Zarathushtra believed that Ahura Mazda was unchanging, unknowable, and the source of all that was good in the world.

Based on this belief, Zarathushtra taught that everything that Ahura Mazda had created was pure and good and deserved to be treated with respect, including the natural environment. For this reason, Zoroastrians avoid any activities that pollutes the air, land, or water, earning Zoroastrianism the title, among some people, of the world's first ecological religion. Ecological refers to the workings of nature and its many environments. By receiving this title, Zoroastrianism is called an environmentally aware and caring religion. This is one of the central ways that Zoroastrianism serves as a guide for daily life. Zoroastrians tend to take jobs that allow them to avoid harming the earth. The Gathas place heavy emphasis on industry and hard work. Further, Zoroastrians believe that all creatures are sacred. To follow these beliefs Zoroastrians shun any type of violence, discrimination (behaving unfairly to people because of their perceived differences), and persecution (discrimination that results in violence), and they show great respect for people of other religious traditions. Zoroastrians also promote equality of men and women.

history. While most of these texts did not survive, it is believed that much of their content was translated into Arabic and absorbed into Islam. Because of this destruction, many of the Zoroastrian texts that do survive are fragments, or incomplete pieces.

Much of the Avesta, and therefore the Gathas, are written in a language called Avestan, sometimes referred to as Gathic Avestan. This is one of the oldest Indo-European languages and is similar in some ways to Sanskrit, the language of ancient India. Indo-European languages are a series of related languages, including English, Spanish, German, Greek, and many others that descend from a common ancestral language probably spoken in what is now Russia about four thousand years ago. The Avesta had to be reconstructed from scattered texts, some of them in Greek translations. In the early twenty-first century many Zoroastrians continue to recite the Avesta in the Avestan language, although most do not understand the words. The original Avestan is often recited first, and then the text is repeated in the local language.

Zoroastrianism had a great deal of influence on Judaism and Christianity, giving rise to such concepts as the soul, heaven and hell, the savior (one who will show people the way to heaven), resurrection (rising from the dead), final judgment, and others. For example, Zoroastrians believe that the soul, or *urvan,* is given three days to meditate after death. If good thoughts outweigh the bad, the soul is admitted to heaven; if the bad outweighs the good, the soul is sent to hell. Another important concept in Zoroastrianism is that the world passes through three phases. The first is creation. The second, the present world, is one in which good and evil are mixed but people's good actions and thoughts are helping lead the world to a heavenly ideal. In the final state, good and evil will be separated, all will be pure and good, and even the souls that have been sent to hell will be freed.

Things to remember while reading the excerpt from the Avesta in *The Divine Songs of Zarathushtra*:

- The excerpt begins with Yasna 29 and refers to the Ox-Creator. At the time of Zarathushtra, cattle were very important to survival. Every part of the cattle could be used for food, clothing, or other purposes. People were very dependent on cattle, and the animals, in turn, were also dependent on the people for their well-being. The Ox-Creator, representing the most valued creature of the time, asks Ahura Mazda for protection from the surrounding violence.

- The Daevas are demon spirits who follow Angra Mainya, or Ahriman, the Devil. They have "rushed together to Violence." Zarathushtra taught that there was both a good and a bad and that people could choose the good. The Daevas did not choose correctly.

- To fight against the Daevas, one needs to exercise Asha, which includes truth, order, and discipline. Zarathusthra is telling his followers that by this behavior, they can choose good and avoid joining the Daevas in hell.

• • •

Excerpt from the Avesta in *The Divine Songs of Zarathushtra*

Ahunavaiti Gatha

Yasna 29

1. Unto you **wailed** the Ox-soul, "For whom did ye fashion me? Who created me? Violence and **rapine** (and) savagery **hath oppressed** me, and outrage and might. I have no other herdsman than you; prepare for me then the blessings of pasture."

2. Then the Ox-Creator asked of the Right: "**Hast** thou a judge for the Ox, that ye may be able to appoint him **zealous tendance** as well as **fodder?** Whom do ye will to be his lord, who may drive off violence together with the followers of the Lie?" . . .

Wailed: Cried.

Rapine: Plunder, the use of force to take property, especially in time of war.

Hath: Has.

Oppressed: To dominate harshly or by force.

Hast: Have.

Zealous: Enthusiastic.

Tendance: The act of taking care or being in charge.

Fodder: An animal's food.

*The Zoroastrian god Ahura
Mazda is depicted on the
façade of the Old Majlis
Building in Tehran, Iran.
Zarathushtra wrote the
Gathas in praise of Ahura
Mazda.* © ROGER WOOD/
CORBIS.

Twain: Two.

Aright: Correctly.

Infatuation: An intense and
usually brief obsession for an
idea or person.

Enfeeble: Weaken.

Dominion: Control,
authority.

Karapan and the Usij: Classes of priests.

Kavi: A king of ancient Iraq.

Yasna 30

6. Between these **twain** the Daevas also chose not **aright,** for **infatuation** came upon them as they took counsel together, so that they chose the Worst Thought. Then they rushed together to Violence, that they might **enfeeble** the world of men. . . .

Ushtavaiti Gatha

Yasna 44

20. Have the Daevas ever exercised good **dominion?** And I ask of those who see how for the Daevas' sake the **Karapan and the Usij** give cattle to violence, and how the **Kavi** made them continually to mourn, instead of taking care that they make the pastures prosper through Right. . . .

Spentamainyush Gatha

Yasna 48

7. Violence must be put down! against cruelty make a stand, ye who would make sure of the reward of Good Thought through Right, to whose company the holy man belongs. His dwelling place shall be in thy House, O Ahura. . . .

12. These shall be the deliverers of the provinces, who **exert** themselves, O Good Thought in their action, O **Asha,** to fulfill their duty, face to face with thy command, O Mazda. For these are the appointed **smiters** of Violence.

Yasna 49

4. They who make the increase of violence and cruelty with their tongues, the foes of cattle-nurture among its friends; whose ill deeds **prevail,** not their good deeds: these (shall be) in the house of the Daevas, (the place for) the Self of the Liar.

Exert: Make an effort.

Asha: Holiness, order, truth, righteousness.

Smiters: Those who strike hard.

Prevail: Win out, prove to have greater influence.

• • •

What happened next...

Initially, Zarathushtra had only a single follower to his religion, a cousin. The local Iranian leaders felt threatened by Zarathustra's religious ideas and their emphasis on peace and right conduct and the rejection of overly complex rituals. Even the local people resisted his ideas because Zarathushtra reduced the Daevas from demon gods to mere workers on behalf of Angra Mainyu.

After twelve years of trying to persuade the people to accept his ideas, Zarathushtra left Persia. He found refuge in Bactria, an ancient Greek kingdom in ancient Afghanistan and Tajikistan. There, King Vishtaspa and his queen, Hutosa, heard Zarathushtra debate local religious leaders and decided to adopt his ideas. They made Zoroastrianism the official religion of the kingdom.

Did you know...

- The most prominent symbol of Zoroastrianism is the *Faravahar,* sometimes spelled *Farohar.* The name comes from an Avestan word *fravarane,* meaning "I choose," suggesting the idea that a person freely chooses to follow the religion. The *Faravahar* depicts a bird with its wings spread and a human figure appearing to sit atop it.
- Because of their emphasis on "Good thoughts, good words, good deeds," Zoroastrians make significant contributions to charity and have a reputation for honesty and tolerance for other religious beliefs.
- A strong similarity between Zoroastrianism, Judaism, Christianity, and Islam is that a savior, in Zoroastrianism a descendant of Zarathushtra called Saoshyant, will be born of a virgin (a woman

who has never had sex). He will raise the dead and evaluate everyone's life in the final judgment.

Consider the following...

- Summarize the resemblances you see between Zoroastrianism's belief in "Good thoughts, good speech, good deeds" and the ethical codes of other religious traditions you may be familiar with.

- Explain specifically how violence runs counter to the Zoroastrian faith.

- Explain what a Zoroastrian would mean by "good mind" and how a good mind is part of the religion's belief system.

For More Information

BOOKS

Boyce, Mary. *Zoroastrians: Their Religious Beliefs and Practices.* New York: Routledge, 2001.

Mehr, Farheng. *The Zoroastrian Tradition: An Introduction to the Ancient Wisdom of Zarathushtra.* Costa Mesa, CA: Mazda Publishers, 2003.

Nanavutty, Piloo. *The Gathas of Zarathushtra: Hymns in Praise of Wisdom.* Middletown, NJ: Grantha Corporation, 1999.

"Yasna." In *The Divine Songs of Zarathushtra,* translated by Irach J. S. Taraporewala. Bombay, India: D. S. Taraporevala Sons, 1951. This excerpt can also be found online at http://www.sacred-texts.com/zor/sbe31/yasnae.htm.

WEB SITES

"Religion and Ethics: Zoroastrianism." *bbc.co.uk.* http://www.bbc.co.uk/religion/religions/zoroastrian/index.shtml (accessed on June 5, 2006).

"The Gathas." *Zoroastriankids.com.* http://www.zoroastriankids.com/gathas.html (accessed on June 5, 2006).

"Zoroastrianism." *ReligiousTolerance.org* http://www.religioustolerance.org/zoroastr.htm (accessed on June 5, 2006).

"The Philosophy of Atheism"

"The Philosophy of Atheism," available online from Spunk Library at
http://www.spunk.org/library/writers/goldman/sp001502.html
By Emma Goldman
Published in 1916 in Mother Earth

"It is the earth, not heaven, which man must rescue if he is truly to be saved."

Emma Goldman (1869–1940) is remembered as one of the most out-spoken American atheists of the late nineteenth and early twentieth centuries. An atheist is someone who does not believe in God. She rejected belief in such religious ideas as heaven, hell, sin, and other principles, and she outlined her views in a 1916 essay called "The Philosophy of Atheism." Goldman was also a prominent anarchist. Anarchism is a political theory that considers government to be unnecessary and even harmful. Anarchists call for a society based on voluntary cooperation and free association of individuals and groups.

Goldman was a controversial figure whose beliefs were not very popular in the United States of the early twentieth century. She was in favor of equality of the sexes, sexual freedom, birth control, and labor organization into unions, as well as many other issues that were considered radical at that time. "The Philosophy of Atheism" described another of Goldman's controversial beliefs: that God did not exist. A philosophy is an idea or theory that gives greater understanding to how the world works. Goldman's philosophy first appeared in the journal *Mother Earth,* which she founded. She later gave speeches on this philosophy.

In addition to stating in her essay that God did not exist, Goldman believed that religion could not provide people with a guide for living. Religion, she said, was designed to make man dependent and without

Weak Versus Strong Atheism

Sometimes the terms "weak atheist" and "strong atheist" are used to refer to different types of atheists. Weak atheists do not find the evidence for the existence of gods persuasive. While theists say that deities, or gods, do exist, weak atheists do not necessarily disagree. Some simply hold no opinion on the matter. Others more actively have doubts that gods exist. They consider it likely that gods do not exist because no one can prove that they do. In this respect, weak atheism is similar to agnosticism, or the view that gods might or might not exist but no one can know for certain.

In contrast to weak atheism is strong atheism. Strong atheism describes the position Emma Goldman takes in her essay, "The Philosophy of Atheism." Strong atheists positively deny that deities exist. Goldman states that it is only by rejecting the idea of God altogether that mankind can break away from the crutch of religion and achieve true freedom. Strong atheists tend to believe in rationalism, the philosophy that truth can be reached through human reason and factual analysis rather than through religious faith or the teachings of a church.

Strong atheists are critical of any belief system that demands from people faith or simple acceptance instead of relying on reasoning and critical thinking. Atheists of this type, including Goldman, argue that religion and belief in God are not just irrational, or unreasonable, but also destructive and harmful because of the influence of religious institutions over people's lives. Atheists believe that only by freeing themselves from religious beliefs can people likewise free themselves from superstition and realize their true potential.

free will (self-determination). Therefore, any guidelines from religion on how to live life also had this same aim. Goldman also discussed what philosophers call the "problem of evil." This says that a powerful, kind, and loving god would have arranged the world in a way that reflects his (or her) goodness, and would not have allowed evil to exist. Belief in such a god, Goldman said, ignores the existence of evil and suffering in the world. It is in part by this reasoning that Goldman concluded that a loving god does not exist.

Goldman believed that only humans could create a world in which people live lives of freedom and peace rather than lives of suffering, war, and mistreatment. Guides for living have to come from universal principles of social justice rather than from religion and its sacred writings. Social justice is the belief that all people should receive the same rights, from opportunities in education and economy, to equality in treatment. Goldman states that the solution to the problems that torment mankind is with man himself, not through reliance on a divine being. "No, not the gods, but MAN must rise in his mighty wrath. He . . . himself, must undertake to usher in justice upon the earth." In other words, only humans, with their own passion for justice and humanity, can solve the problems of injustice in the world.

Emma Goldman was born in Russia but in her teens immigrated to the United States. She was drawn to anarchist beliefs by the events surrounding the Haymarket Square bombing in Chicago, Illinois, in 1886. During a workers' rally a bomb was tossed into the crowd, killing a number of policemen and wounding many more, including bystanders. Many people, including Goldman, believed that the four men who were later hanged for the crime had been convicted because of their political views rather than by the evidence.

In the decades that followed, Goldman dedicated herself to revolutionary ideals, equality of the sexes, and the rights of workers. She was imprisoned for distributing literature about birth control at a time when it was illegal to do so. In 1892 she came under suspicion because the police believed she had taken part in an attempt to assassinate the wealthy industrialist Henry Clay Finch. An industrialist is someone who owns or operates a manufacturing business. She was later a vocal opponent of U.S. entry into World War I (1914–18; a war in which Great Britain, France, the United States and their allies defeated Germany, Austria-Hungary, and their allies). After she was convicted of openly opposing the military draft, she was sentenced to prison, stripped of her U.S. citizenship, and deported to the Soviet Union.

Consistent with her social beliefs and her distrust of institutions, which she believed robbed people of their freedom, Goldman was a firm atheist. Her views were by no means new. Atheism, from the Greek word *atheos,* meaning "without gods," can be traced back to ancient Greece and Rome. For many centuries, people who opposed the official religion of the country in which they lived faced charges of atheism and were often executed for their beliefs. It was not until the dawn of the Age of Reason in Europe (roughly the seventeenth and eighteenth centuries) that philosophers in such countries as France, Germany, Russia, and England began to take openly atheistic positions. These views were still often considered criminal by the state. One of the most prominent Age of Reason atheists was Francis Bacon (1561–1626), a British philosopher who wrote: "Atheism leaves a man to sense, to philosophy, to natural piety [devotion], to laws, to reputation; all of which may be guides to an outward moral virtue, even if religion vanished; but religious superstition dismounts [takes down] all these and erects an absolute monarchy in the minds of men." This is a viewpoint very similar to Goldman's, who argues that people have to provide their own guides for living, not take them from religious beliefs.

Things to remember while reading "The Philosophy of Atheism":

- Atheism is a philosophy, a set of ideas about understanding the universe and the ways to live appropriately. Philosophies can

Emma Goldman believed that people needed to rely on themselves to improve their lives rather than putting their faith in a God. Only humans, she said, could create the changes they sought.
© BETTMANN/CORBIS.

address the workings of nature, the meaning of life, and religion, as well as other topics in the arts and sciences. Atheism's philosophy is that there is no God and humankind must rely only on itself to improve human life and solve the world's problems.

- Goldman's argument in favor of atheism looks to science as the source of reason, rather than to faith. As man's knowledge of science and the natural world has increased over time, the concept of God, she says, has become more unclear. It is precisely such advances in knowledge that cause many people to doubt or deny the existence of God.

- The essay talks strongly about people giving power to themselves instead of appealing to a divine being with positive and negative qualities found in the world. By assigning powers such as punishment and reward for bad and good behavior to a god, people lose their free will and surrender control over their lives. Goldman believes that people themselves have the power to take charge of their lives and even to help address the problems and reduce the suffering in the world.

- Religious revivals, which Goldman attacks, are large gatherings of people who come to hear compelling speakers, such as Billy Sunday (1862–1935), preach about religion. In the early twentieth century such revivals were common and resulted in many people becoming newly religious. Revivalism was responsible for a large growth in U.S. religious participation.

● ● ●

Excerpt from "The Philosophy of Atheism"

Exposition: Explanation.

To give an adequate **exposition** of the Philosophy of Atheism, it would be necessary to go into the historical changes of the belief in a Deity, from its earliest beginning to the present day. But that is not within the scope of the present paper. However, it is not out of place to mention, in passing, that the concept God, Supernatural Power, Spirit, Deity, or in whatever other term the essence of Theism may have found expression, has become more indefinite and **obscure** in the course of time and progress. In other words, the God idea is growing more impersonal and **nebulous** in proportion as the human mind is learning to understand natural phenomena and in the degree that science progressively **correlates** human and social events.

God, today, no longer represents the same forces as in the beginning of His existence; neither does He direct human destiny with the same Iron hand as of **yore.** Rather does the God idea express a sort of spiritualistic **stimulus** to satisfy the **fads** and **fancies** of every shade of human weakness. In the course of human development the God idea has been forced to adapt itself to every phase of human affairs, which is perfectly **consistent** with the origin of the idea itself.

The conception of gods originated in fear and curiosity. Primitive man, unable to understand the phenomena of nature and **harassed** by them, saw in every terrifying **manifestation** some **sinister** force **expressly** directed against him; and as ignorance and fear are the parents of all **superstition,** the troubled fancy of primitive man wove the God idea.

Very **aptly,** the world-renowned atheist and anarchist, Michael Bakunin, says in his great work *God and the State:* "All religions, with their gods, their **demi-gods,** and their prophets, their **messiahs** and their saints, were created by the prejudiced fancy of men who had not **attained** the full development and full possession of their **faculties.** . . . The history of religions, of the birth, grandeur, and the decline of the gods who had succeeded one another in human belief, is nothing, therefore, but the development of the collective intelligence and conscience of mankind. As fast as they discovered, in the course of their historically-progressive advance, either in themselves or in external nature, a quality, or even any great **defect** whatever, they **attributed** it to their gods, after having exaggerated and enlarged it beyond measure, after the manner of children, by an act of their religious fancy. . . . The idea of God implies the **abdication** of human reason and justice; it is the most decisive **negation** of human liberty, and necessarily ends in the enslavement of mankind, both in theory and practice."

Thus the God idea . . . has dominated humanity and will continue to do so until man will raise his head to the sunlit day, unafraid and with an awakened will to himself. In proportion as man learns to realize himself and mold his own destiny theism becomes **superfluous.** How far man will be able to find his relation to his fellows will depend entirely upon how much he can outgrow his dependence upon God. . . .

It is the earth, not heaven, which man must rescue if he is truly to be saved. . . .

Obscure: Difficult to understand.

Nebulous: Unclear.

Correlates: Makes a relationship between.

Yore: Olden days.

Stimulus: Something that encourages an activity or interest.

Fads: Fashions or trends that are popular for a short period of time.

Fancies: Whims or sudden likings.

Consistent: In agreement.

Harassed: Bothered, disturbed.

Manifestation: Appearance.

Sinister: Threatening.

Expressly: Deliberately.

Superstition: False idea.

Aptly: Appropriately.

Demi-gods: Beings who are part human and part god.

Messiahs: Those who rescue or save from harm.

Attained: Achieved.

Faculties: Mental abilities.

Defect: Flaw.

Attributed: Credited.

Abdication: Giving up.

Negation: Denial.

Superfluous: Unnecessary.

Billy Sunday: A well-known American baseball player turned evangelist, or an enthusiastic preacher of Christianity.

It is characteristic of theistic "tolerance" that no one really cares what the people believe in, just so they believe or pretend to believe. To accomplish this end, the crudest...methods are being used. Religious...revivals with **Billy Sunday** as their champion—methods which must outrage every refined sense, and which in their effect upon the ignorant and curious often tend to create a mild state of insanity....All these frantic efforts find approval and support from the earthly powers....

Consciously or unconsciously, most theists see in gods and devils, heaven and hell; reward and punishment, a whip to lash the people into obedience, meekness and contentment....

Squalor: Dirtiness.

Jahve or Jehovah: A name for the god of the Hebrew Old Testament.

Have not all theists painted their Deity as the god of love and goodness? Yet after thousands of years of such preachments the gods remain deaf to the agony of the human race. Confucius cares not for the poverty, **squalor** and misery of people of China. Buddha remains undisturbed in his philosophical indifference to the famine and starvation of outraged Hindoos; **Jahve** continues deaf to the bitter cry of Israel; while Jesus refuses to rise from the dead against his Christians who are butchering each other.

Wrath: Anger.

Deceived: Tricked.

Emissaries: Representatives.

Usher: Lead.

Oracles: Predictions of the future.

Mean: Lowly.

Degradation: Poverty, terrible life conditions.

The burden of all song and praise "unto the Highest" has been that God stands for justice and mercy. Yet injustice among men is ever on the increase; the outrages committed against the masses in this country alone would seem enough to overflow the very heavens. But where are the gods to make an end to all these horrors, these wrongs, this inhumanity to man? No, not the gods, but MAN must rise in his mighty **wrath.** He, **deceived** by all the deities, betrayed by their **emissaries,** he, himself, must undertake to **usher** in justice upon the earth....

The philosophy of Atheism represents a concept of life without any metaphysical Beyond or Divine Regulator. It is the concept of an actual, real world with its liberating, expanding and beautifying possibilities, as against an unreal world, which, with its spirits, **oracles,** and **mean** contentment has kept humanity in helpless **degradation.**

Paradox: Contradiction.

Speculation: Guesswork.

Demonstrable: Provable.

Immolation: Killing as a sacrifice, usually by burning.

Ascertain: Learn.

Futile: Useless.

Omnipotence: All-powerfulness.

It may seem a wild **paradox,** and yet it is pathetically true, that this real, visible world and our life should have been so long under the influence of metaphysical **speculation,** rather than of physical **demonstrable** forces. Under the lash of the theistic idea, this earth has served no other purpose than as a temporary station to test man's capacity for **immolation** to the will of God. But the moment man attempted to **ascertain** the nature of that will, he was told that it was utterly **futile** for "finite human intelligence" to get beyond the all-powerful infinite will. Under the terrific weight of this **omnipotence,** man has been bowed into the dust—a will-less creature, broken and sweating in the dark. The triumph of the philosophy of Atheism is to free man from the nightmare of gods...Again and again the light of

MOTHER EARTH
BULLETIN

VOL. I.   OCTOBER, 1917, NEW YORK   NO. 1.

Freedom of Criticism and Opinion

EMMA GOLDMAN

Under the "Trading With the Enemy Act," the Postmaster General has become the absolute dictator over the press. Not only is it impossible now for any publication with character to be circulated through the mails, but every other channel, such as express, freight, newsstands, and even distribution has been stopped. As MOTHER EARTH will not comply with these regulations and will not appear in an emasculated form, it prefers to take a long needed rest until the world has regained its sanity.

The MOTHER EARTH BULLETIN has been decided upon largely as a means of keeping in touch with our friends and subscribers, and for the purpose of keeping them posted about our movements and activities.

FORBIDDEN

DEDICATION

This is the wee Babe of Mother Earth. It was conceived during the greatest human crisis — born into a tragic, disintegrating world. To give it life, Mother Earth had to choose death, yet out of Death must come Life again. The Babe is frail of body, but it comes with a heritage of strength, determination and idealism to be worthy of her who gave it birth.

To bring a child into the world these days is almost an unpardonable luxury. But the child of Mother Earth comes to you for a share of the beautiful love and devotion you gave its mother. Assured of that, it will make a brave effort to Live and to Do.—*E. G.*

EMMA GOLDMAN - - - - - Publisher and Editor

Office: 226 Lafayette Street, New York City

Telephone, Spring 8711

10c per copy   *$1.00 per year*

reason has dispelled the theistic nightmare, but poverty, misery and fear have recreated the phantoms.... Atheism, on the other hand, in its philosophic aspect refuses allegiance not merely to a definite concept of God, but it refuses all servitude to the God idea, and opposes the theistic principle as such. Gods in their individual function are not half as **pernicious** as the principle of theism which represents the belief in a supernatural, or even omnipotent, power to rule the earth and man upon it. It is the **absolutism**

Pernicious: Harmful.

Absolutism: Unquestionable.

Emancipation: Freeing.

Fetters: Restraints.

Consciousness: Awareness.

Fidelity: Faithfulness, devotion.

Vile: Evil.

Imbued: Filled.

Hypocrisy: Insincerity, a false claim to having high principles.

Exponents: Supporters.

Conditioned: Made strong or readied.

Precepts: Guidelines.

Vitality: Strength.

Disintegrating: Decaying.

Suffices: Is enough.

Sterility: Unproductiveness.

Affirmation: Positive statement in support.

Yea: Positive statement in support.

of theism, its pernicious influence upon humanity, its paralyzing effect upon thought and action, which Atheism is fighting with all its power.

The philosophy of Atheism has its root in the earth, in this life; its aim is the **emancipation** of the human race from all Godheads, be they Judaic, Christian, Mohammedan, Buddhistic, Brahministic, or what not. Mankind has been punished long and heavily for having created its gods; nothing but pain and persecution have been man's lot since gods began. There is but one way out of this blunder: Man must break his **fetters** which have chained him to the gates of heaven and hell, so that he can begin to fashion out of his reawakened and illumined **consciousness** a new world upon earth. . . .

Atheism is already helping to free man from his dependence upon punishment and reward as the heavenly bargain-counter for the poor in spirit.

Do not all theists insist that there can be no morality, no justice, honesty or **fidelity** without the belief in a Divine Power? Based upon fear and hope, such morality has always been a **vile** product, **imbued** partly with self-righteousness, partly with **hypocrisy.** As to truth, justice, and fidelity, who have been their brave **exponents** and daring proclaimers? Nearly always the godless ones: the Atheists; they lived, fought, and died for them. They knew that justice, truth, and fidelity are not **conditioned** in heaven, but that they are related to and interwoven with the tremendous changes going on in the social and material life of the human race. . . .

Thoughtful people are beginning to realize that moral **precepts,** imposed upon humanity through religious terror, have become stereotyped and have therefore lost all **vitality.** A glance at life today, at its **disintegrating** character, its conflicting interests with their hatreds, crimes, and greed, **suffices** to prove the **sterility** of theistic morality. . . .

Atheism in its negation of gods is at the same time the strongest **affirmation** of man, and through man, the eternal **yea** to life, purpose, and beauty.

• • •

What happened next . . .

Goldman's views did not fall on deaf ears. In 1925 the American Association for the Advancement of Atheism was formed to attack all religious beliefs by distributing atheistic literature. Then, in 1929, a successor organization was formed, the League of Militant Atheists. This organization, which claimed to have 5.5 million members, worked actively to weaken the influence of religion. It established centers where lectures on atheism could be presented and tried to place atheists as university professors. In the later twentieth century American Atheists, Inc. (1963) and Atheists United (1982) were formed to protect the civil rights of atheists and promote the constitutional doctrine of separation of church and state, that religion and the government should operate separately from one another.

Did you know . . .

- J. Edgar Hoover (1895–1972), the first director of the Federal Bureau of Investigation (FBI), called Emma Goldman "the most dangerous woman in America."
- In 1901 Goldman was arrested and charged for having planned the attempt by Leon Czolgosz (1873–1901) to assassinate President William McKinley (1843–1901; served 1896–1901) on September 6 of that year. She was held in jail but later released because of lack of evidence.
- Although Emma Goldman was convicted of crimes and served three separate prison terms, many people regard her as a heroine, especially because of her opposition to war, her defense of the rights of workers, and her belief in the equality of the sexes. Institutions such as schools and family-planning clinics are named after her.
- Scientists are more likely to be atheists than are people in other professions. In 1996 a survey found that about 60 percent of scientists expressed disbelief or doubt about the existence of God. In contrast, in a 2001 survey of Americans, less than 0.5 percent identified themselves as atheists.

Consider the following . . .

- Explain why, in Goldman's view, religion cannot provide people with a useful guide to living.
- Compare how atheists examine the "problem of evil" with the way this problem is examined in a religious tradition you may be familiar with.
- Goldman refers to organized religion as "the most powerful and lucrative [profitable] industry in the world." Explain what she means by this statement, and express agreement or disagreement.

For More Information

BOOKS

Glassgold, Peter. *Anarchy!: An Anthology of Emma Goldman's Mother Earth.* New York: Counterpoint Press, 2001.

Goldman, Emma. *Living My Life,* vol. 1. New York: Dover Press, 1930.

Moritz, Theresa, and Albert Moritz. *The World's Most Dangerous Women: A New Biography of Emma Goldman.* Vancouver, British Columbia, Canada: Subway Books, 2002.

PERIODICALS

Goldman, Emma. "The Philosophy of Atheism." *Mother Earth* (February 1916): 410–416. This article can also be found online at http://www.spunk.org/library/writers/goldman/sp001502.html.

WEB SITES

Beverly, Christopher Thomas, and David Wilson Cary. "Atheism." *Religious Movements Page.* http://religiousmovements.lib.virginia.edu/nrms/atheism.html (accessed on June 5, 2006).

"Religion and Ethics: Atheism." *bbc.co.uk.* http://www.bbc.co.uk/religion/religions/atheism/ (accessed on June 5, 2006).

Bible

Sermon on the Mount, chapters 5–7 of the book of Matthew, King James Bible
Available online from the Internet Sacred Text Archive at
http://www.sacred-texts.com/bib/kjv/mat005.htm;
http://www.sacred-texts.com/bib/kjv/mat006.htm;
http://www.sacred-texts.com/bib/kjv/mat007.htm
Compiled between 1400 BCE and 90 CE

"Wherefore by their fruits ye shall know them."

The Bible is the sacred text of Christianity. It is composed of two major parts: the Old Testament and the New Testament. The Old Testament is the Jewish sacred scripture, but "Old Testament" is a Christian term, and Jews refer to their scripture as the Tanakh. It is also often called the Hebrew Bible. While Christians believe in the authority of the Old Testament, the core of Christianity is found in the New Testament, which features accounts of the life and teachings of the religion's founder, Jesus Christ (c. 6 BCE–c. 33 CE). These accounts are broken up into "books" named after important early figures in Christianity and contain chapters. The biblical book of Matthew contains what is commonly called the Sermon on the Mount in chapters 5 through 7. The Sermon on the Mount records the actual teachings of Jesus Christ. A shorter version of the sermon also can be found in the sixth chapter of the book of Luke.

Jesus's political and spiritual roles

The word *Christ* comes from a Greek word meaning something like "the chosen one." The Jewish people of the time of Christ (around the first century CE) looked forward to the arrival of a messiah, a savior who would be the last of God's prophets. The coming of this messiah was foretold in the Jewish scripture. Most people believed that the long-awaited messiah would establish a kingdom on Earth. They believed that he would free the Jewish people from the Roman Empire, which ruled the region during the time that Christ lived. They saw their expected messiah as an earthly ruler who would lead the Jewish people and make them strong again. Christians regard Christ as the expected messiah. Christ, however, taught a very different message in the Sermon on the Mount than the one the Jews were waiting for. He made clear to his followers that he was on Earth to establish God's heavenly kingdom, not an earthly kingdom. The Sermon on the Mount was a guide to earthly living for his Christian followers. Those who followed Christ's teachings could earn a place in the heavenly kingdom.

The basic message that Christ taught was that to enter the kingdom of heaven a person had to do more than simply follow the letter of the law or practice traditional rituals. Christ taught that a person's inward spirit, outlook, and attitude, towards both God and other people, were more important. As he said in verse 17 of chapter 5 in the book of Matthew, "Think not that I am come to destroy the law, or the prophets: I am not come to destroy, but to fulfil." Through his preaching, Christ was creating a new guide for living for his followers, one based not on legal traditions but on the state of a person's heart.

The Sermon on the Mount contains some of the verses of the New Testament that are most often quoted by Christians. One example is the third verse of chapter 5: "Blessed are the poor in spirit: for theirs is the kingdom of heaven." In this verse, Christ is saying that people should be humble ("poor in spirit"). Only those with an attitude of humility in their hearts can reach heaven. He calls on his followers to be peacemakers and to endure persecution from those who are not ready to accept Christ's message. Persecution is mistreatment, often involving violence. He sets a high standard for his followers, telling them to be meek and merciful. He urges them to be simple and trusting and to avoid outward shows of holiness. He concludes chapter 5 by saying, "Be ye therefore perfect, even as your Father which is in heaven is perfect."

Separating Christianity from Judaism In chapter 5 of the book of Matthew, Christ offers some examples of how his standards differ from those of the Jewish law. In verses 21 through 24, he says that it is not enough simply to follow the law not to kill, which is one of the laws contained in the Ten Commandments of the Old Testament. In Christ's view, reconciliation, meaning compromising and reaching an understanding with others, and forgiveness are more important. He considers the example of someone who goes to the temple (a Jewish house of worship) with an offering but does so while he feels anger against a fellow human being. He tells such a person to "go thy way; first be reconciled to thy brother, and then come and offer thy gift." Christ's emphasis is always on love and forgiveness.

The Sermon on the Mount is rich with statements Christ made that express the essence, or the core and the heart, of Christianity. Chapter 6, verses 9 through 13, contain the well-known "Lord's Prayer," a prayer to the Father in Heaven that is part of most Christian services. This prayer is a simple expression of belief in God and a request for help in becoming a forgiving person. Another often-quoted verse is the first verse of chapter 7, "Judge not that ye not be judged." For Christ, the statement meant that one should look to the state of his or her own heart rather than worrying about the behavior of others. He also urges that people should treat others as they would wish to be treated themselves.

Things to remember while reading the excerpt from the Bible:

- Although Christ was the founder of Christianity, it must be remembered that he was born as a Jew, lived as a Jew, and was educated in the traditions and laws of Judaism contained in the Jewish scripture. During his sermon, he makes reference to the "scribes and Pharisees." These are the names of sects, or subgroups, of early Judaism, but, more important, they serve as representatives of a strict obedience to tradition, law, and ritual, as outlined in the Old Testament.

- The numbers in the excerpt follow the usual method for identifying passages from the Bible. For example, Matthew 5:3 refers to the third verse of the fifth chapter of Matthew. A verse generally, but not always, corresponds to a sentence.

- Christ makes reference to the ancient Mesopotamian law of Hammurabi, "an eye for an eye, a tooth for a tooth," as behavior that is not acceptable. The Sermon on the Mount urges Christians to act with kindness, charity, and forgiveness towards all, even if those others cause harm. Christ did not just urge his followers to behave this way. He himself acted in accordance with his words, as the story of his life told through the New Testament reveals.

The Ten Commandments

Christians regard the Sermon on the Mount as, in a sense, a New Testament version of the Ten Commandments. These commandments, the basic requirements of Judaism and Christianity, are found in chapter 20 of Exodus, the second book of the Jewish scripture. They were given to the prophet Moses as part of God's "covenant," or agreement, with the Israelites, the Jewish people.

The Ten Commandments became the basis for all Jewish law. They provided Jews with a guide to ethical, or moral, living. The first four commandments, verses 2 through 11, deal with people's relationship with God. The remaining six commandments, verses 12 through 17, have to do with people's relationships with others, covering such matters as family relationships; regard for human life and honesty; and standards for sex, property, speech, and thought.

20:2 I am the LORD thy God, which have brought thee out of the land of Egypt, out of the house of bondage. [slavery]

20:3 Thou shalt have no other gods before me.

20:4 Thou shalt not make unto thee any graven [carved] image, or any likeness of any thing that is in heaven above, or that is in the earth beneath, or that is in the water under the earth.

20:5 Thou shalt not bow down thyself to them, nor serve them: for I the LORD thy God am a jealous God, visiting the iniquity [sin] of the fathers upon the children unto the third and fourth generation of them that hate me;

20:6 And shewing [showing] mercy unto thousands of them that love me, and keep my commandments.

20:7 Thou shalt not take the name of the LORD thy God in vain; for the LORD will not hold him guiltless that taketh his name in vain.

20:8 Remember the sabbath day [day of worship], to keep it holy.

20:9 Six days shalt thou labour, and do all thy work:

20:10 But the seventh day is the sabbath of the LORD thy God: in it thou shalt not do any work, thou, nor thy son, nor thy daughter, thy manservant, nor thy maidservant, nor thy cattle, nor thy stranger that is within thy gates:

20:11 For in six days the LORD made heaven and earth, the sea, and all that in them is, and rested the seventh day: wherefore the LORD blessed the sabbath day, and hallowed [made holy] it.

20:12 Honour thy father and thy mother: that thy days may be long upon the land which the LORD thy God giveth thee.

20:13 Thou shalt not kill.

20:14 Thou shalt not commit adultery [sex with someone other than one's wife or husband].

20:15 Thou shalt not steal.

20:16 Thou shalt not bear false witness [lie] against thy neighbour.

20:17 Thou shalt not covet [desire] thy neighbour's house, thou shalt not covet thy neighbour's wife, nor his manservant, nor his maidservant, nor his ox, nor his ass, nor any thing that is thy neighbour's.

"The Second Book of Moses: Called Exodus" (chapter 20). Available online from the Internet Sacred Text archive at http://www.sacred-texts.com/bib/kjv/exo020.htm.

• • •

Excerpt from the Bible

The Gospel According to Saint Matthew

Chapter 5

5:1 And seeing the multitudes, he went up into a mountain: and when he was set, his disciples came unto him:

5:2 And he opened his mouth, and taught them, saying,

5:3 Blessed are the poor in spirit: for theirs is the kingdom of heaven.

5:4 Blessed are they that that mourn: for they shall be comforted.

5:5 Blessed are the **meek** for they shall inherit the earth.

Meek: Humble.

5:6 Blessed are they which do hunger and thirst after **righteousness** for they shall be filled.

Righteousness: Decency, honesty.

5:7 Blessed are the merciful: for they shall obtain mercy.

5:8 Blessed are the pure in heart: for they shall see God.

5:9 Blessed are the peacemakers: for they shall be called the children of God.

5:10 Blessed are they which are persecuted for righteousness' sake: for theirs is the kingdom of heaven.

5:11 Blessed are ye, when men shall **revile** you, and persecute you, and shall say all manner of evil against you falsely, for my sake.

Revile: Insult, abuse.

5:12 Rejoice, and be exceeding glad: for great is your reward in heaven: for so persecuted they the prophets which were before you.

5:13 Ye are the salt of the earth: but if the salt have lost his **savour, wherewith** shall it be salted? it is **thenceforth** good for nothing, but to be cast out, and to be **trodden** under foot of men.

Savour or savor: Flavor, taste.

Wherewith: With what.

5:14 Ye are the light of the world. A city that is set on an hill cannot be hid.

Thenceforth: From that time on.

5:15 Neither do men light a candle, and put it under a bushel, but on a candlestick; and it giveth light unto all that are in the house.

Trodden: Stepped on.

5:16 Let your light so shine before men, that they may see your good works, and glorify your Father which is in heaven.

5:17 Think not that I am come to destroy the law, or the prophets: I am not come to destroy, but to fulfil.

5:18 For **verily** I say unto you, Till heaven and earth pass, one **jot** or one **tittle** shall in no **wise** pass from the law, till all be fulfilled.

Verily: Truly.

Jot: Bit, speck.

5:19 Whosoever therefore shall break one of these least commandments, and shall teach men so, he shall be called the least in the kingdom of heaven: but whosoever shall do and teach them, the same shall be called great in the kingdom of heaven.

Tittle: A small part.

Wise: Way.

5:20 For I say unto you, That except your righteousness shall exceed the righteousness of the scribes and Pharisees, ye shall in no case enter into the kingdom of heaven.

5:21 Ye have heard that it was said of them of old time, Thou shalt not kill; and whosoever shall kill shall be in danger of the judgment:

5:22 But I say unto you, That whosoever is angry with his brother without a cause shall be in danger of the judgment: . . .

Ought: Anything.

5:23 Therefore if thou bring thy gift to the altar, and there rememberest that thy brother hath **ought** against thee;

5:24 Leave there thy gift before the altar, and go thy way; first be reconciled to thy brother, and then come and offer thy gift.

Adversary: Enemy, opponent.

In the way: In company.

Thence: From there.

Uttermost: Greatest amount.

Farthing: A former British coin, worth about a quarter of a penny.

Lust: Long for, desire.

Forswear: Be guilty of lying or giving false evidence or of breaking an oath.

5:25 Agree with thine **adversary** quickly, whiles thou art **in the way** with him; lest at any time the adversary deliver thee to the judge, and the judge deliver thee to the officer, and thou be cast into prison.

5:26 Verily I say unto thee, Thou shalt by no means come out **thence,** till thou hast paid the **uttermost farthing.**

5:27 Ye have heard that it was said by them of old time, Thou shalt not commit adultery:

5:28 But I say unto you, That whosoever looketh on a woman to **lust** after her hath committed adultery with her already in his heart. . . .

5:33 Again, ye have heard that it hath been said by them of old time, Thou shalt not **forswear** thyself, but shalt perform unto the Lord thine oaths:

5:34 But I say unto you, Swear not at all; neither by heaven; for it is God's throne:

5:35 Nor by the earth; for it is his footstool: neither by Jerusalem; for it is the city of the great King. . . .

5:38 Ye have heard that it hath been said, An eye for an eye, and a tooth for a tooth

5:39 But I say unto you, That ye resist not evil: but whosoever shall smite thee on thy right cheek, turn to him the other also.

5:40 And if any man will sue thee at the law, and take away thy coat, let him have thy cloak also. . . .

5:42 Give to him that asketh thee, and from him that would borrow of thee turn not thou away.

5:43 Ye have heard that it hath been said, Thou shalt love thy neighbour, and hate thine enemy.

5:44 But I say unto you, Love your enemies, bless them that curse you, do good to them that hate you, and pray for them which despitefully use you, and persecute you;

5:45 That ye may be the children of your Father which is in heaven: for he maketh his sun to rise on the evil and on the good, and sendeth rain on the just and on the unjust. . . .

5:48 Be ye therefore perfect, even as your Father which is in heaven is perfect.

Chapter 6

6:1 Take heed that ye do not your **alms** before men, to be seen of them: otherwise ye have no reward of your Father which is in heaven....

6:3 But when thou doest alms, let not thy left hand know what thy right hand doeth:

6:4 That thine alms may be in secret: and thy Father which seeth in secret himself shall reward thee openly.

6:5 And when thou prayest, thou shalt not be as the **hypocrites** are: for they love to pray standing in the synagogues and in the corners of the streets, that they may be seen of men....

6:6 But thou, when thou prayest, enter into thy closet, and when thou hast shut thy door, pray to thy Father which is in secret; and thy Father which seeth in secret shall reward thee openly....

Alms: Money or other contributions made to aid the poor.

Hypocrites: People who claim to have high principles and beliefs but do not.

6:9 After this manner therefore pray ye: Our Father which art in heaven, Hallowed be thy name.

6:10 Thy kingdom come, Thy will be done in earth, as it is in heaven.

6:11 Give us this day our daily bread.

6:12 And forgive us our debts, as we forgive our debtors.

6:13 And lead us not into temptation, but deliver us from evil: For thine is the kingdom, and the power, and the glory, for ever. Amen.

Trespasses: Sins, wrongdoings.

6:14 For if ye forgive men their **trespasses,** your heavenly Father will also forgive you:

6:15 But if ye forgive not men their trespasses, neither will your Father forgive your trespasses. . . .

6:19 Lay not up for yourselves treasures upon earth, where moth and rust doth **corrupt,** and where thieves break through and steal:

Corrupt: To spoil or contaminate.

6:20 But lay up for yourselves treasures in heaven, where neither moth nor rust doth corrupt, and where thieves do not break through nor steal:

6:21 For where your treasure is, there will your heart be also. . . .

6:24 No man can serve two masters: for either he will hate the one, and love the other; or else he will hold to the one, and despise the other. Ye cannot serve God and **mammon.**

Mammon: Riches as an evil influence or an object of worship.

Raiment: Clothing.

6:25 Therefore I say unto you, Take no thought for your life, what ye shall eat, or what ye shall drink; nor yet for your body, what ye shall put on. Is not the life more than meat, and the body than **raiment?** . . .

6:28 And why take ye thought for raiment? Consider the lilies of the field, how they grow; they toil not, neither do they spin:

6:29 And yet I say unto you, That even Solomon in all his glory was not **arrayed** like one of these.

Arrayed: Clothed.

6:30 Wherefore, if God so clothe the grass of the field, which to day is, and to morrow is cast into the oven, shall he not much more clothe you, O ye of little faith? . . .

6:33 But seek ye first the kingdom of God, and his righteousness; and all these things shall be added unto you.

6:34 Take therefore no thought for the morrow: for the morrow shall take thought for the things of itself. Sufficient unto the day is the evil thereof.

Chapter 7

7:1 Judge not, that ye be not judged.

7:2 For with what judgment ye judge, ye shall be judged: and with what measure ye **mete,** it shall be measured to you again.

Mete: Give out or deal out.

Mote: A small fragment of wood.

7:3 And why beholdest thou the **mote** that is in thy brother's eye, but considerest not the beam that is in thine own eye?

7:4 Or how wilt thou say to thy brother, Let me pull out the mote out of thine eye; and, behold, a beam is in thine own eye?

7:5 Thou hypocrite, first cast out the beam out of thine own eye; and then shalt thou see clearly to cast out the mote out of thy brother's eye. . . .

7:7 Ask, and it shall be given you; seek, and ye shall find; knock, and it shall be opened unto you: . . .

7:12 Therefore all things whatsoever ye would that men should do to you, do ye even so to them: for this is the law and the prophets. . . .

7:21 Not every one that saith unto me, Lord, Lord, shall enter into the kingdom of heaven; but he that doeth the will of my Father which is in heaven. . . .

7:28 And it came to pass, when Jesus had ended these sayings, the people were astonished at his **doctrine:**

Doctrine: A set of guidelines.

7:29 For he taught them as one having authority, and not as the scribes.

• • •

What happened next . . .

Each of the four Gospels, including Matthew, records numerous events and teachings from the life of Christ. Chapters 8 through 20 of Matthew go on to detail additional teachings of Christ and note the miracles that he performed, particularly miracles of healing. Chapter 21 tells of Christ's triumphant arrival in the city of Jerusalem. Chapters 22 through 27 describe the events surrounding his arrest, trial, and crucifixion (death by hanging on a cross). The book concludes with Chapter 28, Christ's resurrection from the dead.

Did you know . . .

- Little is known about the life of Matthew. In fact, the Gospel does not identify him as the author of the book. About all that is known is that he had been a tax collector for the Roman Empire before he became a disciple of Jesus Christ. This made him a social outcast. He wrote the book sometimes between the years 50 and 100, and the main source of his information was Peter, another of the apostles. An apostle is a close follower of Christ.

- The Bible exists in numerous translations. The excerpt given here is taken from the King James Version of the Bible. This was a translation made especially for King James I of England early in the seventeenth century. It is thought of as the most "literary" translation of the Bible, meaning that the language is suited more to literature than to everyday speech.

- Christians often refer to verses 3 through 11 of Chapter 5 as the Beatitudes. The word *beatitude* comes from a Latin word that essentially means "happy." The word has come to refer specifically to the "Blessed are" statements that Christ made at the beginning of the Sermon on the Mount. By following these precepts, or guidelines, a person can become happy by entering the kingdom of God.

Consider the following...

- Explain Christ's overall purpose in giving the Sermon on the Mount.
- Summarize how Christ's interpretation of law differed from that of the larger Jewish community.
- An often quoted passage from the Sermon on the Mount is "whosoever shall smite [hit] thee on thy right cheek, turn to him the other also." Explain the meaning of this teaching.

For More Information

BOOKS

Carson, D. A. *Jesus' Sermon on the Mount and His Confrontation with the World.* Grand Rapids, MI: Baker Publishing, 2004.

Hybels, Bill, Kevin G. Harney, and Sherry Harney. *Sermon on the Mount 1.* Grand Rapids, MI: Zondervan, 2002.

WEB SITES

"Book of Matthew," *Internet Sacred Text Archive.* http://www.sacred-texts.com/bib/kjv/mat005.htm; http://www.sacred-texts.com/bib/kjv/mat006.htm; http://www.sacred-texts.com/bib/kjv/mat007.htm (accessed on June 5, 2006).

Palmer, Ken. "Sermon on the Mount." *Life of Christ.* http://www.lifeofchrist.com/teachings/sermons/mount/default.asp (accessed on June 5, 2006).

Where to Learn More

The following list focuses on works written for readers of middle school and high school age. Books aimed at adult readers have been included when they are especially important in providing information or analysis that would otherwise be unavailable.

Books

Armstrong, Karen. *Islam: A Short History,* rev. ed. New York: Modern Library, 2002.

Bottero, Jean. *Religion in Ancient Mesopotamia.* Chicago, IL: University of Chicago Press, 2001.

Boyer, P. *Religion Explained: The Human Instincts That Fashion Gods, Spirits, and Ancestors.* London: William Heinemann, 2001.

Buswell, Robert E., Jr., ed. *Encyclopedia of Buddhism.* 2 vols. New York: Macmillan Reference, 2003.

De Lange, Nicholas. *An Introduction to Judaism.* Cambridge, U.K.: Cambridge University Press, 2000.

Dundas, Paul. *The Jains.* 2nd ed. London and New York, NY: Routledge, 2002.

Flood, Gavin D. *An Introduction to Hinduism.* Cambridge, U.K.: Cambridge University Press, 1996.

Glazier, Stephen D. *Encyclopedia of African and African-American Religions.* New York: Routledge, 2001.

Grimassi, Raven. *Encyclopedia of Wicca and Witchcraft.* St. Paul, MN: Llewellyn Publications, 2000.

Hartz, Paula. *Zoroastrianism,* 2nd ed. New York: Facts On File, 2004.

Higginbotham, Joyce. *Paganism: An Introduction to Earth-centered Religions.* St. Paul, MN: Llewellyn Publications, 2002.

Hirschfelder, Arlene, and Paulette Molin. *Encyclopedia of Native American Religions: An Introduction.* 2nd ed. New York: Facts On File, 2001.

Hoffman, Nancy. *Sikhism.* Detroit, MI: Lucent Books, 2006.

Jones, Lindsay. *Encyclopedia of Religion,* 2nd ed. Detroit, MI: Macmillan Reference USA, 2005.

Keown, Damien. *Dictionary of Buddhism.* New York: Oxford University Press, 2003.

Lace, William W. *Christianity*. San Diego, CA: Lucent Books, Inc., 2005.

Martin, Michael, ed. *The Cambridge Companion to Atheism*. Cambridge, U.K.: Cambridge University Press, 2005.

Momen, Moojan. *A Short Introduction to the Baha'i Faith*. Oxford, U.K.: Oneworld Publications, 1997.

Nasr, Seyyed Hossein. *Islam: Religion, History, Civilization*. San Francisco: Harper San Francisco, 2003.

Oldstone-Moore, Jennifer. *Confucianism: Origins, Beliefs, Practices, Holy Texts, Sacred Places*. New York: Oxford University Press, 2002.

Oldstone-Moore, Jennifer. *Taoism: Origins, Beliefs, Practices, Holy Texts, Sacred Places*. New York: Oxford University Press, 2003.

Robinson, George. *Essential Judaism: A Complete Guide to Beliefs, Customs and Rituals*. Rev. ed. New York: Pocket Books, 2000.

Roochnick, David. *Retrieving the Ancients: An Introduction to Greek Philosophy*. New York: Blackwell, 2004.

Tiele, C. P. *Comparative History of the Egyptian and Mesopotamian Religions*. New York: Routledge, 2001.

Tomkins, Steven. *A Short History of Christianity*. London: Lion Books, 2005.

Web Site

URI Kids: World Religions. United Religions Initiative. http://www.uri.org/kids/world.htm (accessed on July 24, 2006).

Religions, Faith Groups, and Ethical Systems. Ontario Consultants on Religious Tolerance. http://www.religioustolerance.org/var_rel.htm (accessed on July 24, 2006).

World Religions Index. http://wri.leaderu.com/ (accessed on July 24, 2006).

Index

Boldface type indicates main entries and their page numbers; Illustrations are marked by (ill.)